DON'T TOY WITH ME, MISS NAGATORO

③

NANASHI

CONTENTS

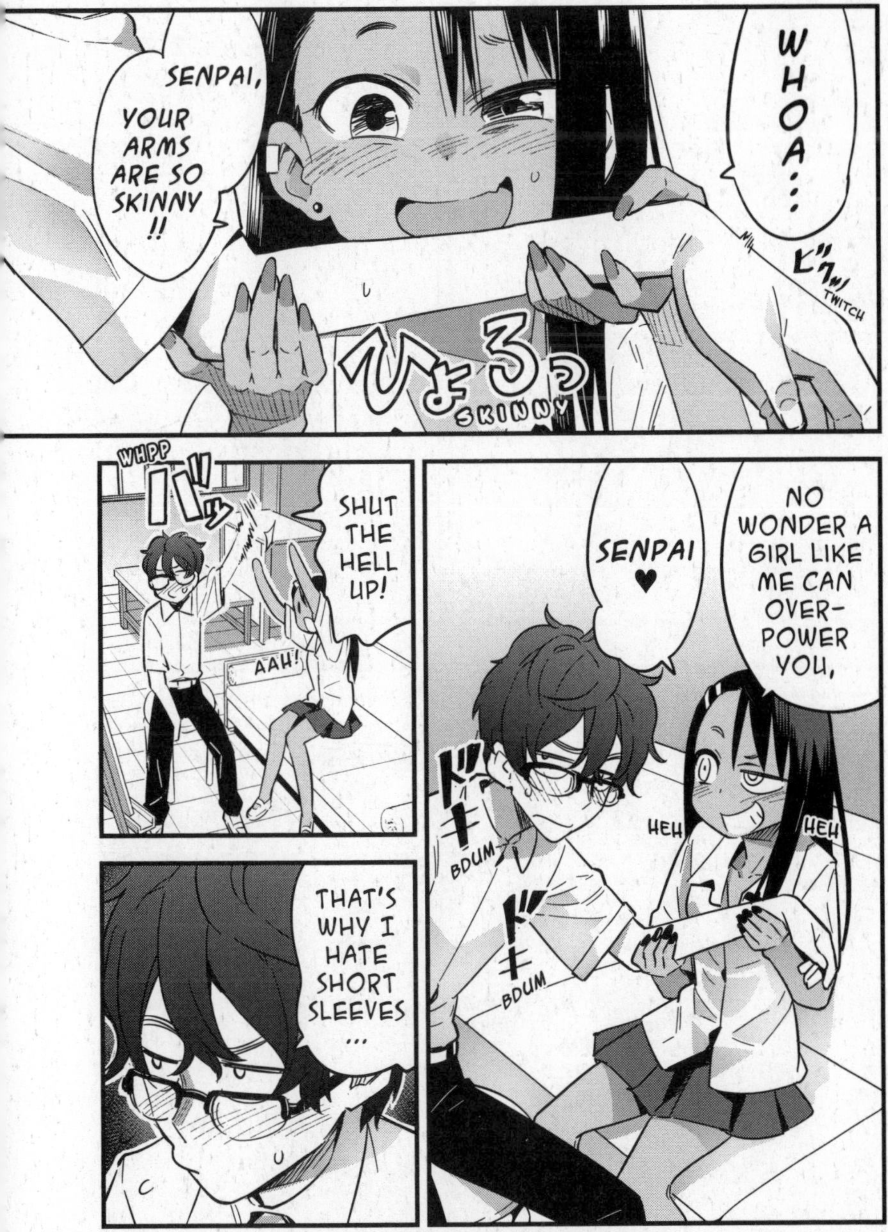
WHOA...
SENPAI, YOUR ARMS ARE SO SKINNY!!
TWITCH
ひょろっ
SKINNY
NO WONDER A GIRL LIKE ME CAN OVER-POWER YOU,
SENPAI ♥
HEH HEH
BDUM
BDUM
WHPP
SHUT THE HELL UP!
AAH!
THAT'S WHY I HATE SHORT SLEEVES...

CHAPTER 15: SENPAI, YOUR ARMS ARE SO SKINNY!!

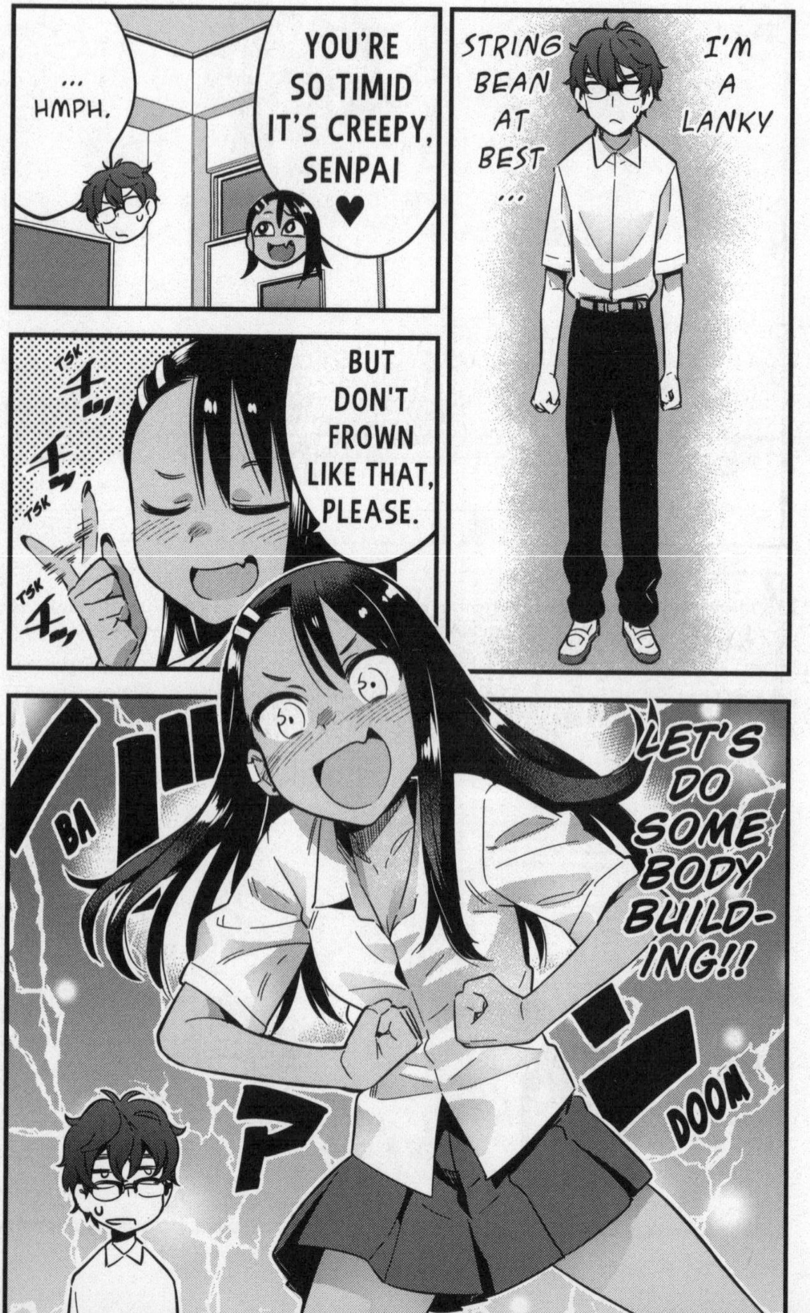

I'M A LANKY
STRING BEAN AT BEST ...
YOU'RE SO TIMID IT'S CREEPY, SENPAI ♥
... HMPH.
BUT DON'T FROWN LIKE THAT, PLEASE.
TSK
TSK
TSK
LET'S DO SOME BODY BUILD-ING!!
BA
DOOM

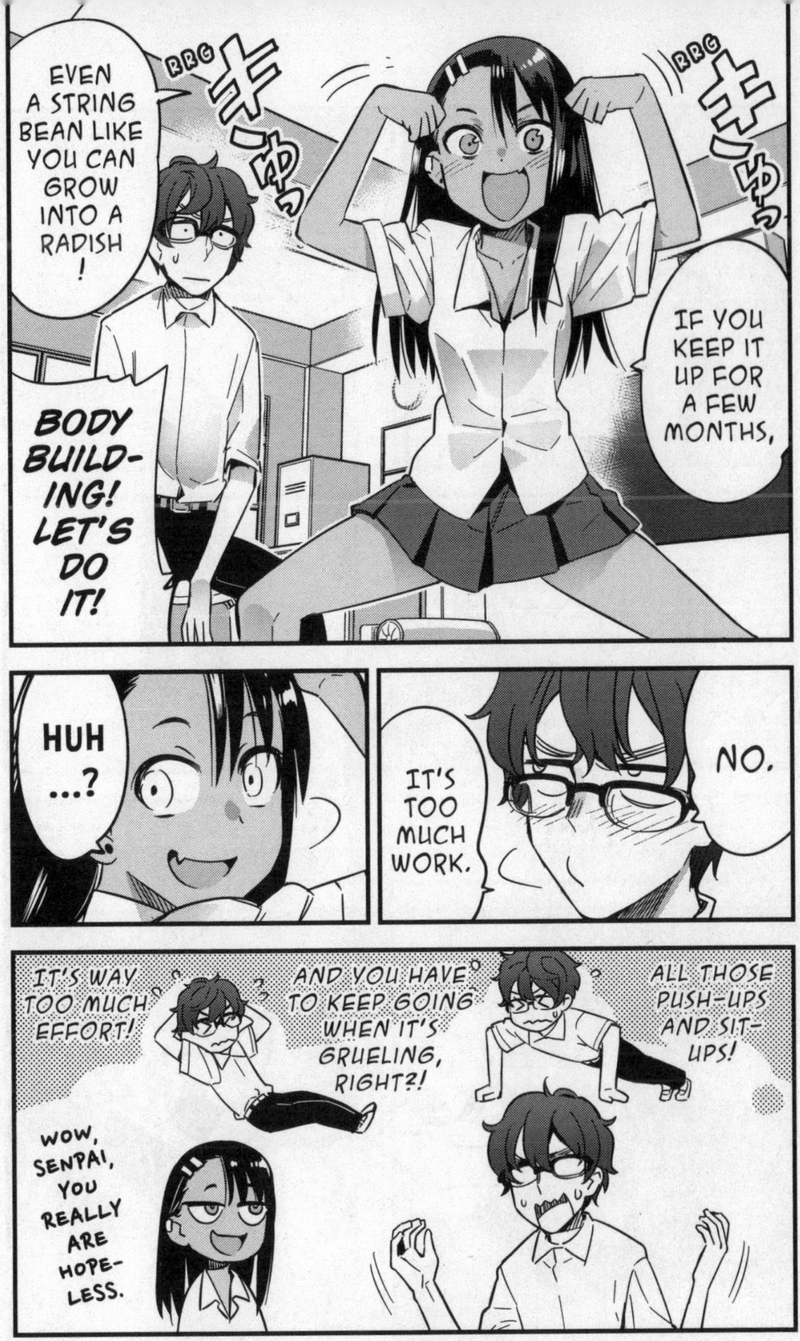
RRG きゅっ
IF YOU KEEP IT UP FOR A FEW MONTHS,
RRG きゅっ
EVEN A STRING BEAN LIKE YOU CAN GROW INTO A RADISH!
BODY BUILD-ING! LET'S DO IT!
NO.
IT'S TOO MUCH WORK.
HUH ...?
ALL THOSE PUSH-UPS AND SIT-UPS!
AND YOU HAVE TO KEEP GOING WHEN IT'S GRUELING, RIGHT?!
IT'S WAY TOO MUCH EFFORT!
WOW, SENPAI, YOU REALLY ARE HOPE-LESS.

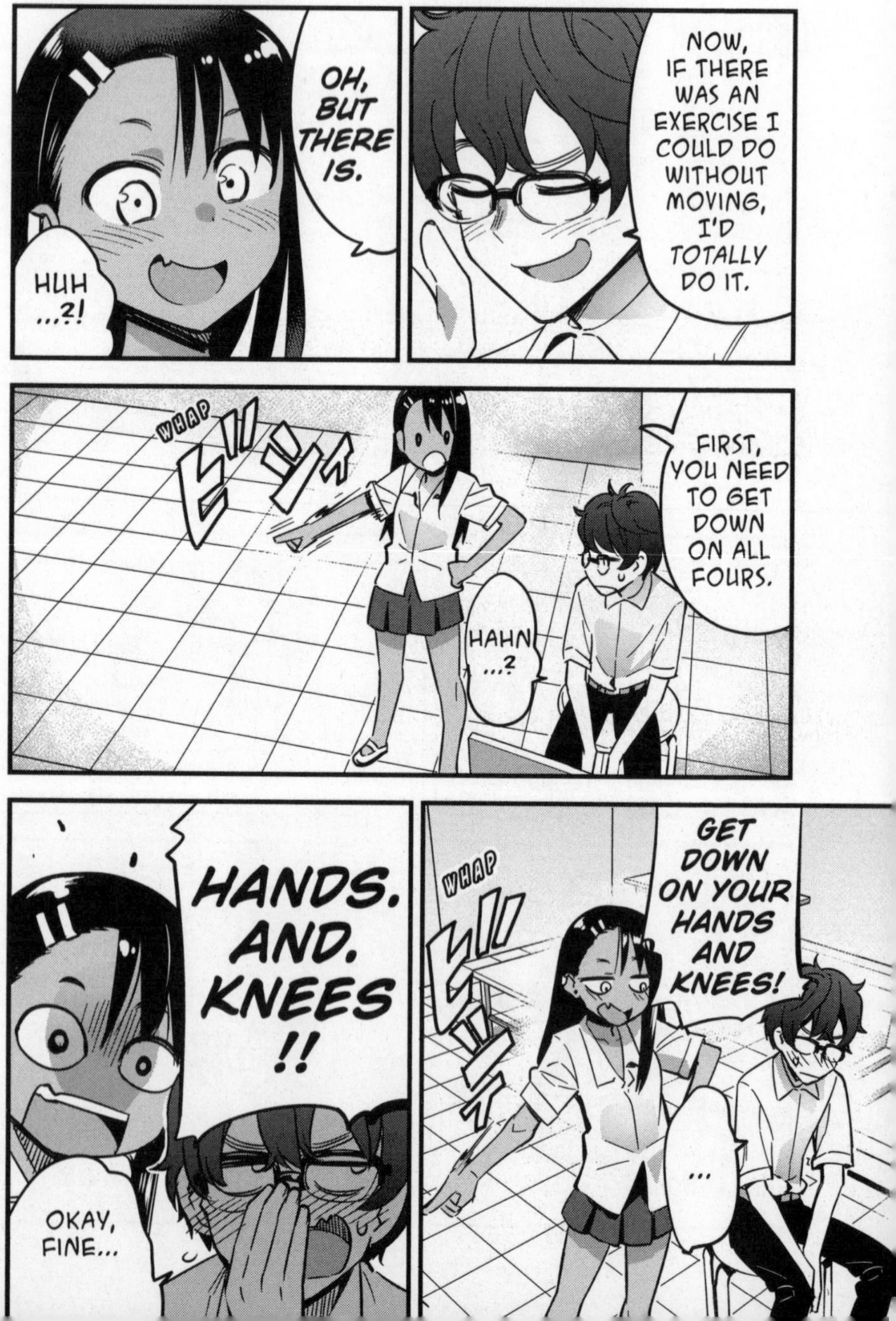
NOW, IF THERE WAS AN EXERCISE I COULD DO WITHOUT MOVING, I'D TOTALLY DO IT.
OH, BUT THERE IS.
HUH...?!
FIRST, YOU NEED TO GET DOWN ON ALL FOURS.
WHAP
HAHN...?
GET DOWN ON YOUR HANDS AND KNEES!
WHAP
...
HANDS. AND. KNEES!!
OKAY, FINE...

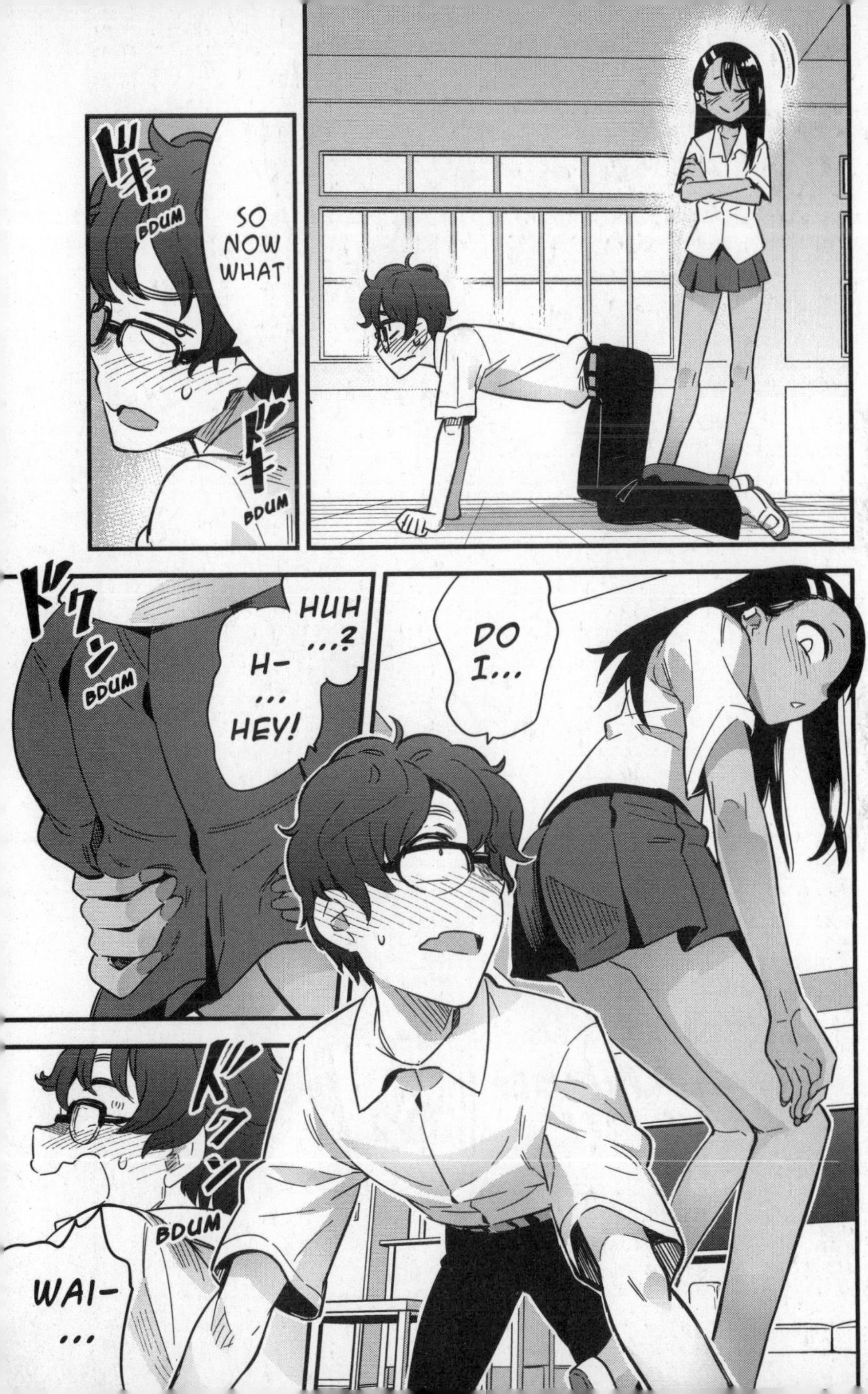
BDUM
SO NOW WHAT
BDUM
DO I...
BDUM
HUH ...?
H- ... HEY!
BDUM
WAI- ...

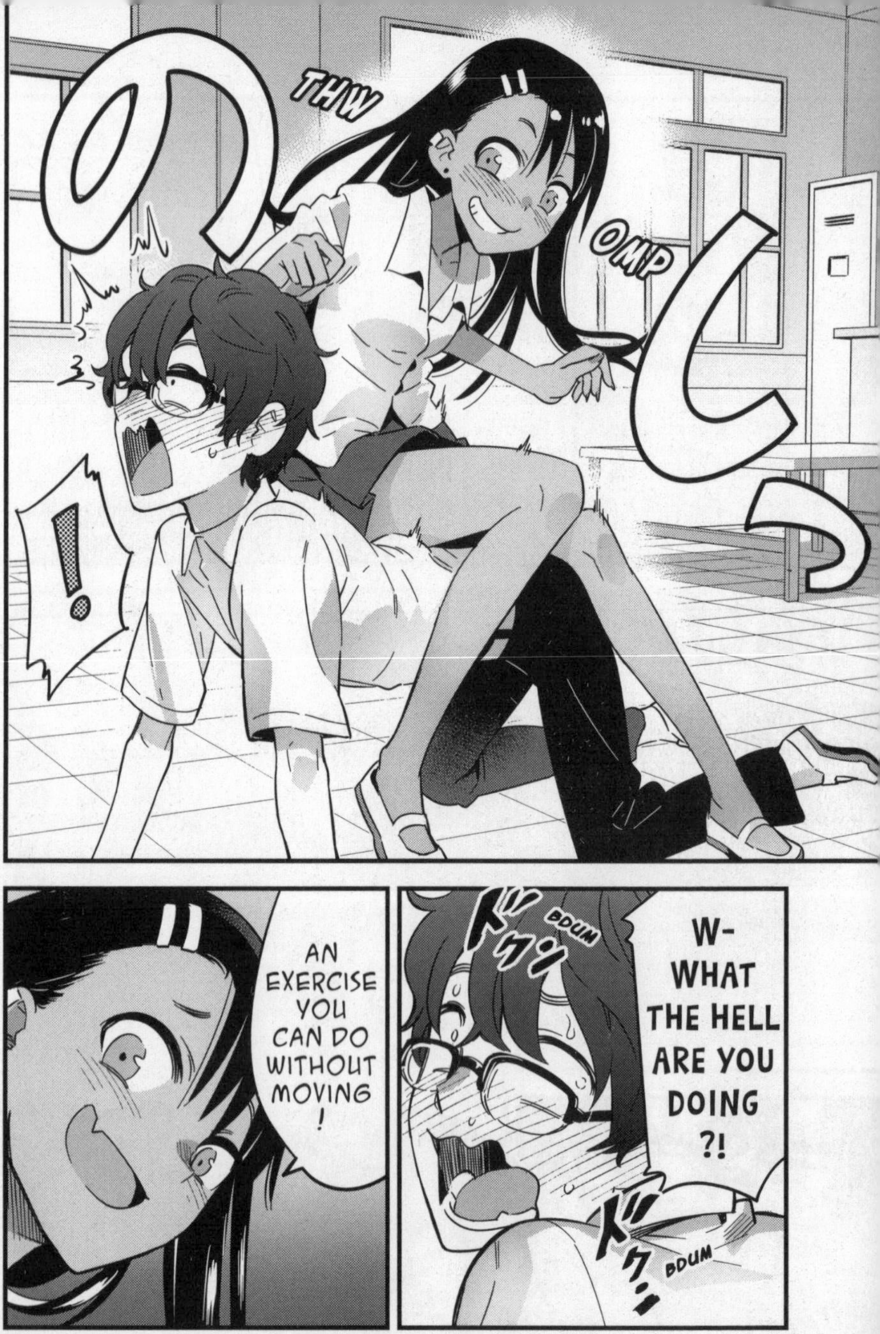
THW
OMP
!
W- WHAT THE HELL ARE YOU DOING ?!
BDUM
BDUM
AN EXERCISE YOU CAN DO WITHOUT MOVING !

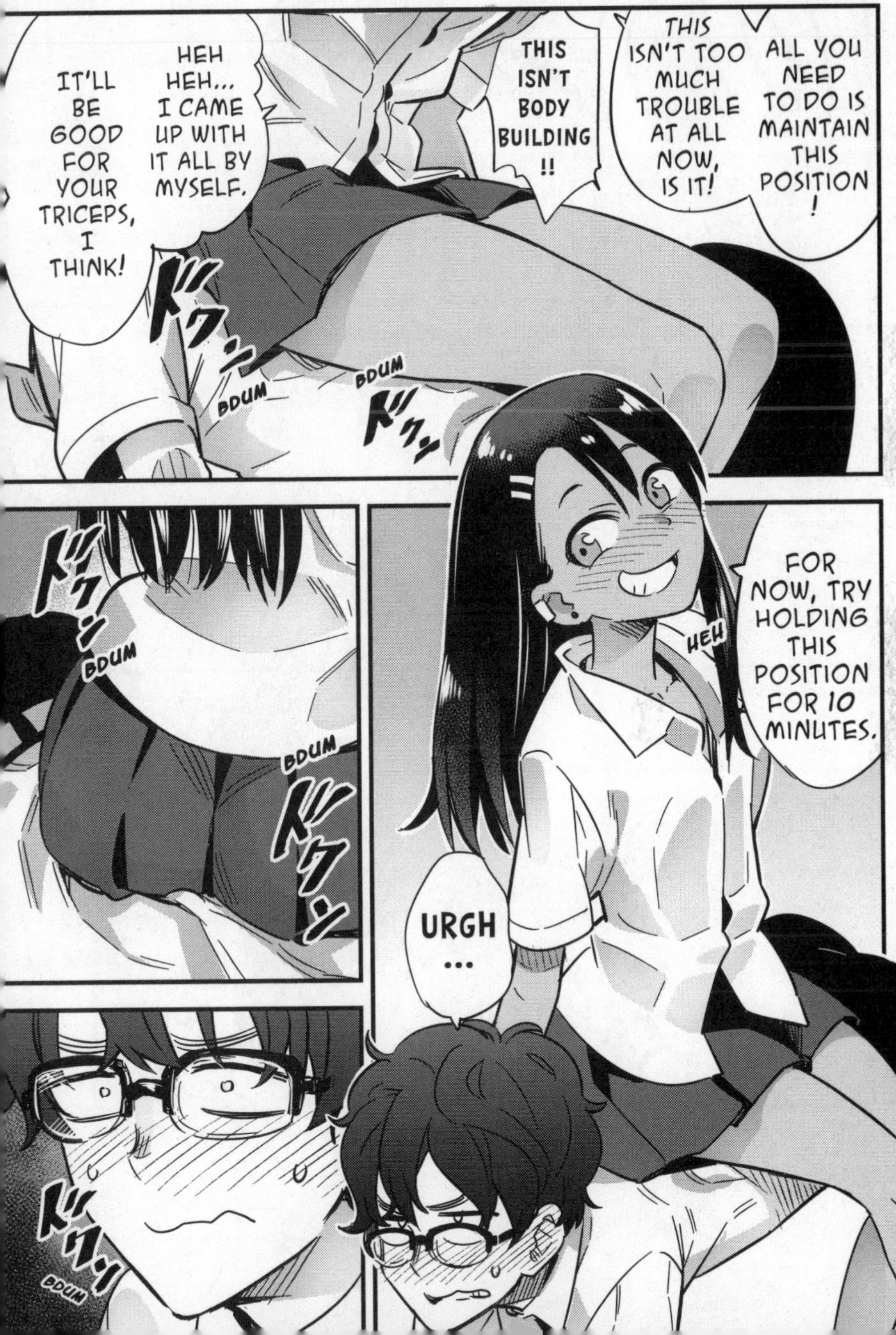
ALL YOU NEED TO DO IS MAINTAIN THIS POSITION!
THIS ISN'T TOO MUCH TROUBLE AT ALL NOW, IS IT!
THIS ISN'T BODY BUILDING!!
HEH HEH... I CAME UP WITH IT ALL BY MYSELF.
IT'LL BE GOOD FOR YOUR TRICEPS, I THINK!
BDUM
BDUM
FOR NOW, TRY HOLDING THIS POSITION FOR 10 MINUTES.
HEH
URGH...
BDUM
BDUM
BDUM

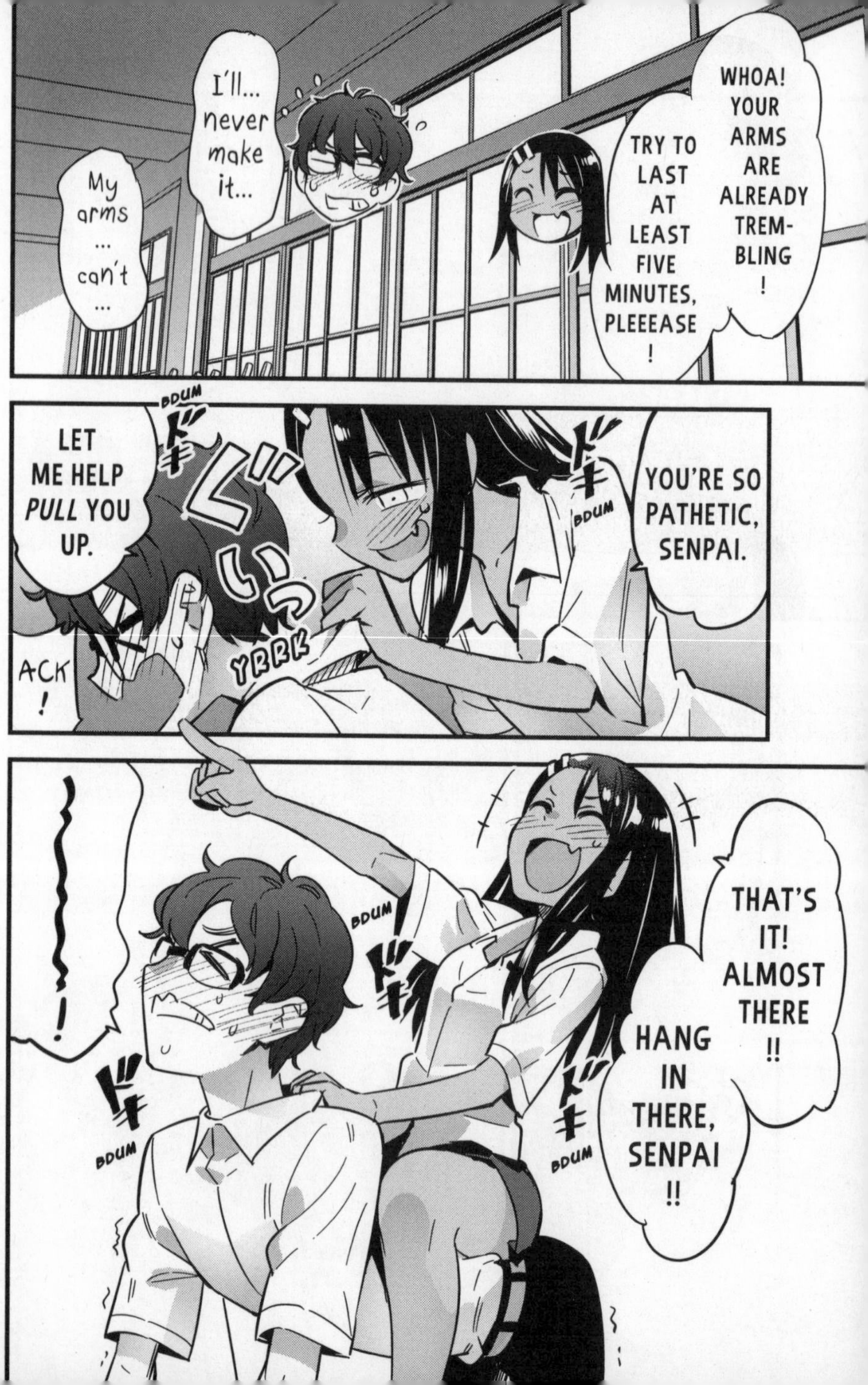
WHOA! YOUR ARMS ARE ALREADY TREM-BLING!
TRY TO LAST AT LEAST FIVE MINUTES, PLEEEASE!
I'll... never make it...
My arms... can't...
BDUM
YOU'RE SO PATHETIC, SENPAI.
BDUM
LET ME HELP *PULL* YOU UP.
YRRK
ACK!
THAT'S IT! ALMOST THERE!!
HANG IN THERE, SENPAI!!
BDUM
BDUM
BDUM
—!

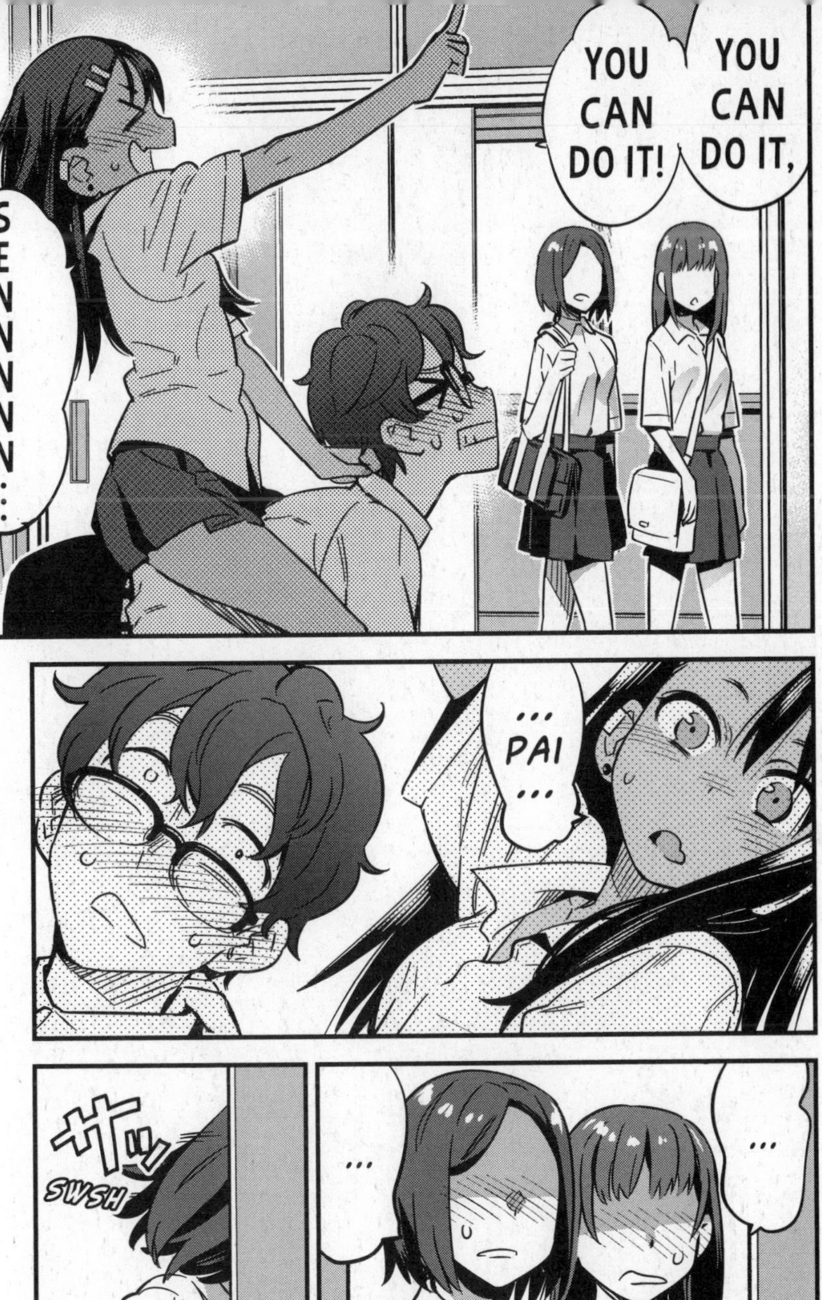

YOU CAN DO IT,
YOU CAN DO IT!
SENNNNN...
...PAI...
...
...
サッ
SWSH

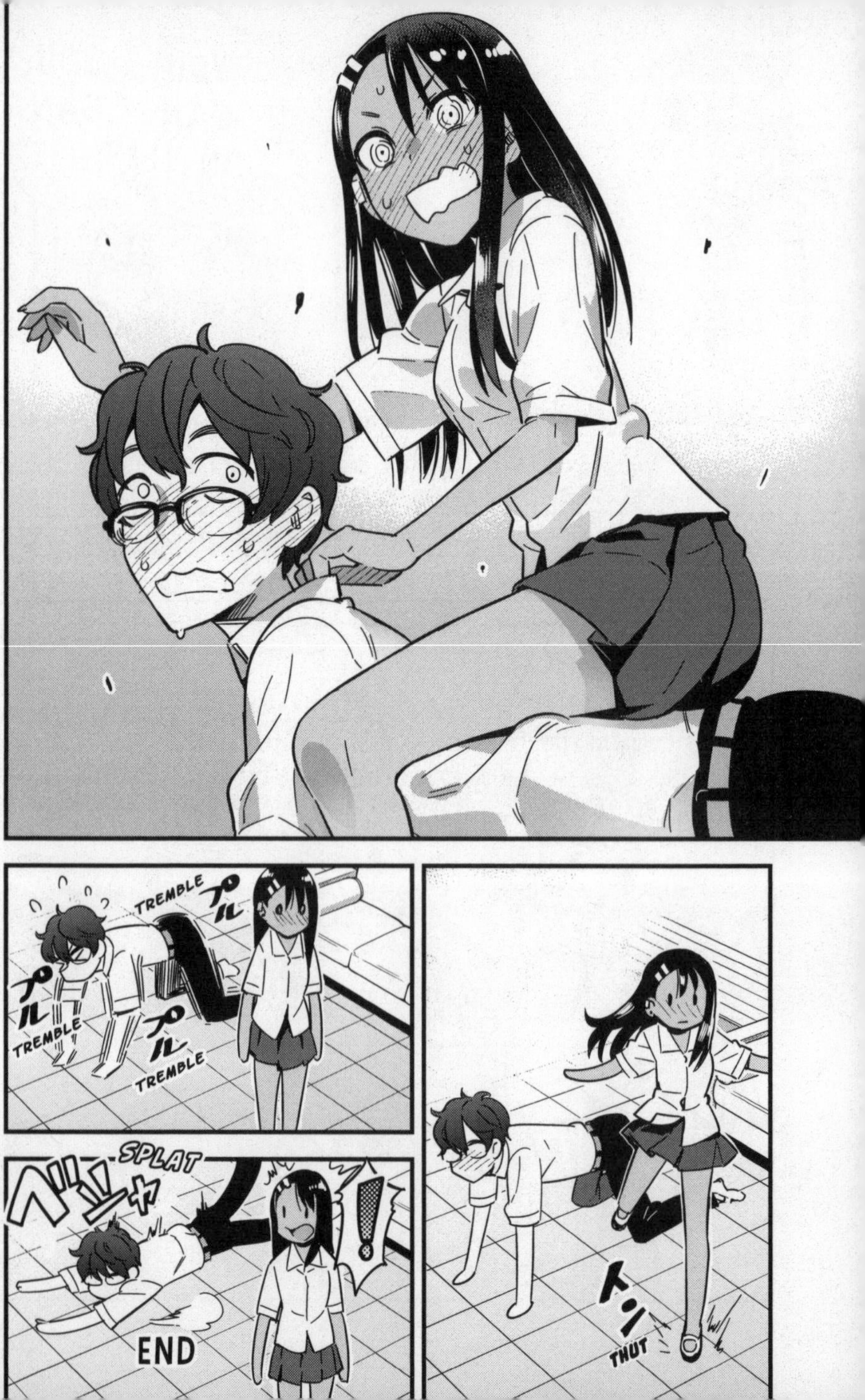
トン
THUT
プル
TREMBLE
プル
TREMBLE
プル
TREMBLE
SPLAT
END

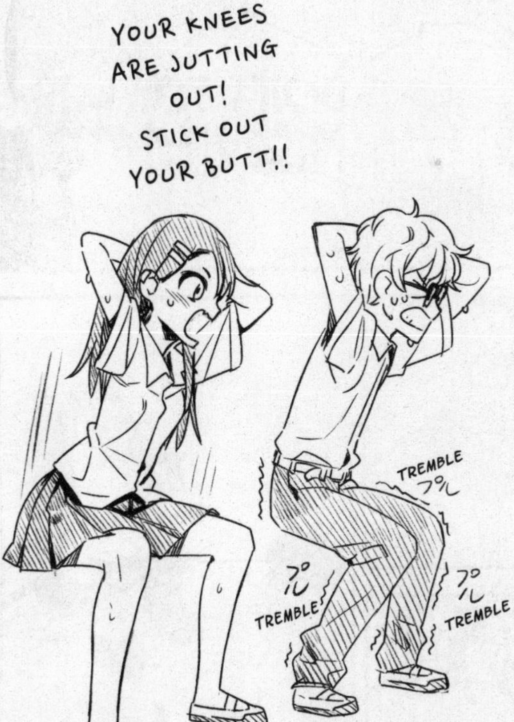
YOUR KNEES ARE JUTTING OUT! STICK OUT YOUR BUTT!!
TREMBLE
プル
プル
TREMBLE
プル
TREMBLE

DON'T TOY WITH ME,
MISS NAGATORO

CHAPTER 16: IF WE BUZZ THAT FLUFF, SENPAI

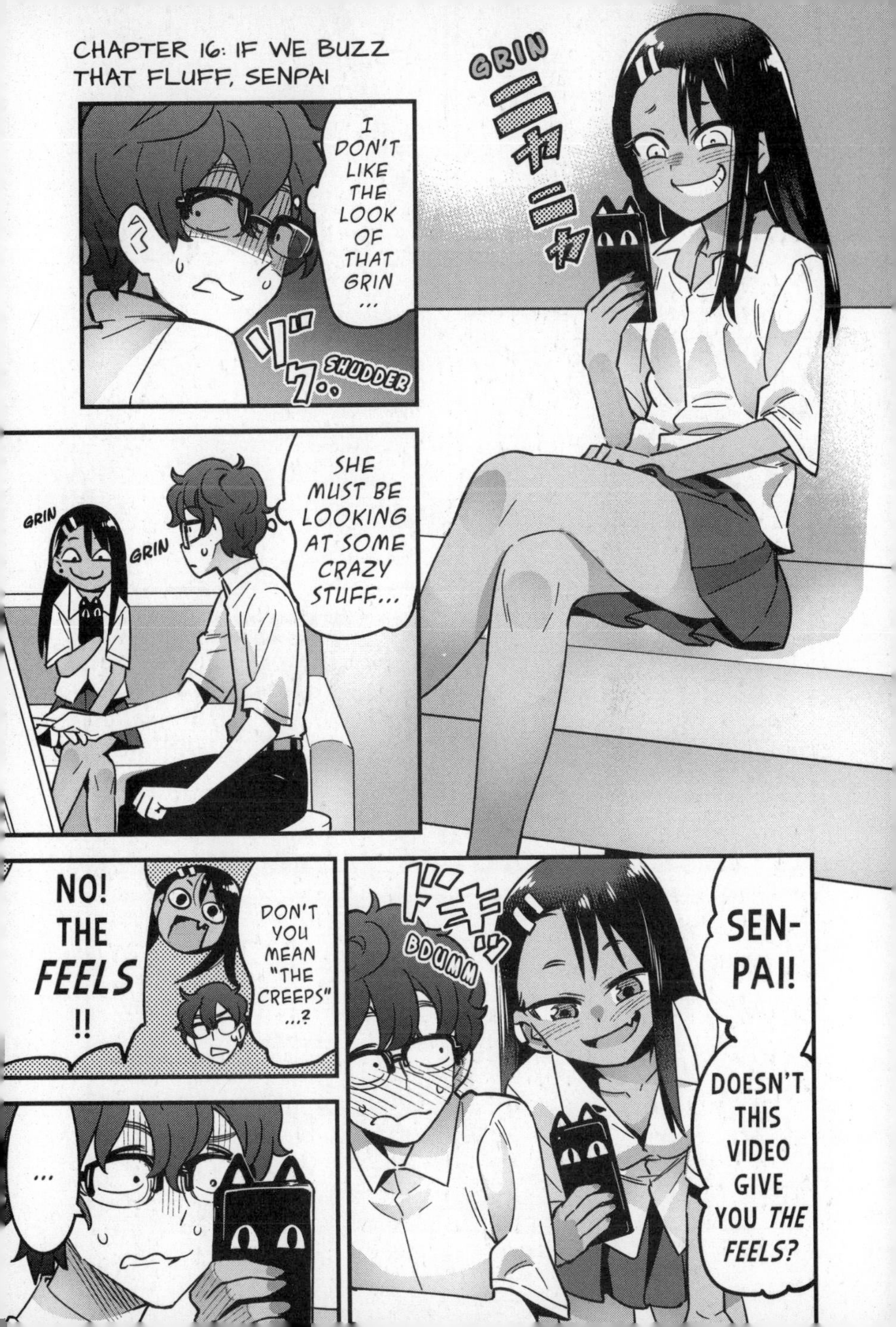
GRIN
I DON'T LIKE THE LOOK OF THAT GRIN ...
SHUDDER
GRIN
GRIN
SHE MUST BE LOOKING AT SOME CRAZY STUFF...
BDUMM
SEN-PAI!
DOESN'T THIS VIDEO GIVE YOU *THE FEELS?*
NO! THE *FEELS* !!
DON'T YOU MEAN "THE CREEPS" ...?
...

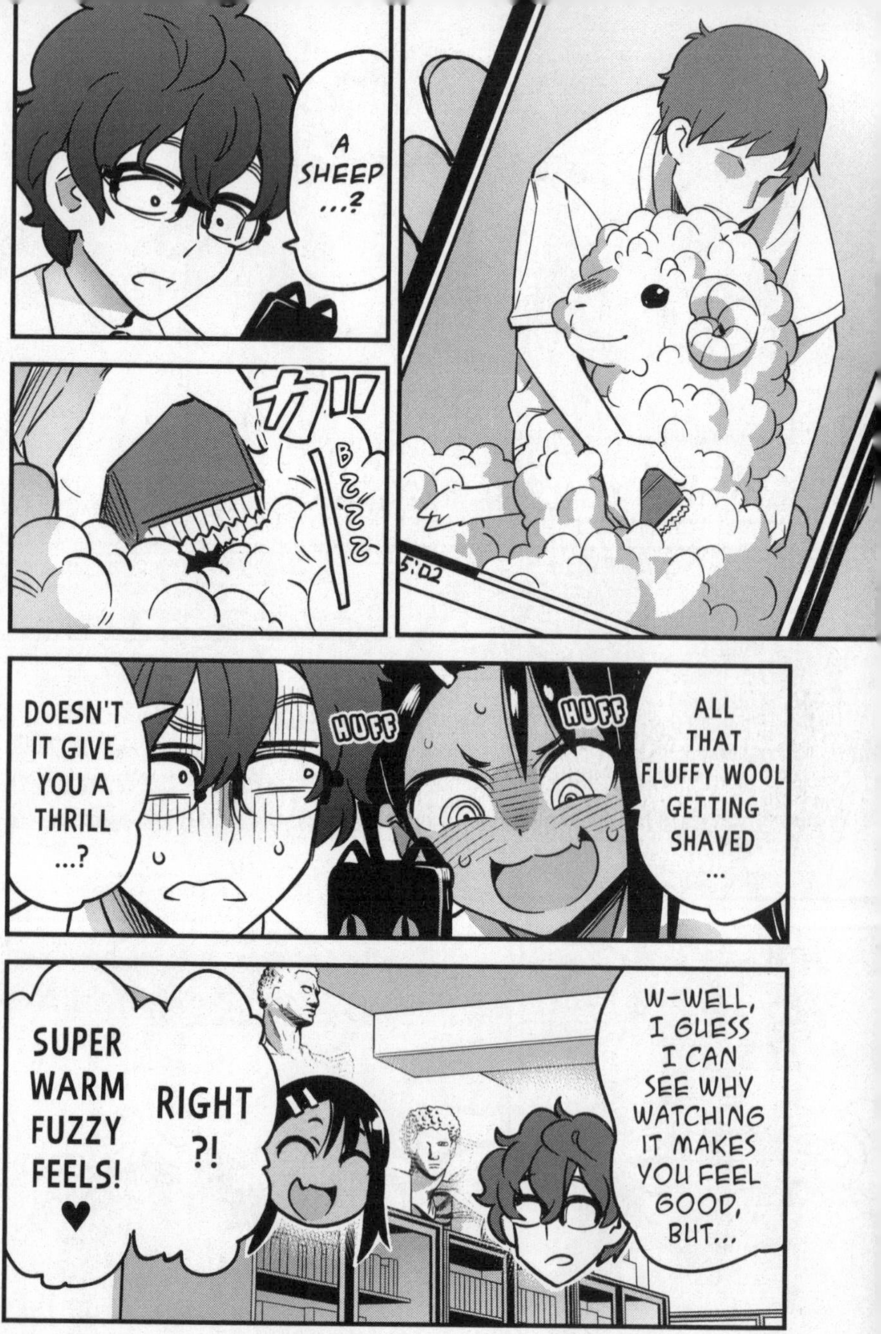
5:02
A SHEEP ...?
カッ
BZZZZ
ALL THAT FLUFFY WOOL GETTING SHAVED ...
HUFF
HUFF
DOESN'T IT GIVE YOU A THRILL ...?
W-WELL, I GUESS I CAN SEE WHY WATCHING IT MAKES YOU FEEL GOOD, BUT...
RIGHT ?!
SUPER WARM FUZZY FEELS! ♥

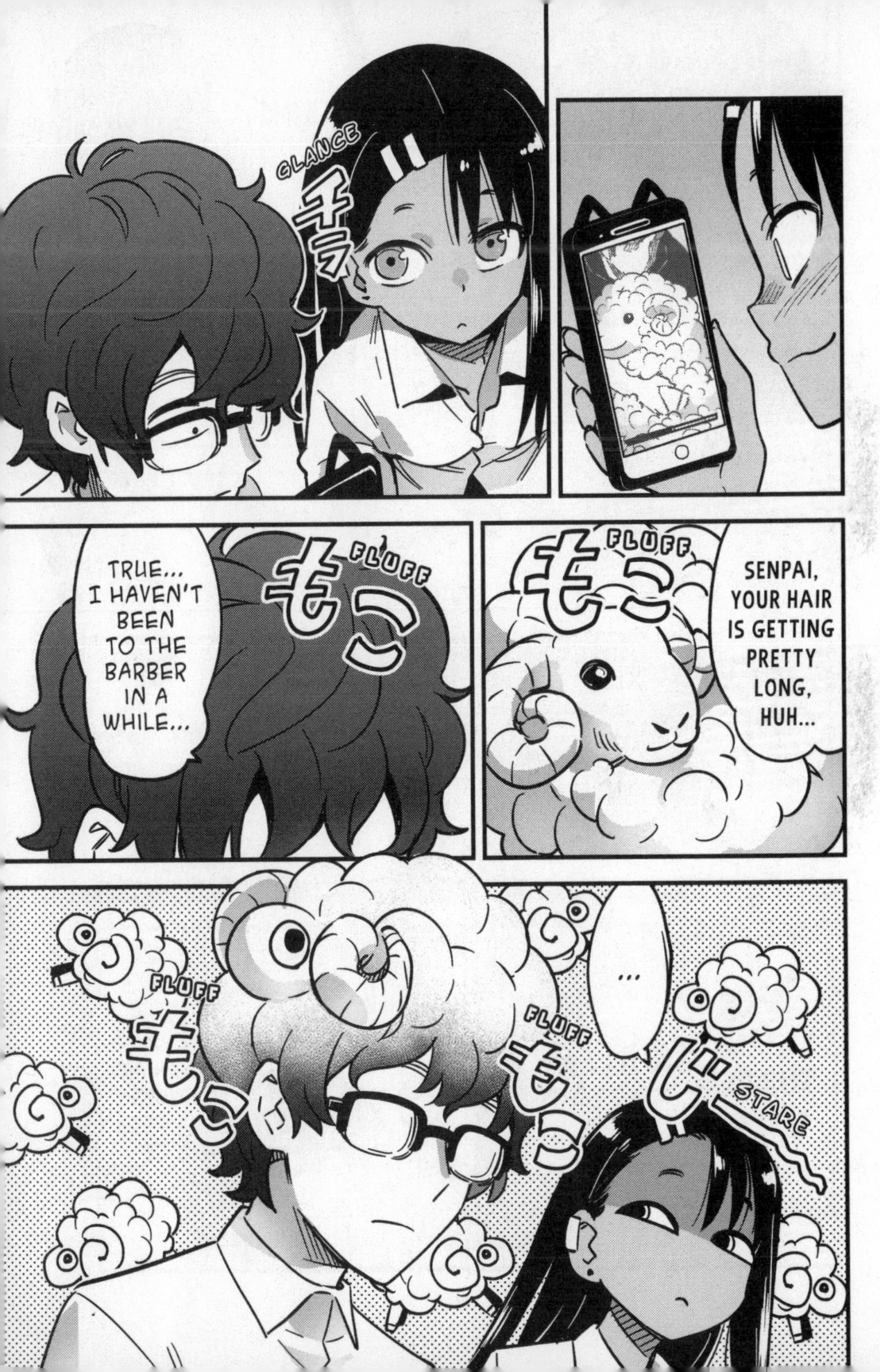
チラ
GLANCE
もこ
FLUFF
SENPAI, YOUR HAIR IS GETTING PRETTY LONG, HUH...
もこ
FLUFF
TRUE... I HAVEN'T BEEN TO THE BARBER IN A WHILE...
...
じー
STARE
もこ
FLUFF
もこ
FLUFF

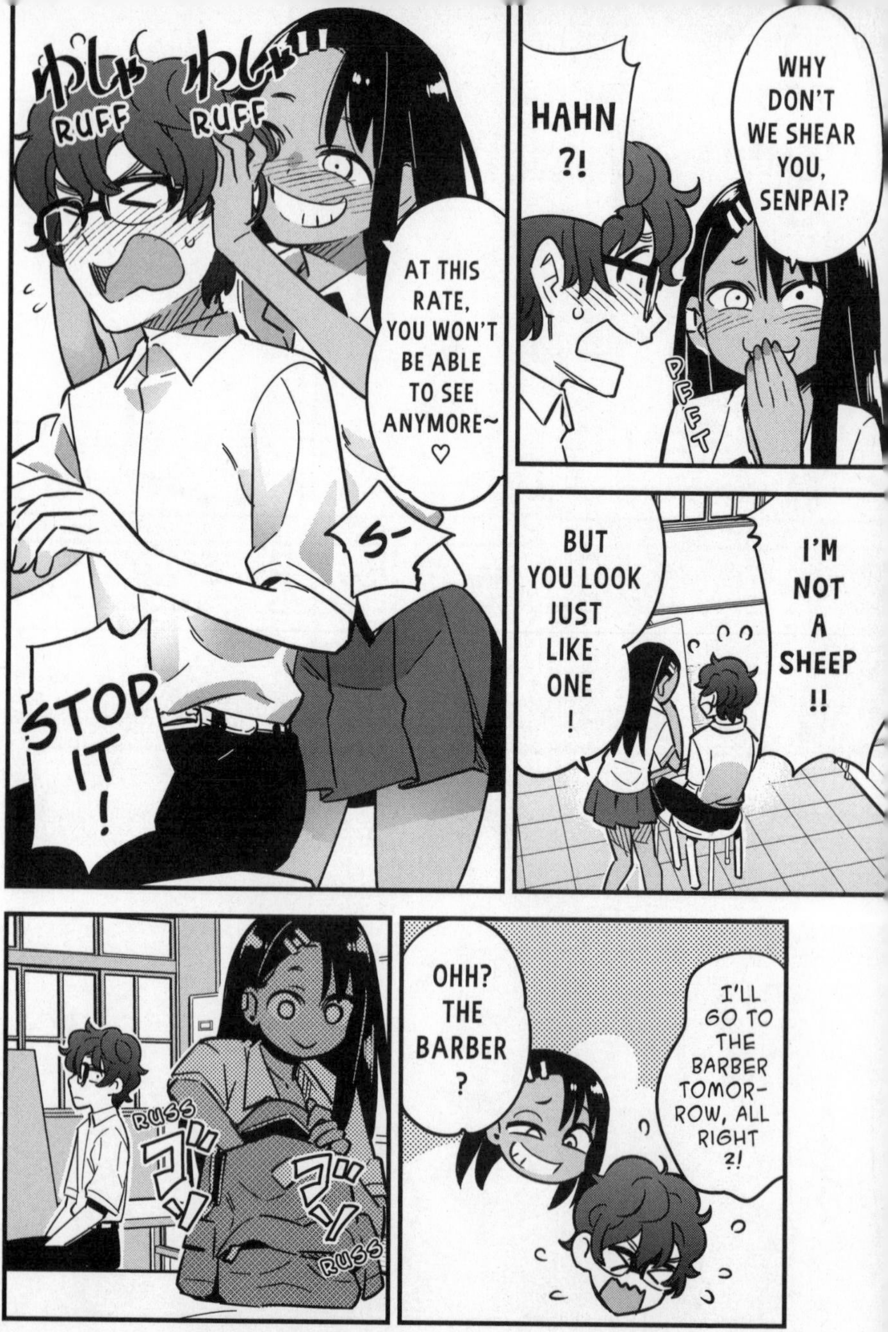
WHY DON'T WE SHEAR YOU, SENPAI?
HAHN ?!
PFFFT
I'M NOT A SHEEP !!
BUT YOU LOOK JUST LIKE ONE !
わしゃ わしゃ!!
RUFF RUFF
AT THIS RATE, YOU WON'T BE ABLE TO SEE ANYMORE~ ♡
S-
STOP IT !
I'LL GO TO THE BARBER TOMORROW, ALL RIGHT ?!
OHH? THE BARBER ?
RUSS
RUSS

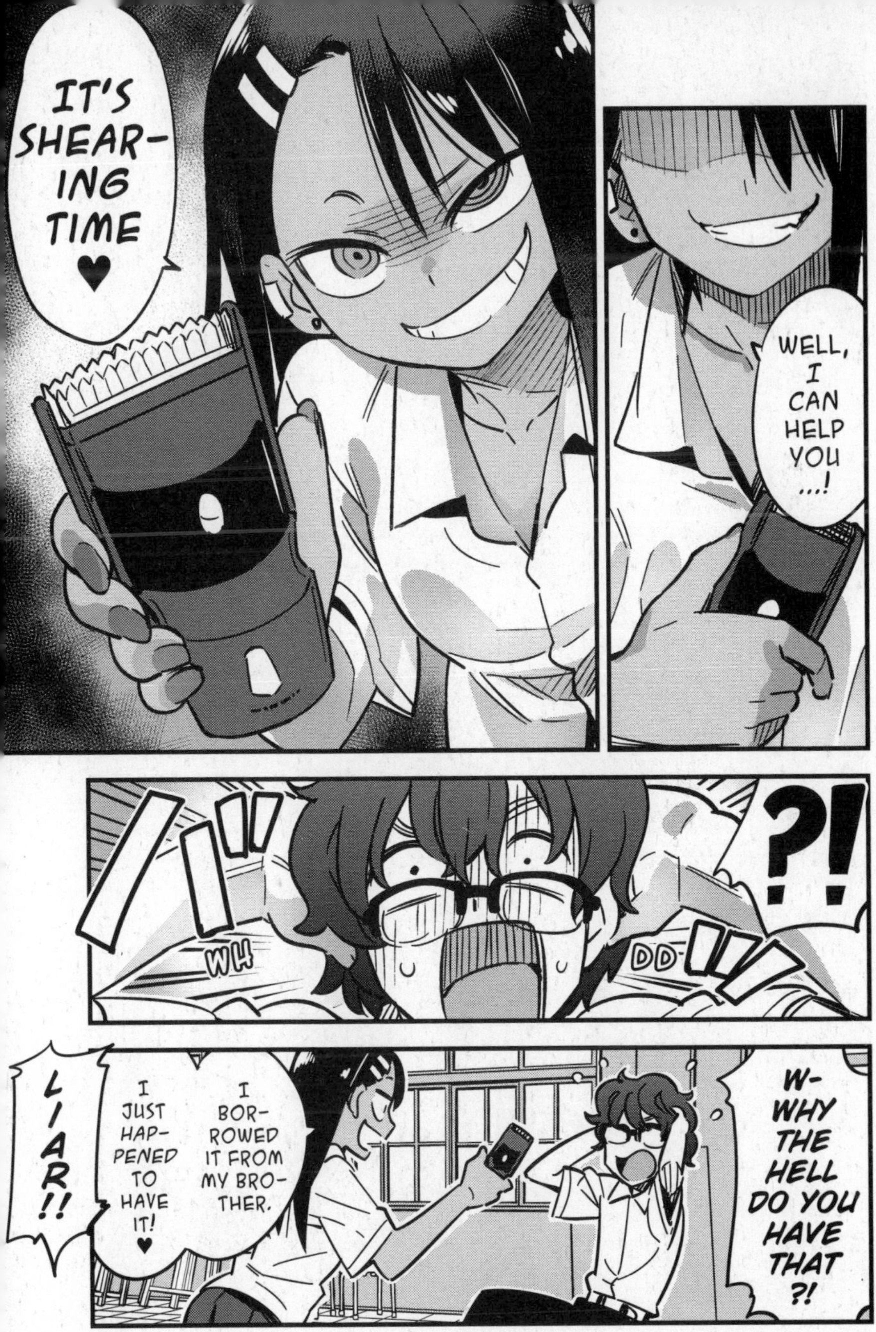
WELL, I CAN HELP YOU ...!
IT'S SHEAR-ING TIME ♥
?!
WH DD !!
W-WHY THE HELL DO YOU HAVE THAT?!
I BOR-ROWED IT FROM MY BRO-THER.
I JUST HAP-PENED TO HAVE IT! ♥
LIAR!!

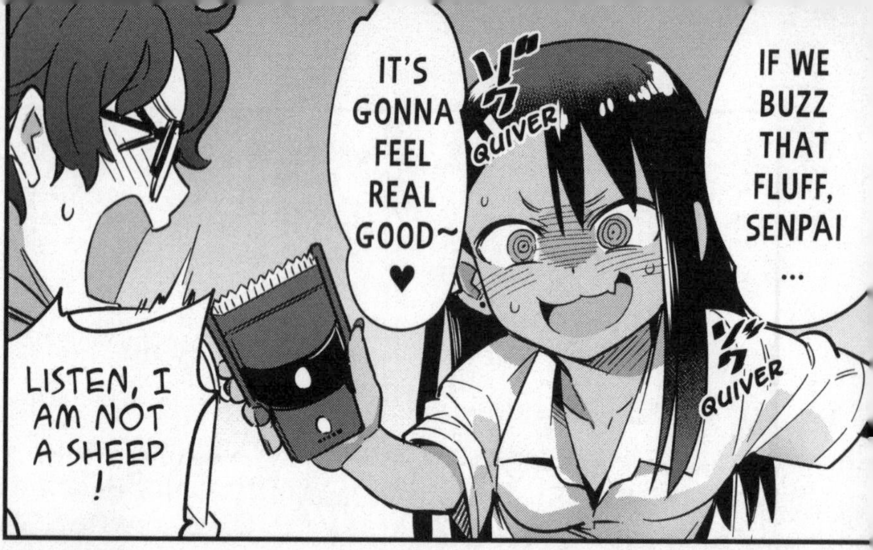
IF WE BUZZ THAT FLUFF, SENPAI...
QUIVER
IT'S GONNA FEEL REAL GOOD~ ♥
QUIVER
LISTEN, I AM NOT A SHEEP!

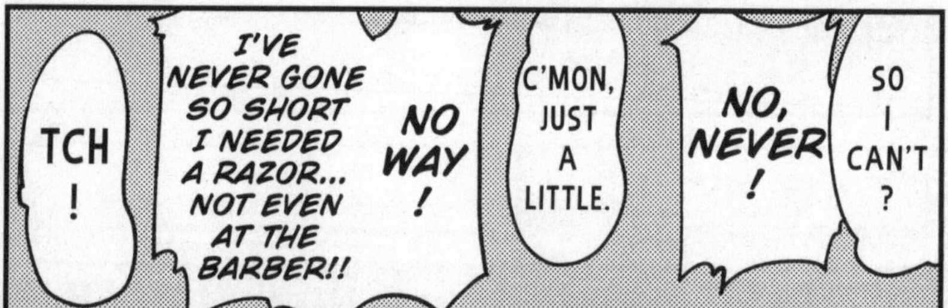
SO I CAN'T?
NO, NEVER!
C'MON, JUST A LITTLE.
NO WAY!
I'VE NEVER GONE SO SHORT I NEEDED A RAZOR... NOT EVEN AT THE BARBER!!
TCH!

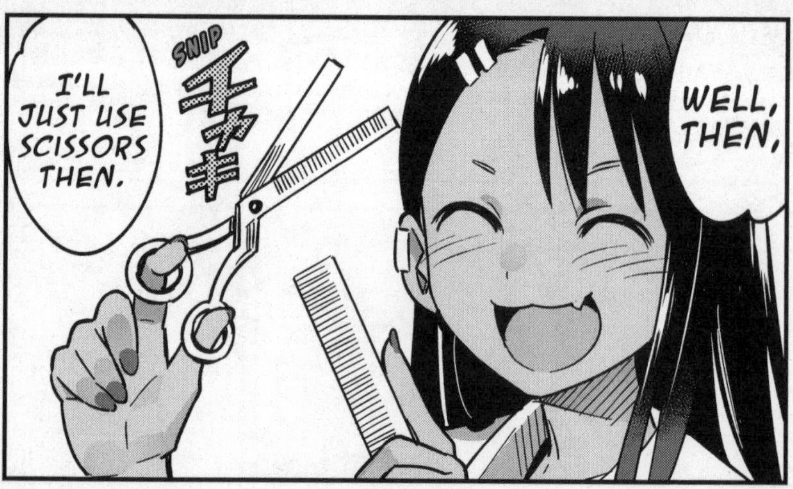
WELL, THEN,
SNIP
I'LL JUST USE SCISSORS THEN.

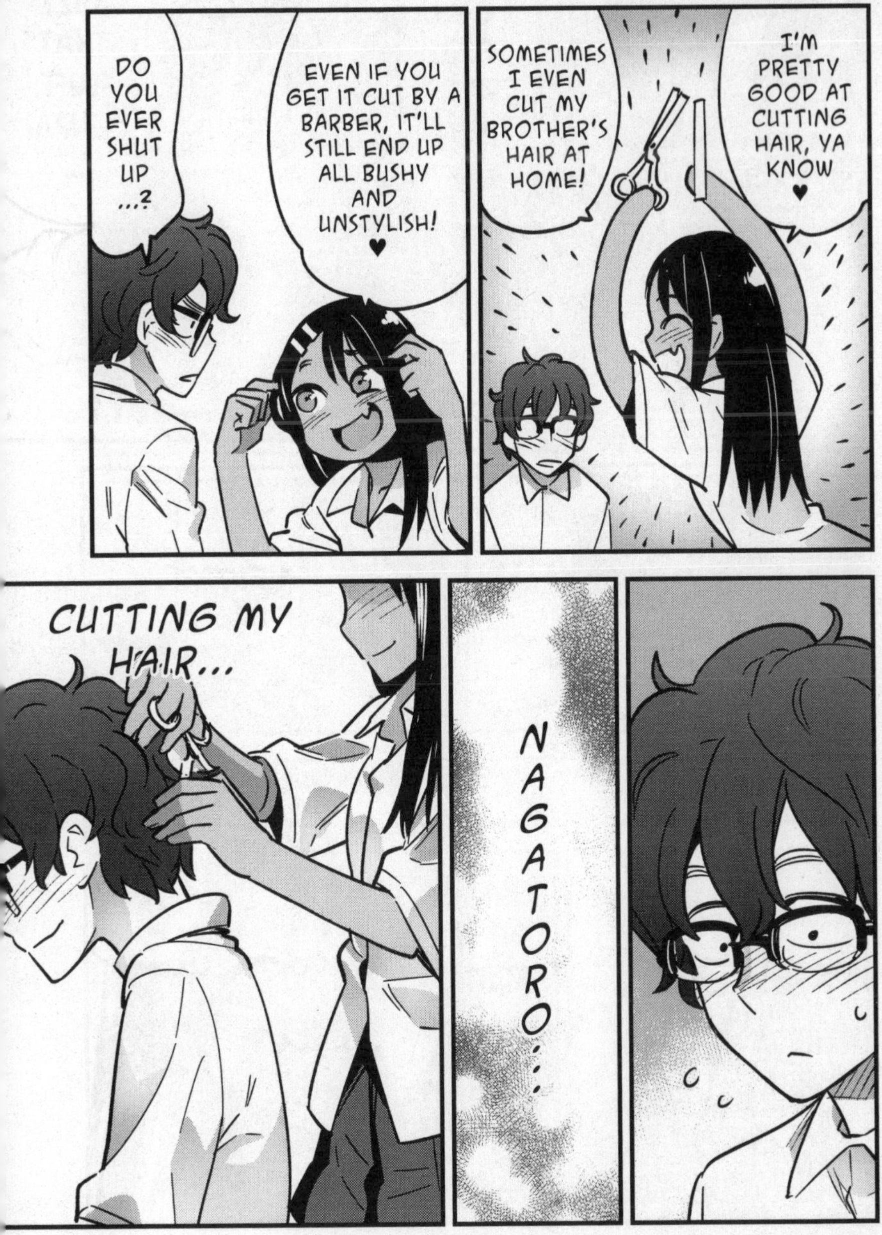
I'M PRETTY GOOD AT CUTTING HAIR, YA KNOW ♥
SOMETIMES I EVEN CUT MY BROTHER'S HAIR AT HOME!
EVEN IF YOU GET IT CUT BY A BARBER, IT'LL STILL END UP ALL BUSHY AND UNSTYLISH! ♥
DO YOU EVER SHUT UP ...?
NAGATORO...
CUTTING MY HAIR...

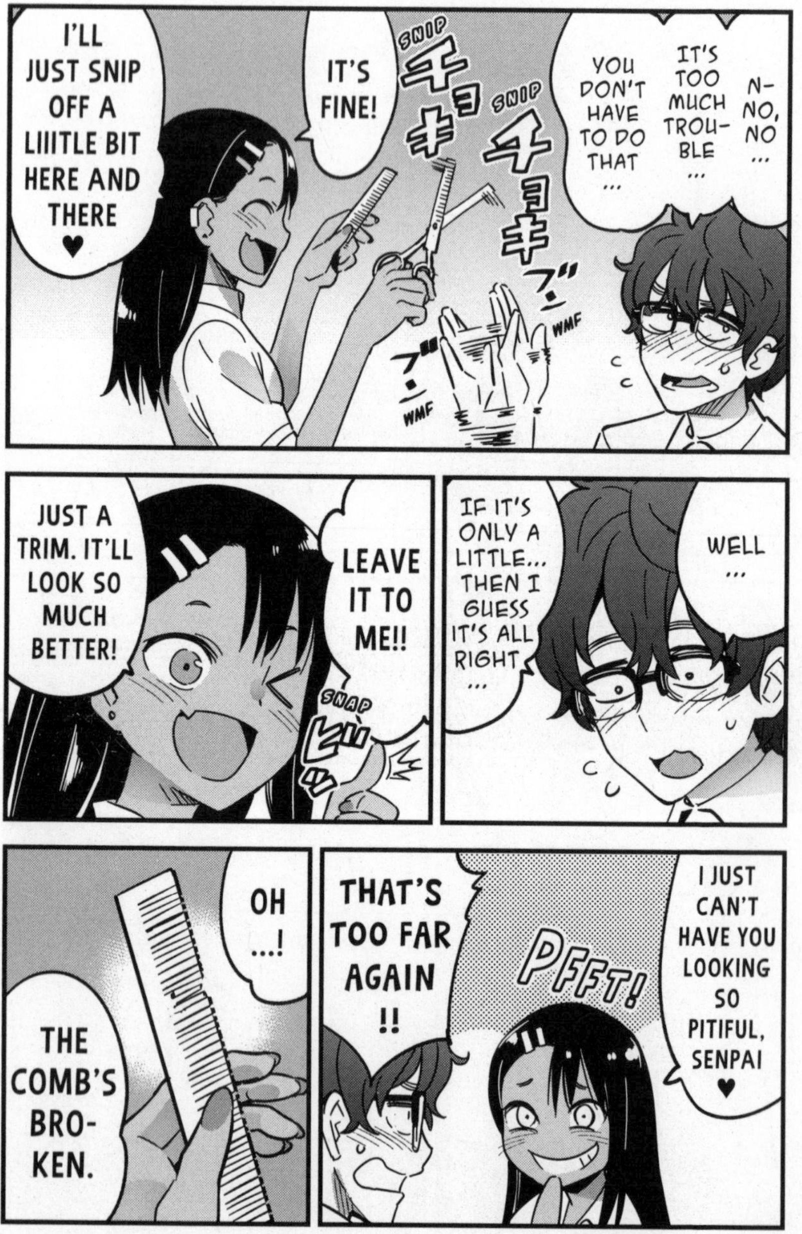
N-NO, NO ...
IT'S TOO MUCH TROU-BLE ...
YOU DON'T HAVE TO DO THAT ...
SNIP
SNIP
IT'S FINE!
I'LL JUST SNIP OFF A LIIITLE BIT HERE AND THERE ♥
WMF
WMF
WELL ...
IF IT'S ONLY A LITTLE... THEN I GUESS IT'S ALL RIGHT ...
LEAVE IT TO ME!!
JUST A TRIM. IT'LL LOOK SO MUCH BETTER!
SNAP
I JUST CAN'T HAVE YOU LOOKING SO PITIFUL, SENPAI ♥
PFFT!
THAT'S TOO FAR AGAIN !!
OH ...!
THE COMB'S BRO-KEN.

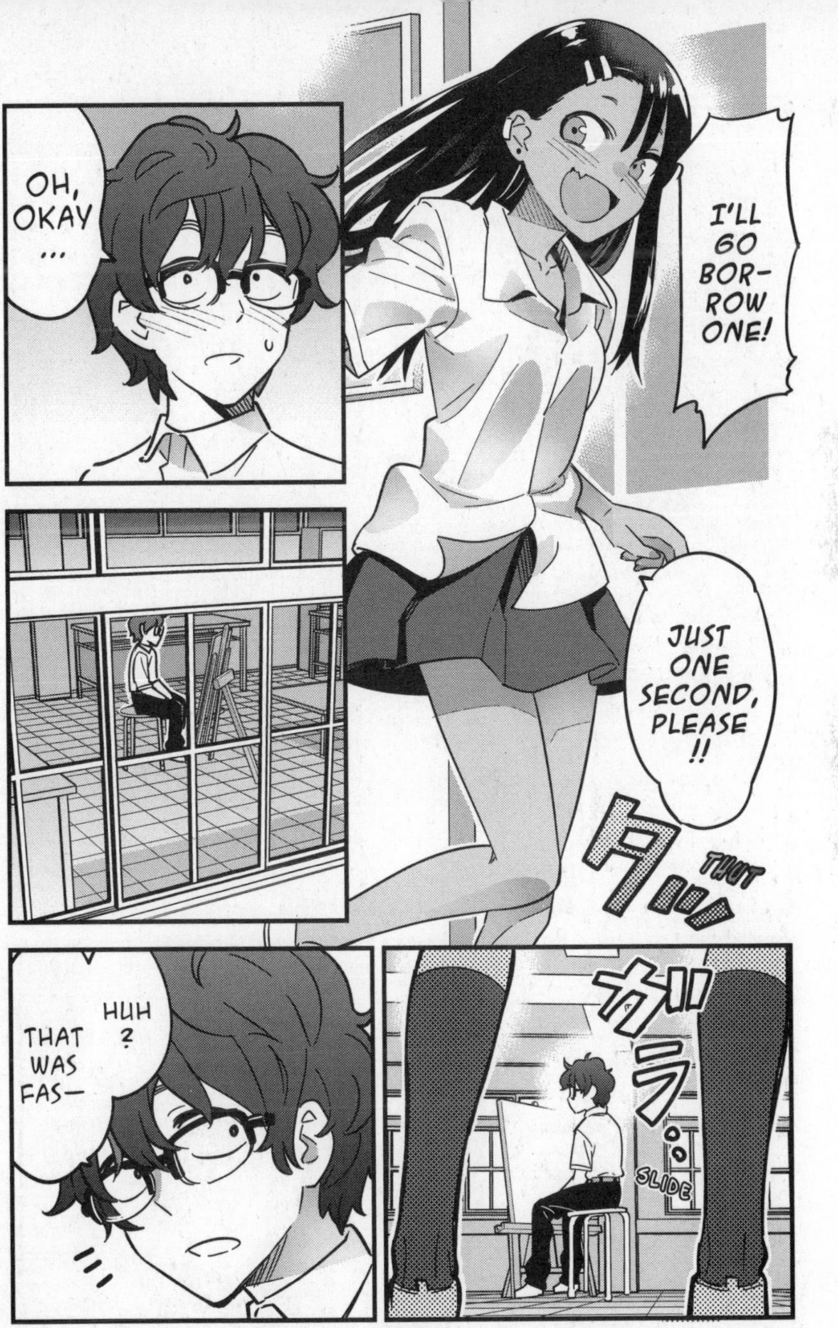
I'LL GO BORROW ONE!
JUST ONE SECOND, PLEASE !!
タッ
THUT
OH, OKAY ...
ガラ
SLIDE
HUH ?
THAT WAS FAS—

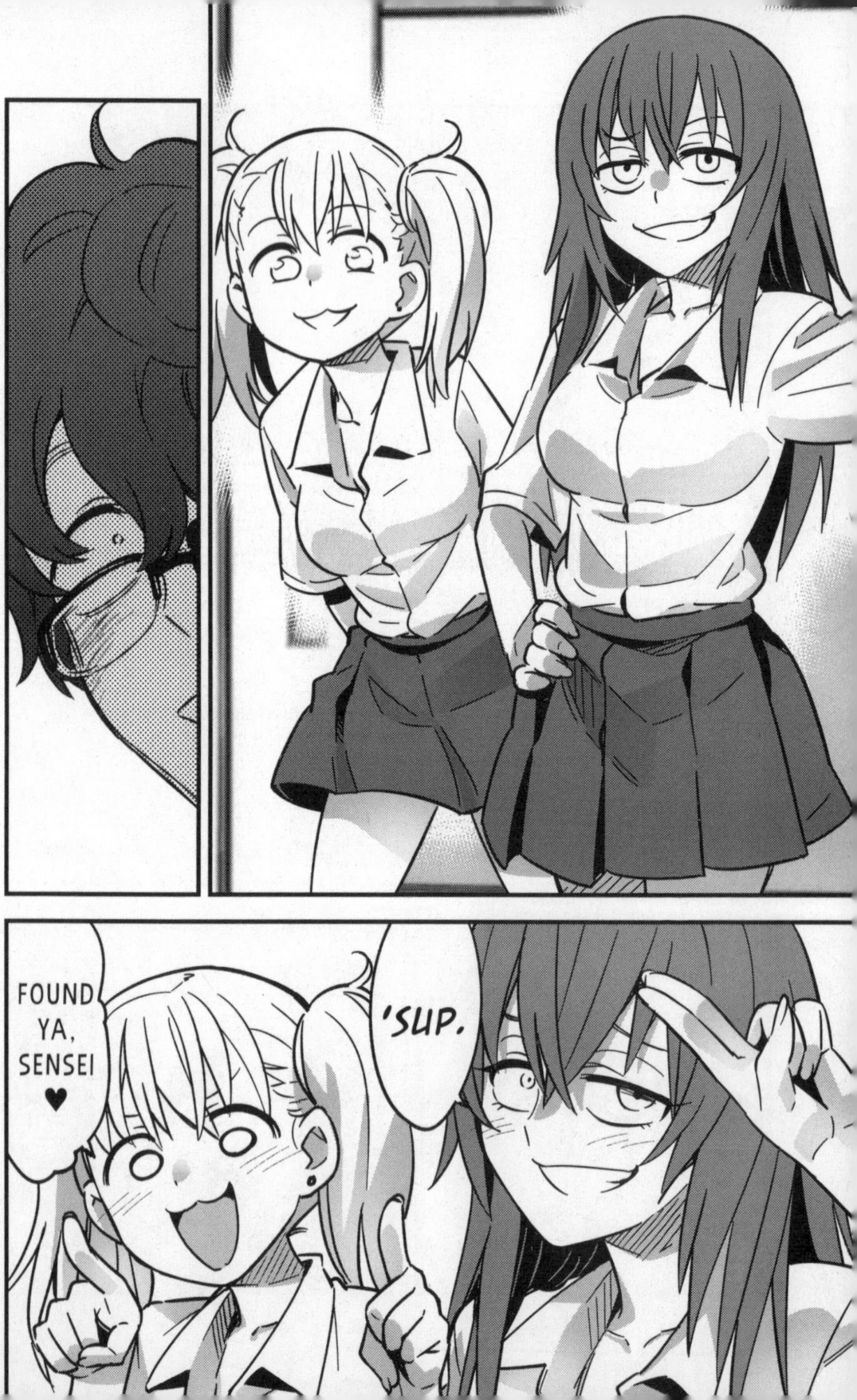
'SUP.
FOUND YA, SENSEI ♥

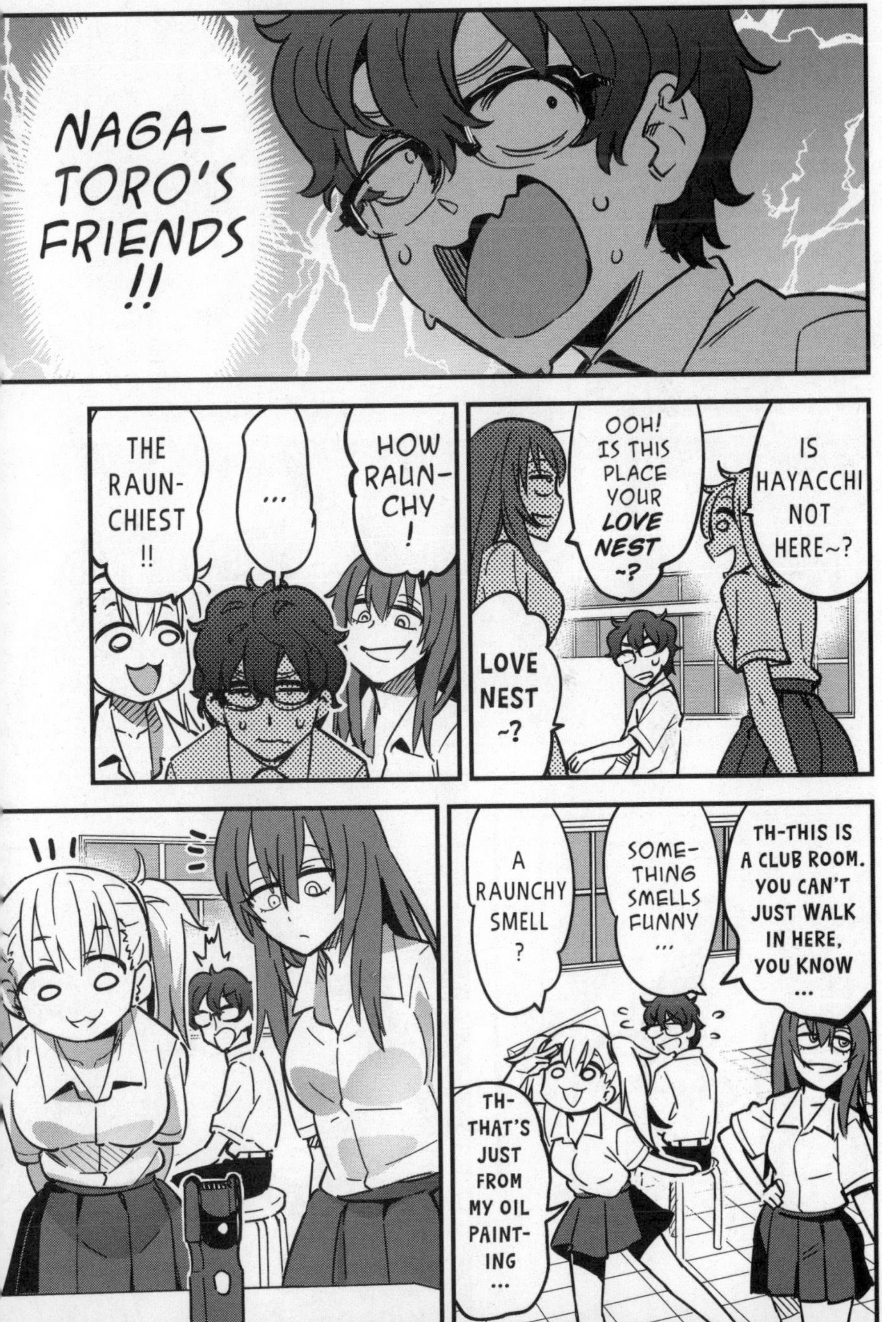
NAGA-TORO'S FRIENDS!!
IS HAYACCHI NOT HERE~?
OOH! IS THIS PLACE YOUR ***LOVE NEST*** ~?
LOVE NEST ~?
HOW RAUN-CHY!
...
THE RAUN-CHIEST!!
TH-THIS IS A CLUB ROOM. YOU CAN'T JUST WALK IN HERE, YOU KNOW...
SOME-THING SMELLS FUNNY...
A RAUNCHY SMELL?
TH-THAT'S JUST FROM MY OIL PAINT-ING...

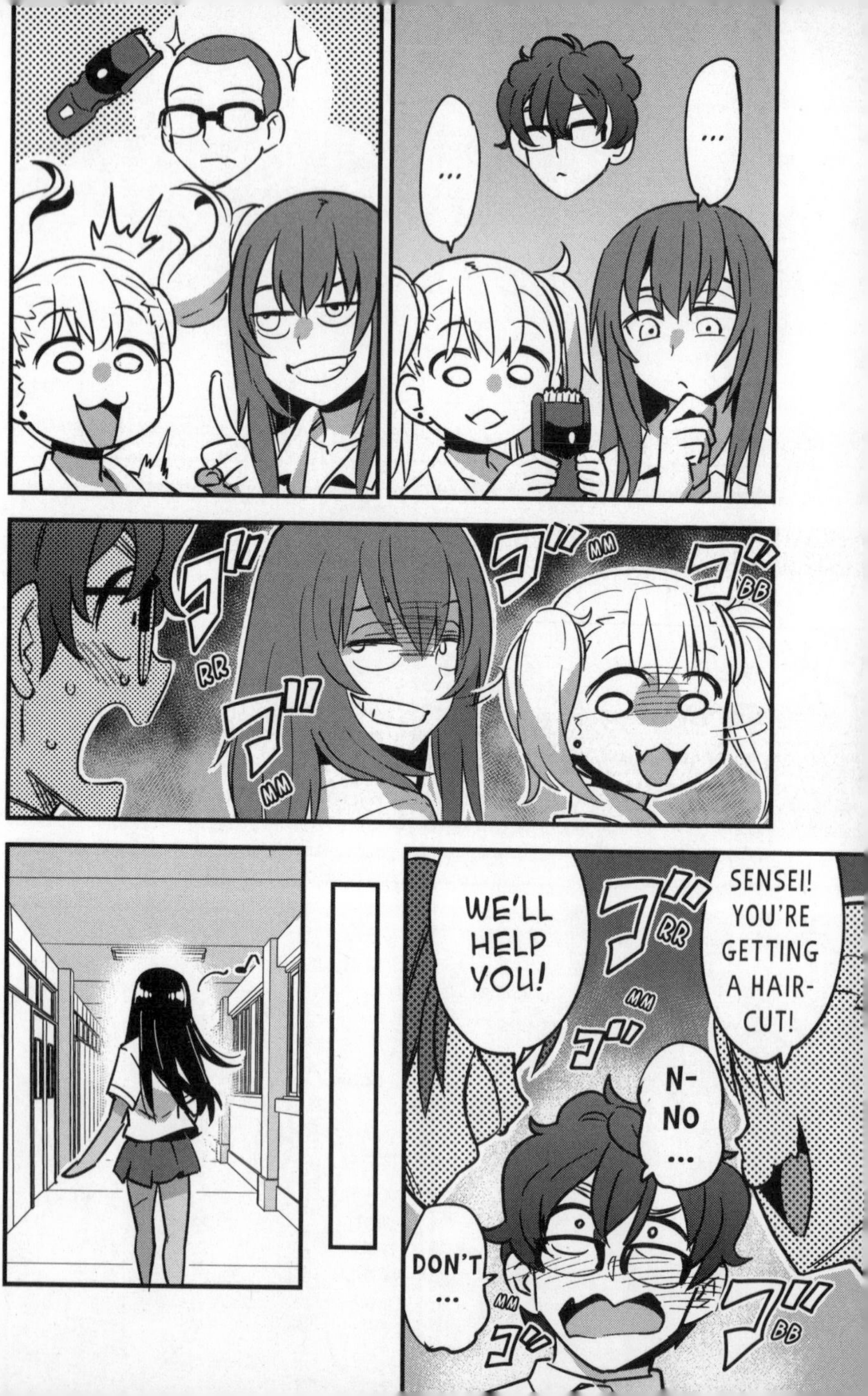
...
...
ゴゴ BB
ゴゴ MM
ゴゴ RR
ゴゴ MM
SENSEI! YOU'RE GETTING A HAIR-CUT!
WE'LL HELP YOU!
ゴゴ RR
ゴゴ MM
N-NO ...
ゴゴ BB
DON'T ...
ゴゴ MM

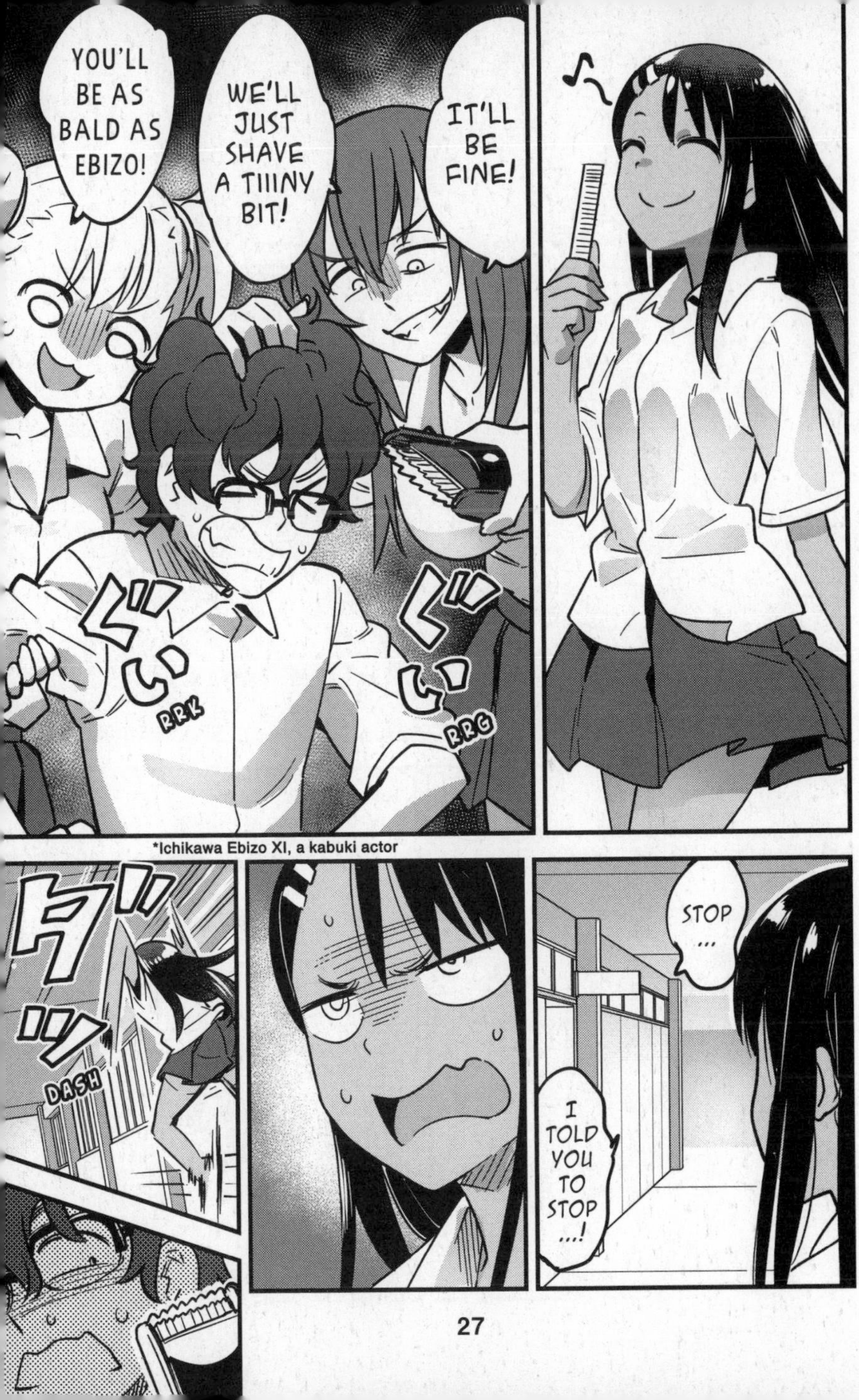
IT'LL BE FINE!
WE'LL JUST SHAVE A TIIINY BIT!
YOU'LL BE AS BALD AS EBIZO!
RRG
RRK
STOP ...
I TOLD YOU TO STOP ...!
DASH

*Ichikawa Ebizo XI, a kabuki actor

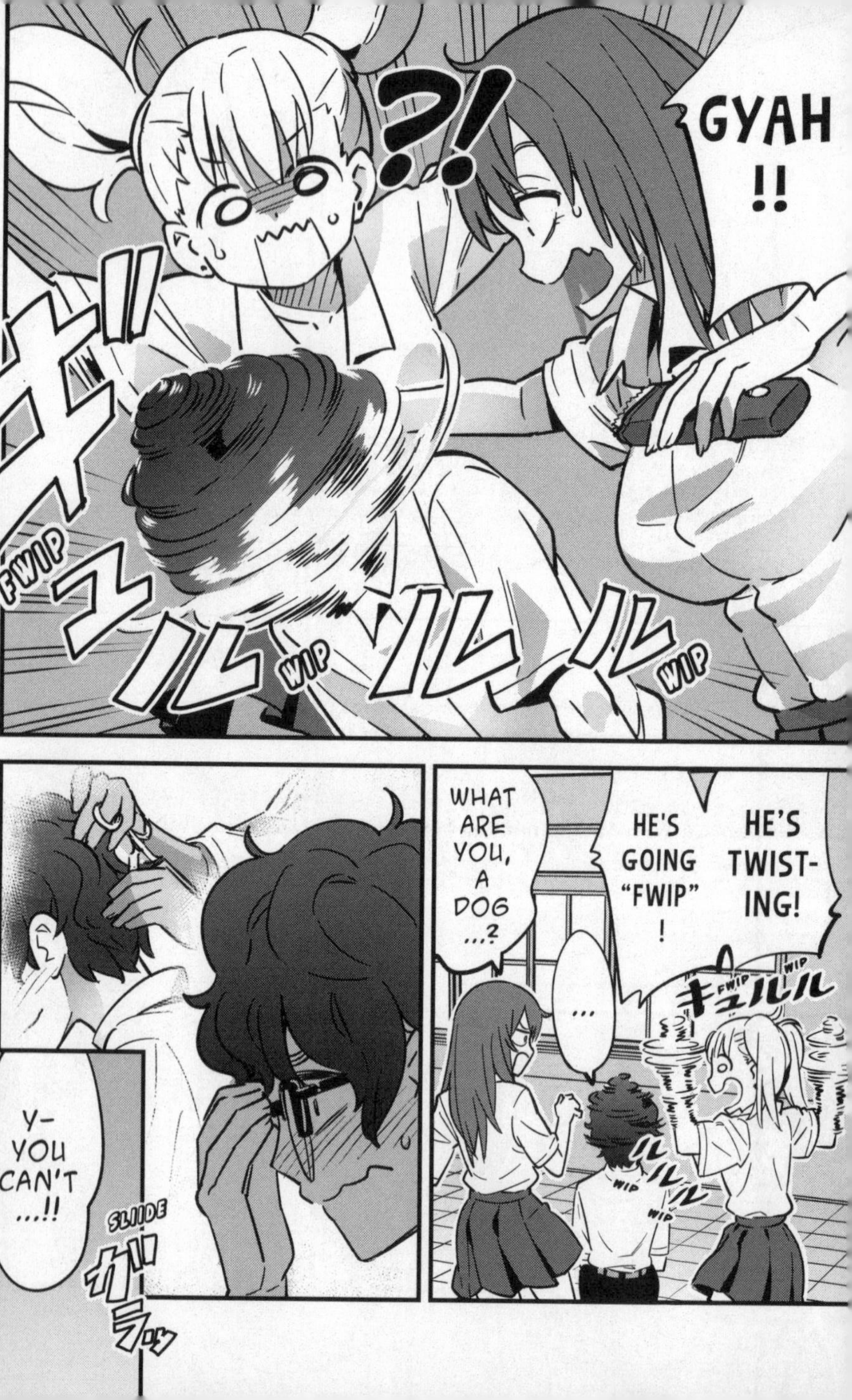
?!
GYAH !!
FWIP
WIP
WIP
HE'S TWIST-ING!
HE'S GOING "FWIP" !
WHAT ARE YOU, A DOG ...?
...
FWIP
WIP
WIP
WIP
Y-YOU CAN'T ...!!
SLIIDE

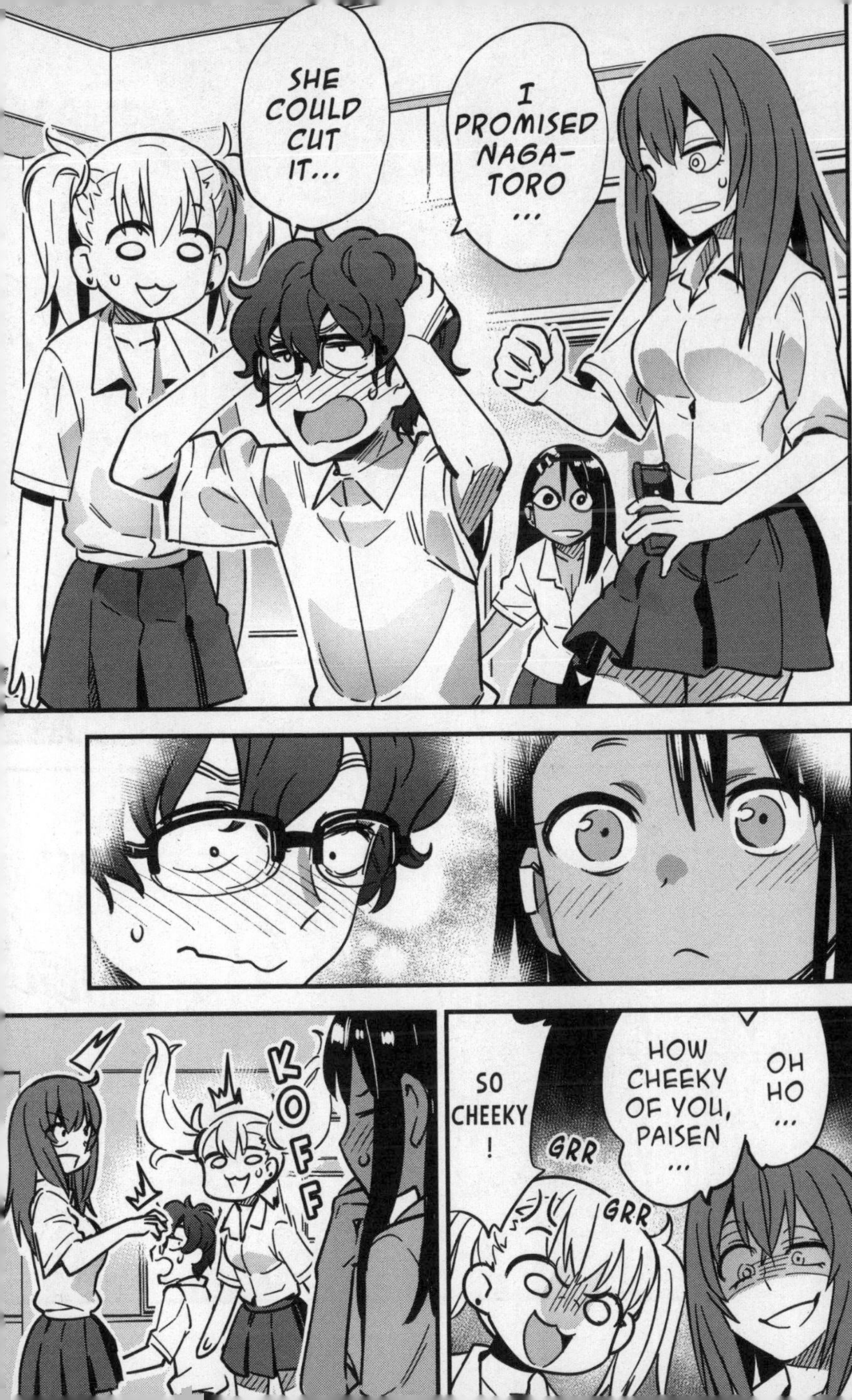
I PROMISED NAGA-TORO ...
SHE COULD CUT IT...
OH HO ...
HOW CHEEKY OF YOU, PAISEN ...
SO CHEEKY !
GRR
GRR
KOFF

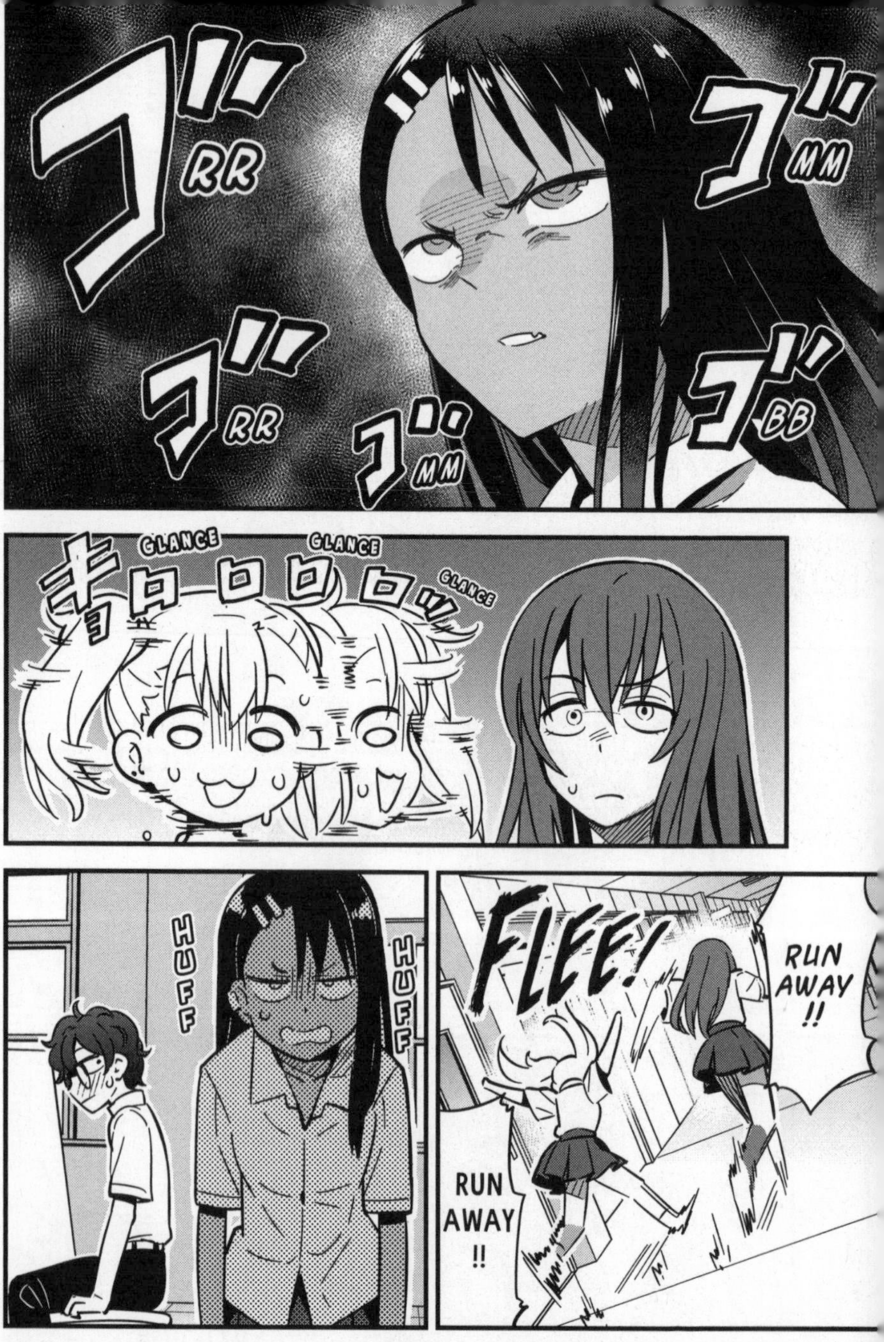
ゴMM
ゴRR
ゴBB
ゴMM
ゴRR
キョロロロロッ
GLANCE
GLANCE
GLANCE
RUN AWAY !!
FLEE!
RUN AWAY !!
HUFF
HUFF

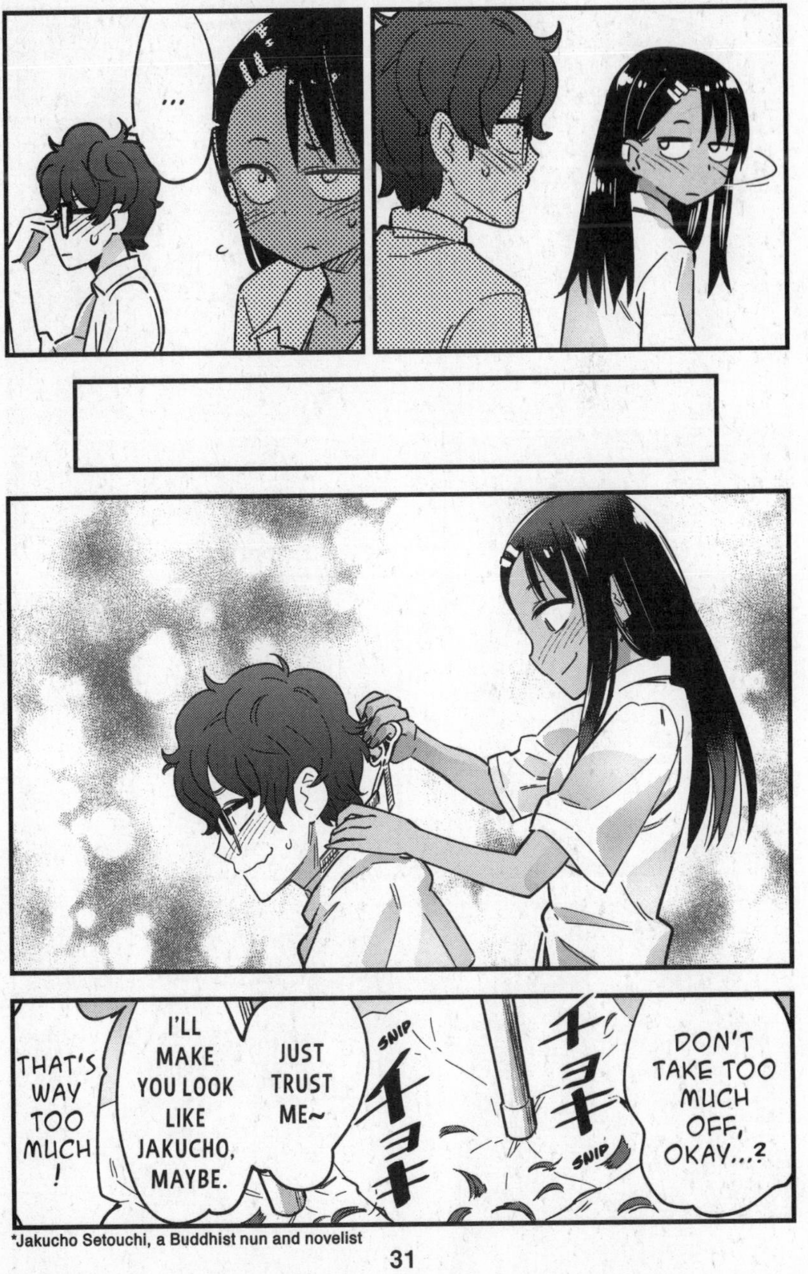
...
DON'T TAKE TOO MUCH OFF, OKAY...?
SNIP
チョキ
SNIP
チョキ
JUST TRUST ME~
I'LL MAKE YOU LOOK LIKE JAKUCHO, MAYBE.
THAT'S WAY TOO MUCH!

*Jakucho Setouchi, a Buddhist nun and novelist

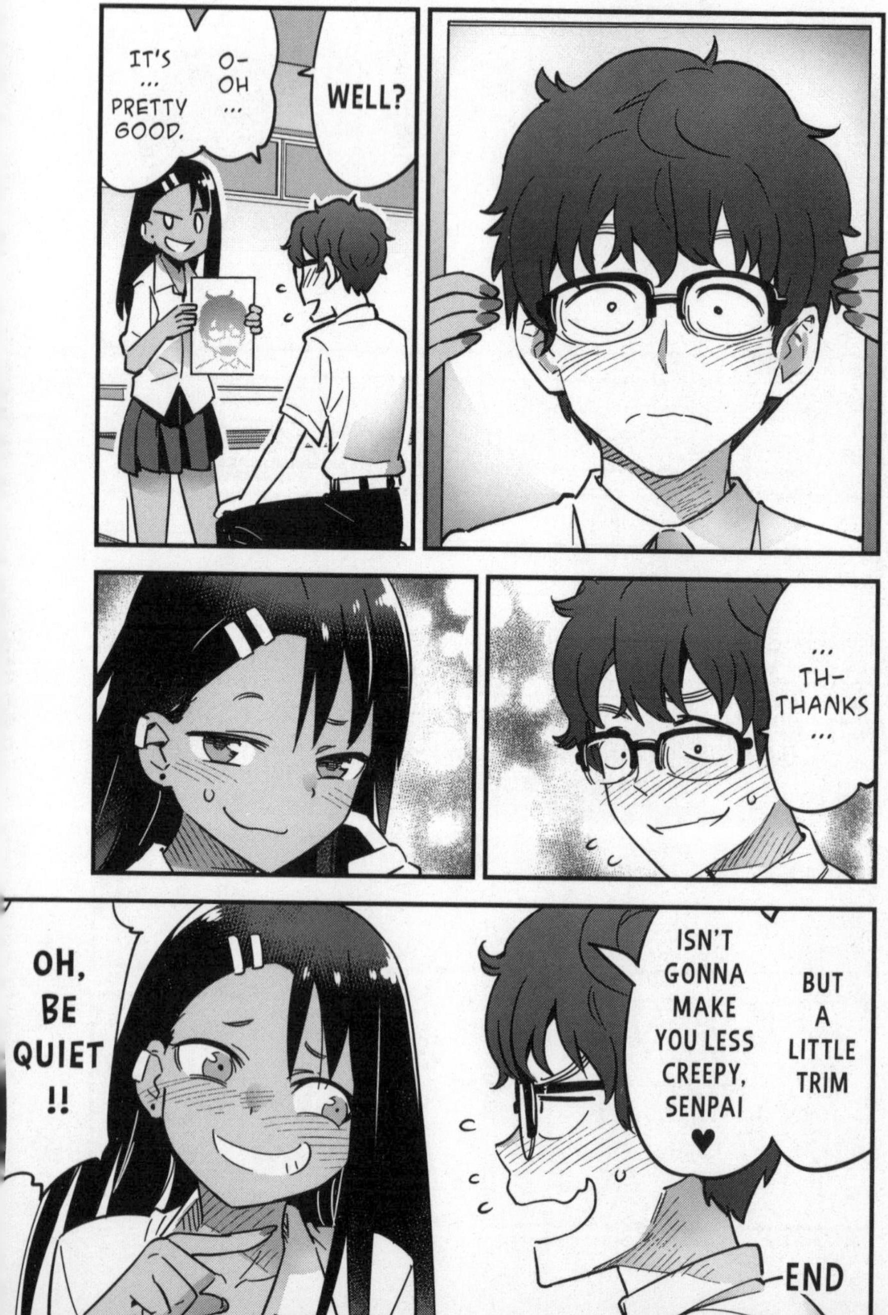
WELL?
O-OH ...
IT'S ... PRETTY GOOD.
... TH-THANKS ...
BUT A LITTLE TRIM
ISN'T GONNA MAKE YOU LESS CREEPY, SENPAI ♥
OH, BE QUIET !!
END

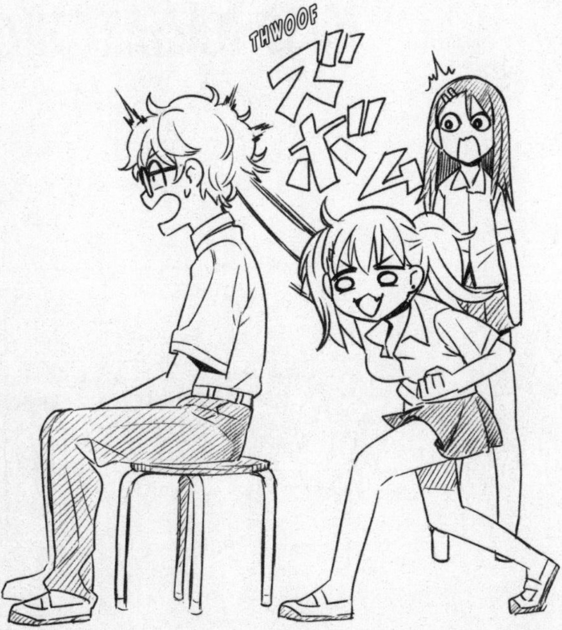
THWOOF
ズボム

DON'T TOY WITH ME,
MISS NAGATORO

Chapter 17: Say, Senpai

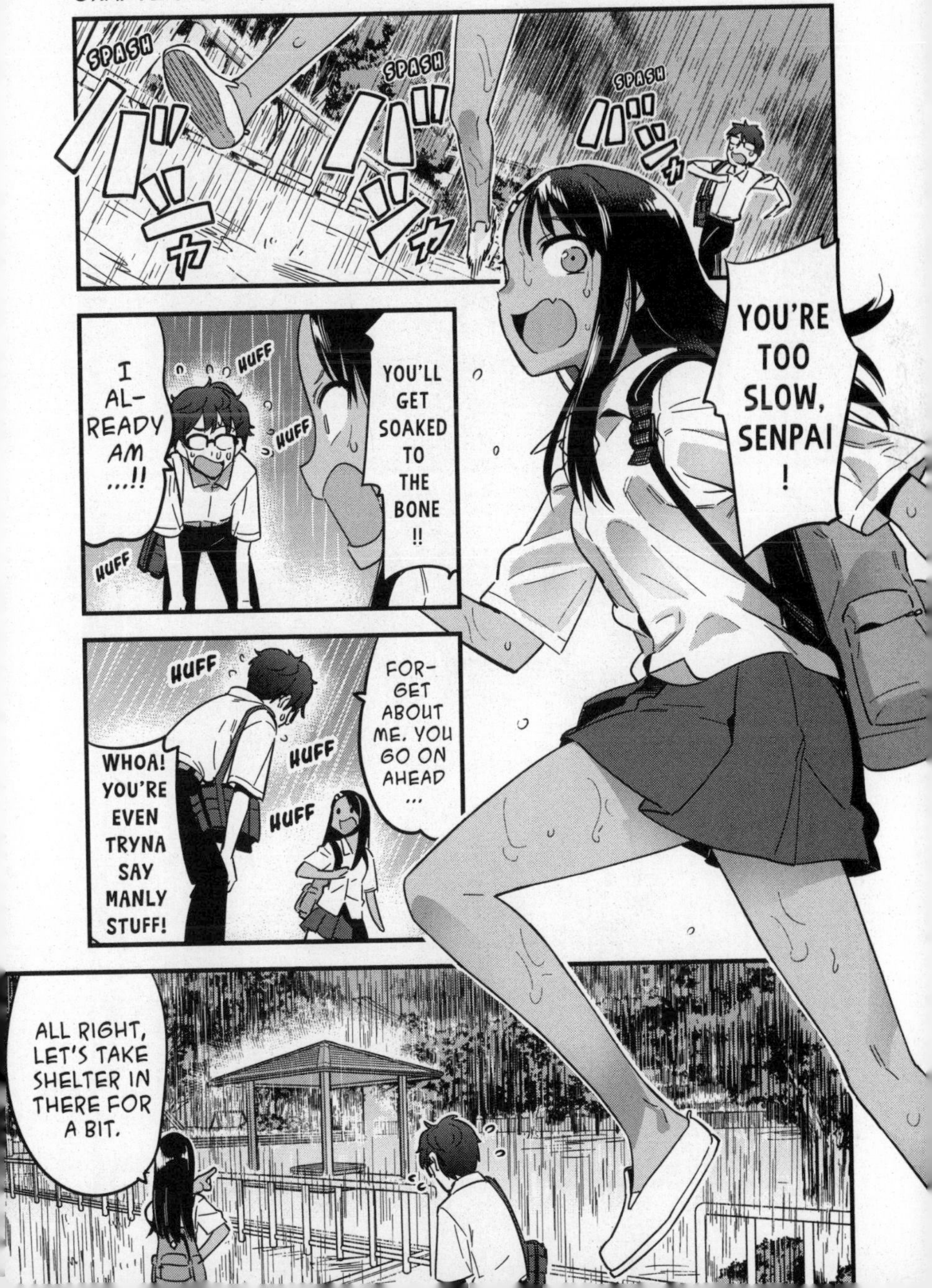
SPASH
SPASH
SPASH
YOU'RE TOO SLOW, SENPAI!
YOU'LL GET SOAKED TO THE BONE!!
HUFF
HUFF
I AL-READY AM ...!!
HUFF
FOR-GET ABOUT ME. YOU GO ON AHEAD ...
HUFF
HUFF
WHOA! YOU'RE EVEN TRYNA SAY MANLY STUFF!
HUFF
ALL RIGHT, LET'S TAKE SHELTER IN THERE FOR A BIT.

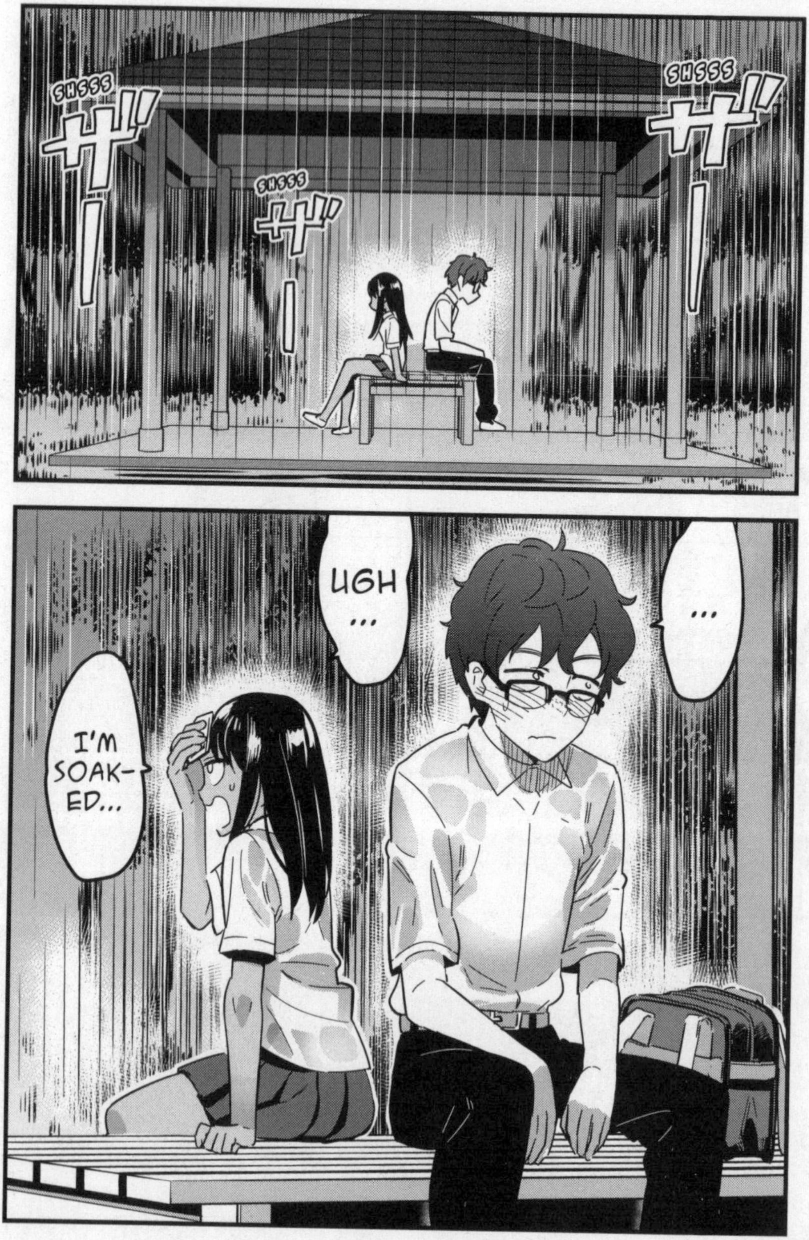
SHSSS
SHSSS
SHSSS
...
UGH ...
I'M SOAK-ED...

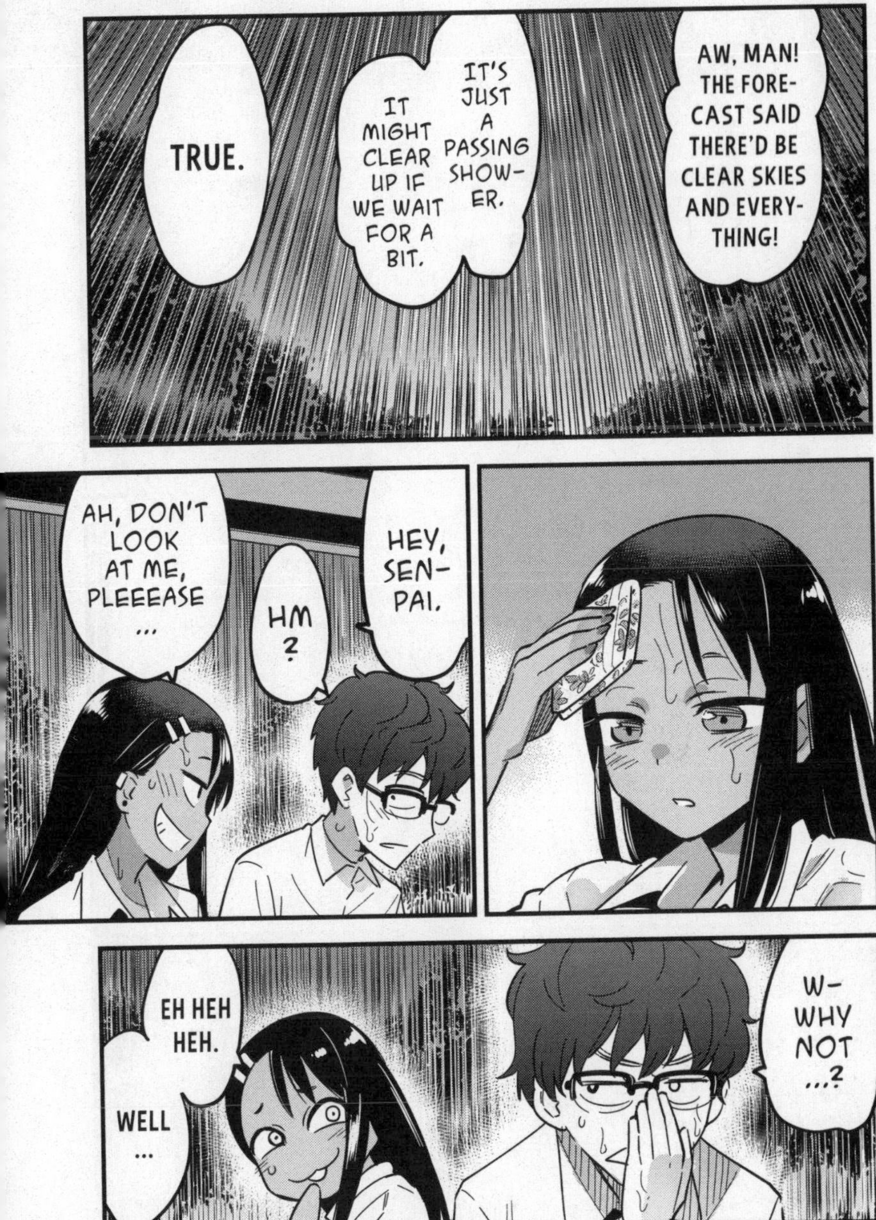
AW, MAN! THE FORE-CAST SAID THERE'D BE CLEAR SKIES AND EVERY-THING!
IT'S JUST A PASSING SHOW-ER.
IT MIGHT CLEAR UP IF WE WAIT FOR A BIT.
TRUE.
HEY, SEN-PAI.
HM?
AH, DON'T LOOK AT ME, PLEEEASE ...
W-WHY NOT ...?
EH HEH HEH.
WELL ...

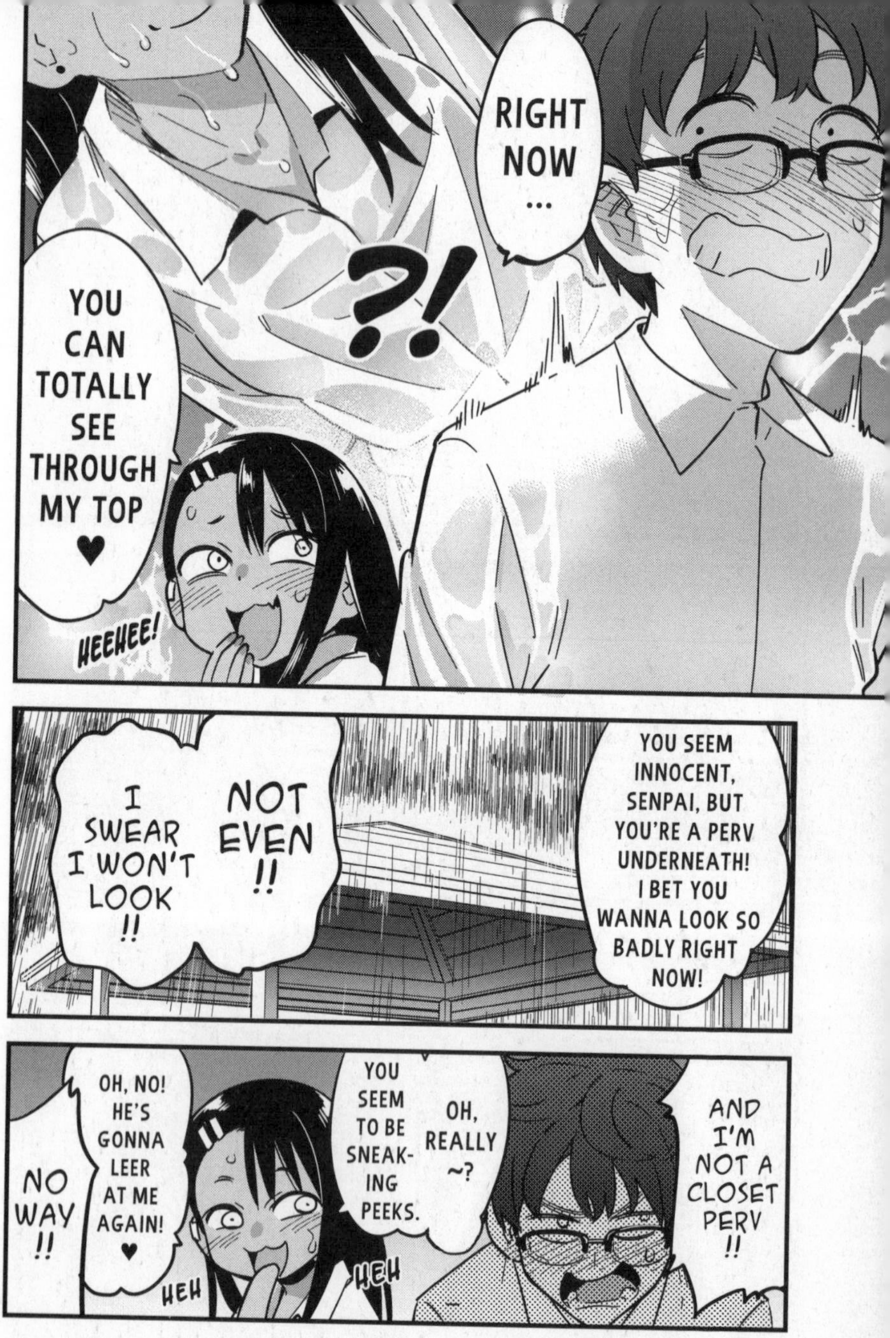

RIGHT NOW ...
?!
YOU CAN TOTALLY SEE THROUGH MY TOP ♥
HEEHEE!
YOU SEEM INNOCENT, SENPAI, BUT YOU'RE A PERV UNDERNEATH! I BET YOU WANNA LOOK SO BADLY RIGHT NOW!
NOT EVEN !!
I SWEAR I WON'T LOOK !!
AND I'M NOT A CLOSET PERV !!
OH, REALLY ~?
YOU SEEM TO BE SNEAK-ING PEEKS.
HEH
OH, NO! HE'S GONNA LEER AT ME AGAIN! ♥
HEH
NO WAY !!

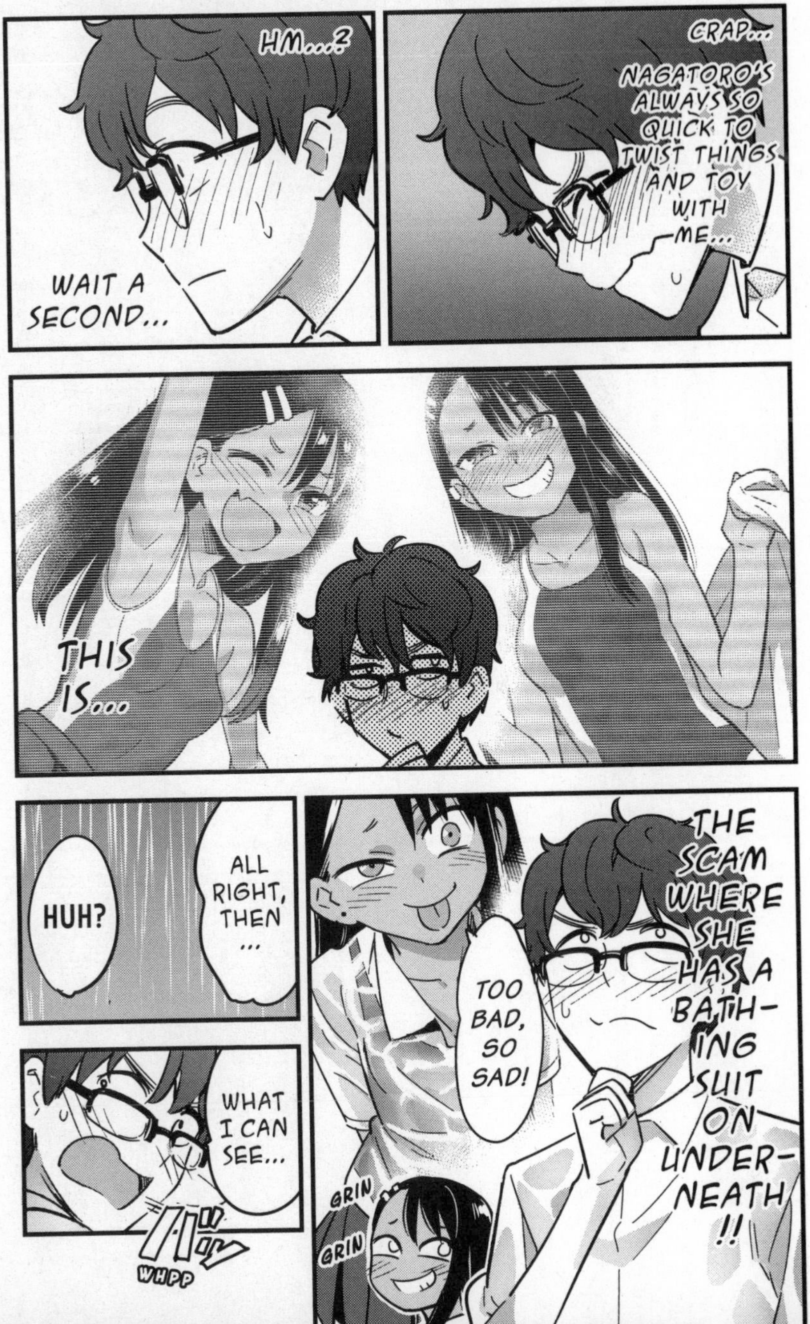
CRAP...
NAGATORO'S ALWAYS SO QUICK TO TWIST THINGS AND TOY WITH ME...
HM...?
WAIT A SECOND...
THIS IS...
THE SCAM WHERE SHE HAS A BATHING-SUIT ON UNDER-NEATH!!
TOO BAD, SO SAD!
GRIN
GRIN
ALL RIGHT, THEN ...
HUH?
WHAT I CAN SEE...
WHPP

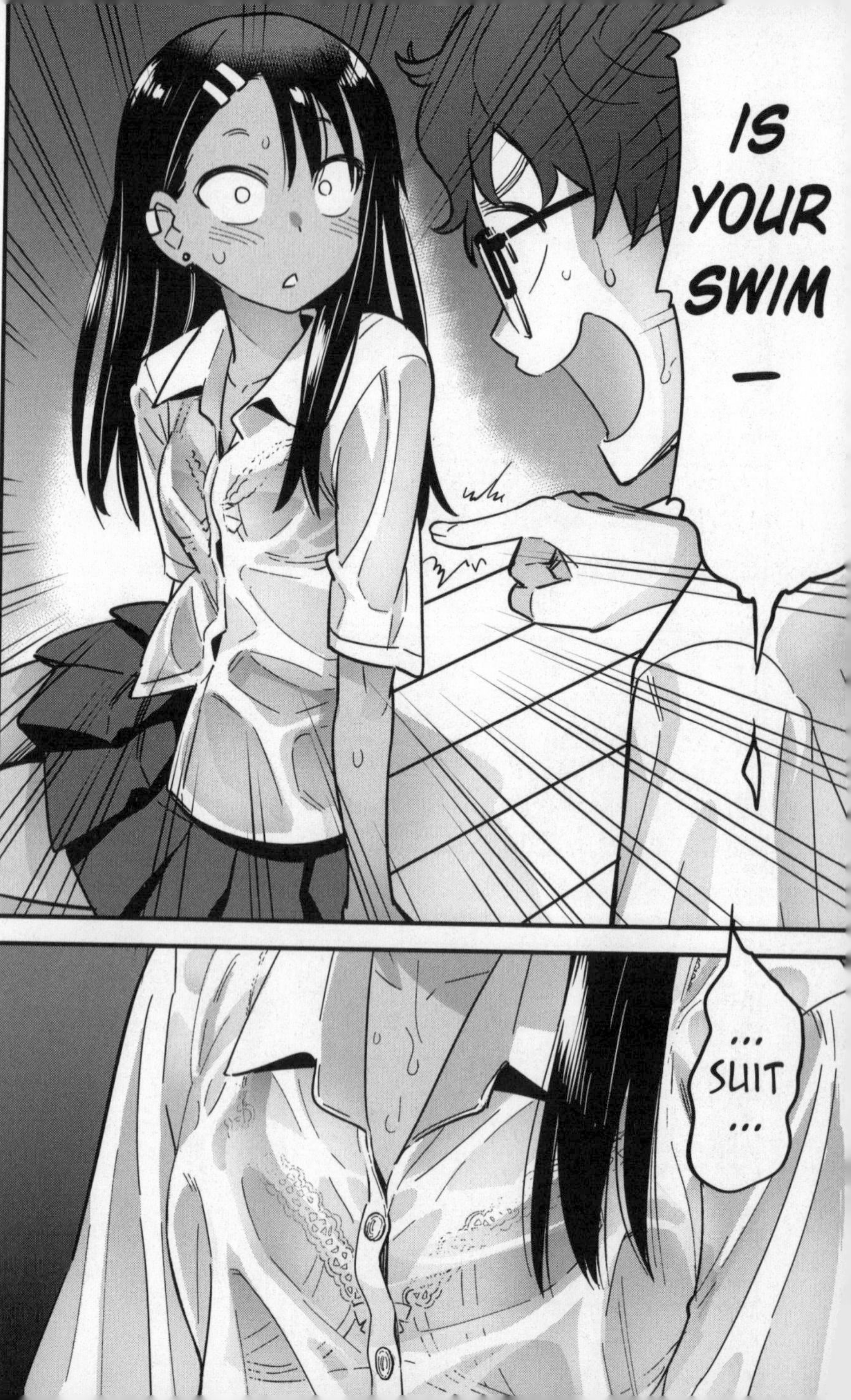
IS YOUR SWIM —
... SUIT ...

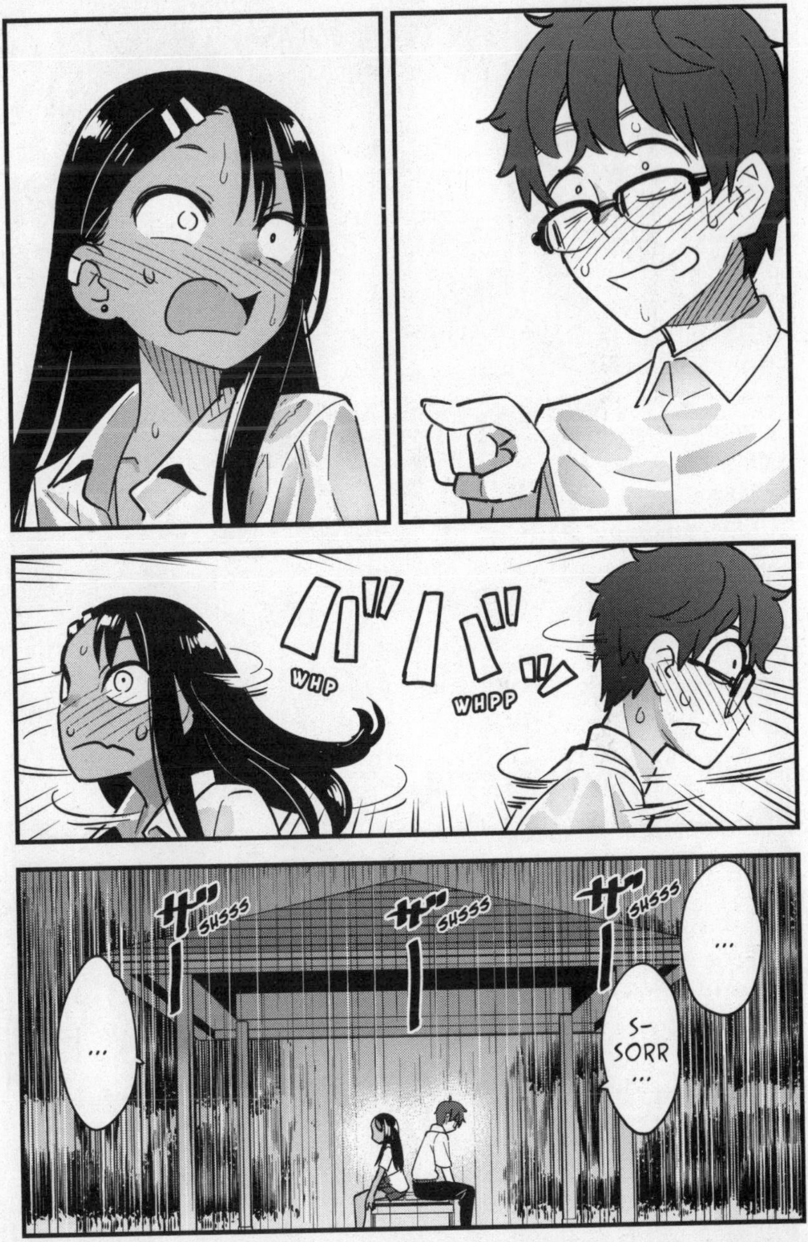
WHPP
WHP
SHSSS
SHSSS
SHSSS
...
S-SORR...
...

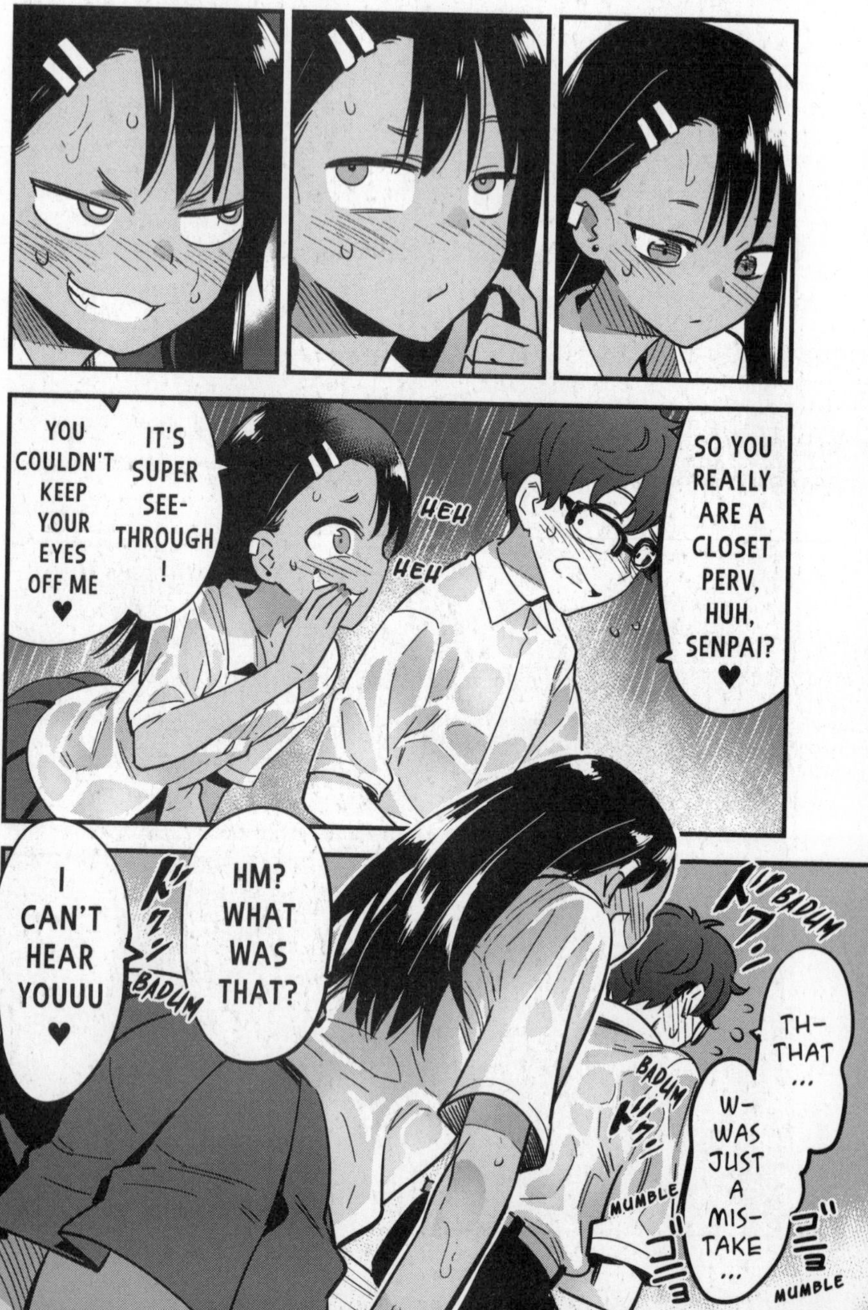
SO YOU REALLY ARE A CLOSET PERV, HUH, SENPAI? ♥
HEH HEH
IT'S SUPER SEE-THROUGH!
YOU COULDN'T KEEP YOUR EYES OFF ME ♥
BADUM
TH-THAT... W-WAS JUST A MIS-TAKE...
MUMBLE
MUMBLE
BADUM
HM? WHAT WAS THAT?
BADUM
I CAN'T HEAR YOUUU ♥

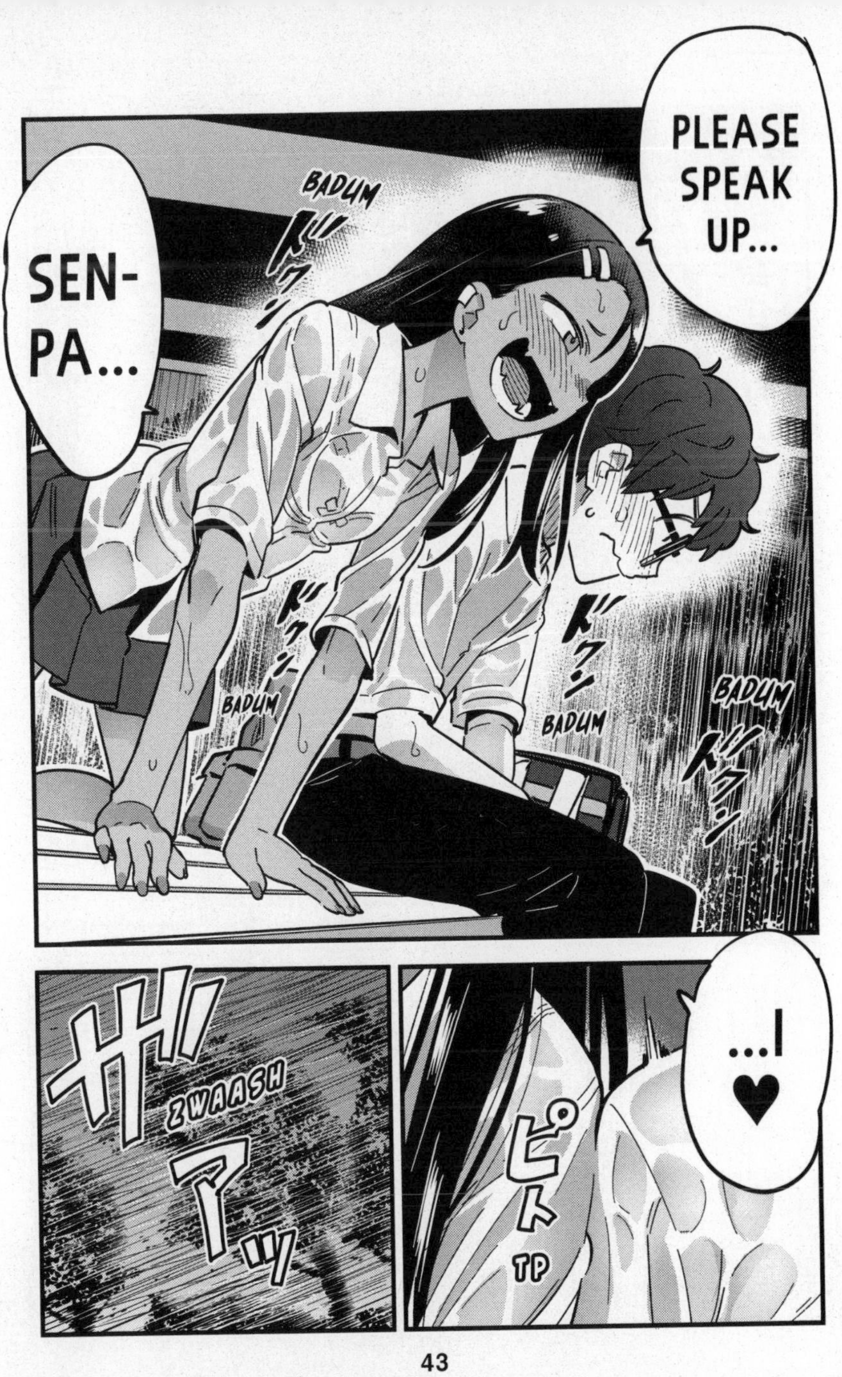
PLEASE SPEAK UP...
BADUM
BADUM
BADUM
SEN-PA...
BADUM
...I ♥
TP
ZWAASH

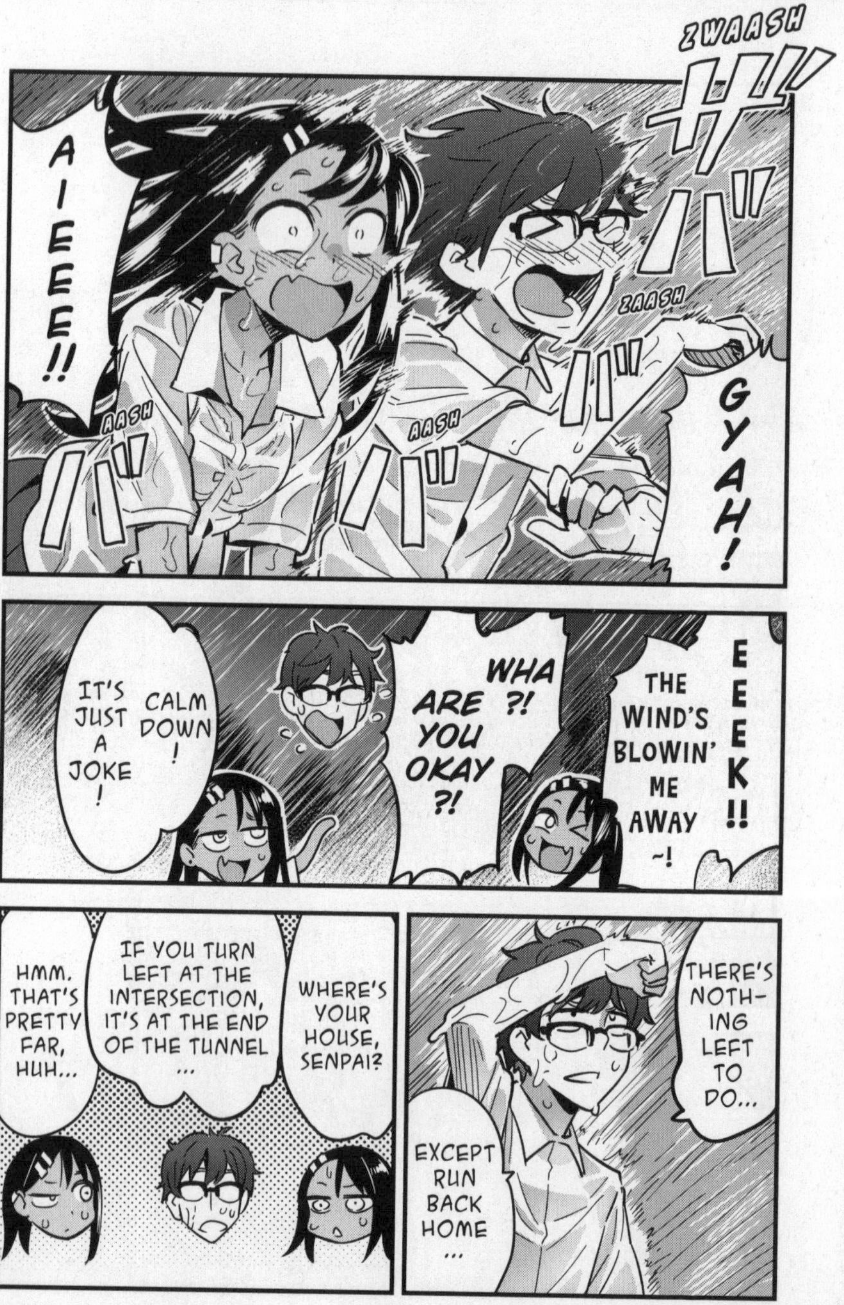
ZWAASH
ZAASH
GYAH!
AIEEE!!
AASH
AASH
EEEK!!
THE WIND'S BLOWIN' ME AWAY ~!
WHA ?!
ARE YOU OKAY ?!
CALM DOWN!
IT'S JUST A JOKE!
THERE'S NOTH-ING LEFT TO DO...
EXCEPT RUN BACK HOME...
WHERE'S YOUR HOUSE, SENPAI?
IF YOU TURN LEFT AT THE INTERSECTION, IT'S AT THE END OF THE TUNNEL...
HMM. THAT'S PRETTY FAR, HUH...

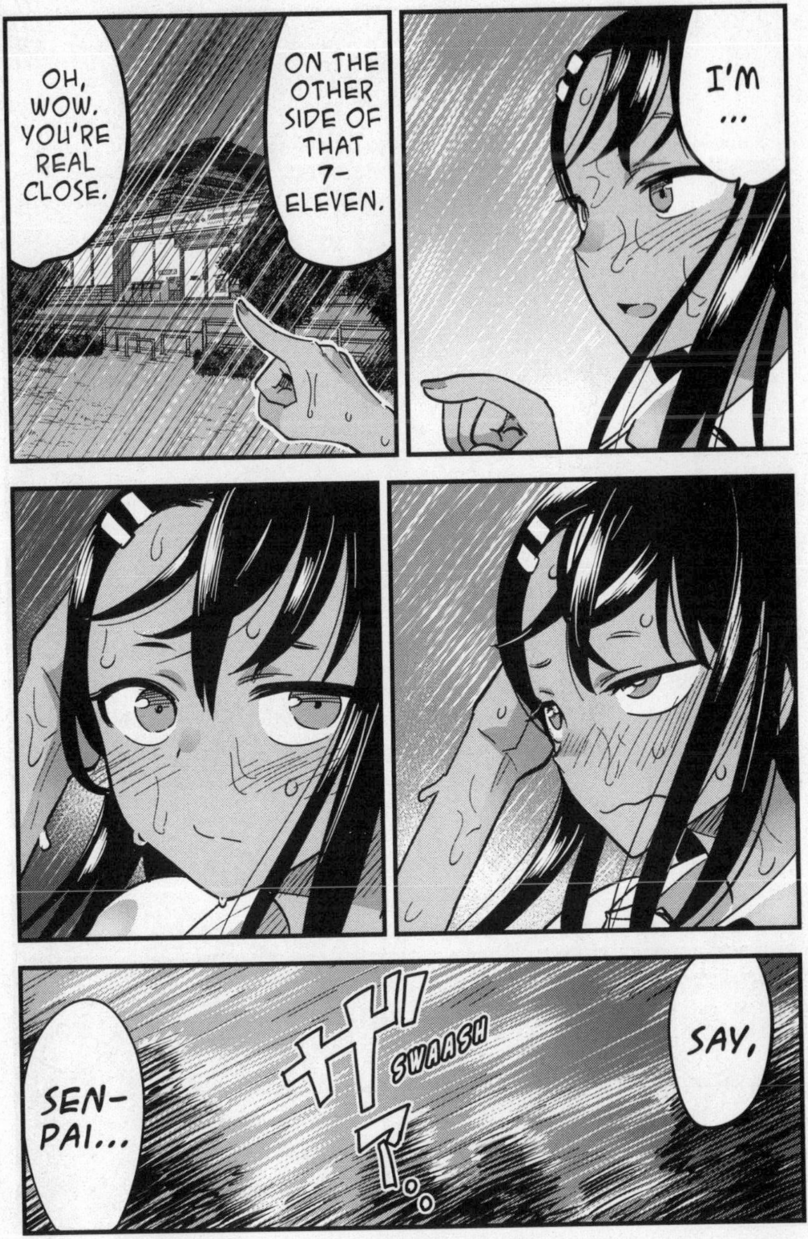
I'M ...
ON THE OTHER SIDE OF THAT 7-ELEVEN.
OH, WOW. YOU'RE REAL CLOSE.
SAY,
SWAASH
SEN-PAI...

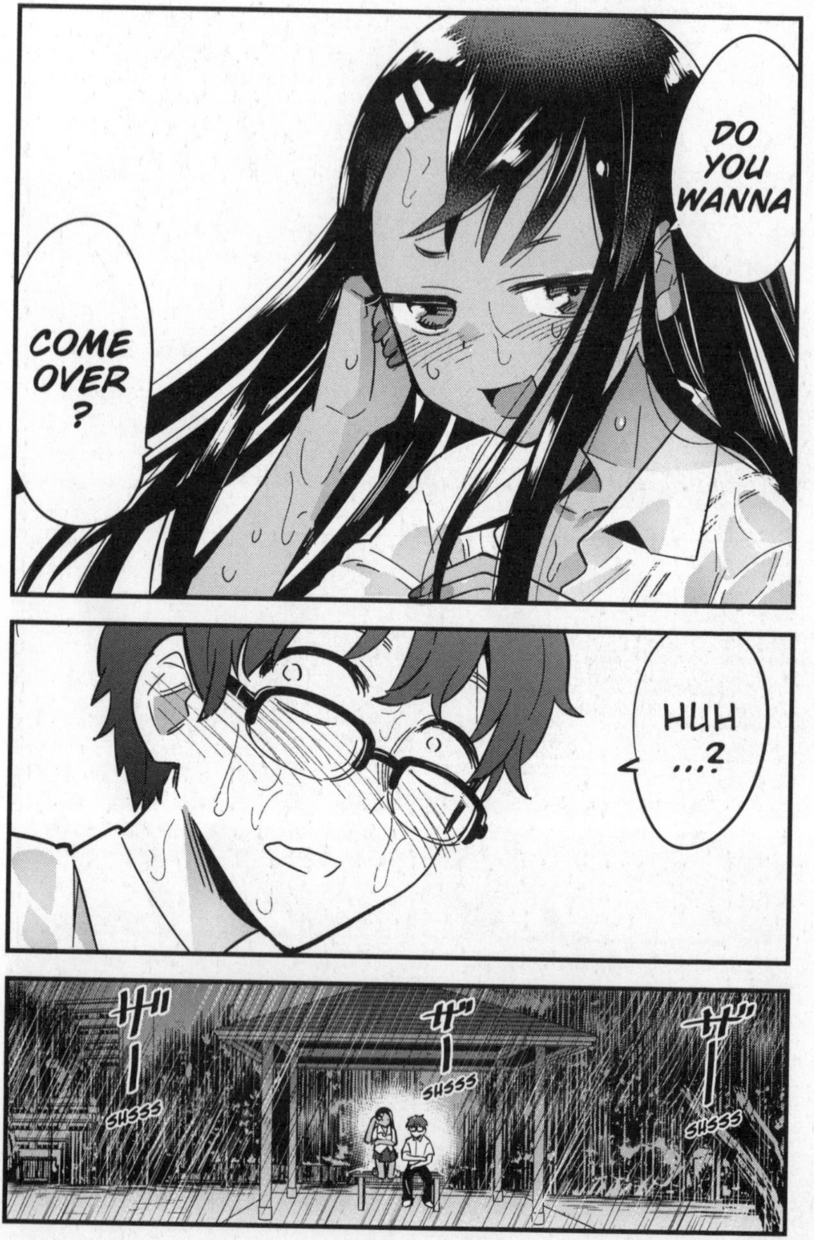
DO YOU WANNA
COME OVER ?
HUH ...?
ザー
SHSSS
ザー
SHSSS
ザー
SHSSS

DON'T TOY WITH ME, MISS NAGATORO

Chapter 18: Let's Do It Again Sometime, Senpai

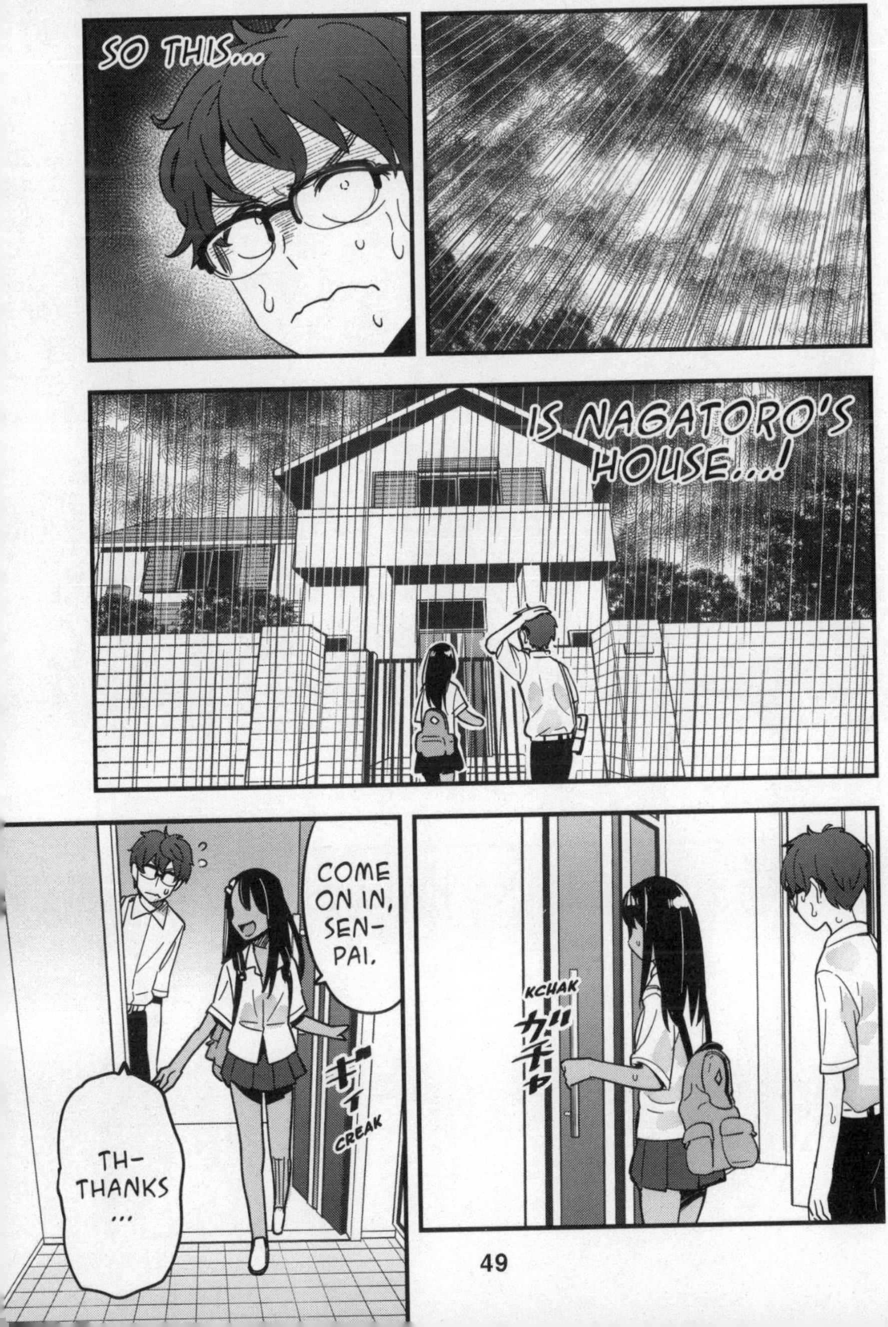
SO THIS...
IS NAGATORO'S HOUSE...!
KCHAK
COME ON IN, SEN-PAI.
CREAK
TH-THANKS ...

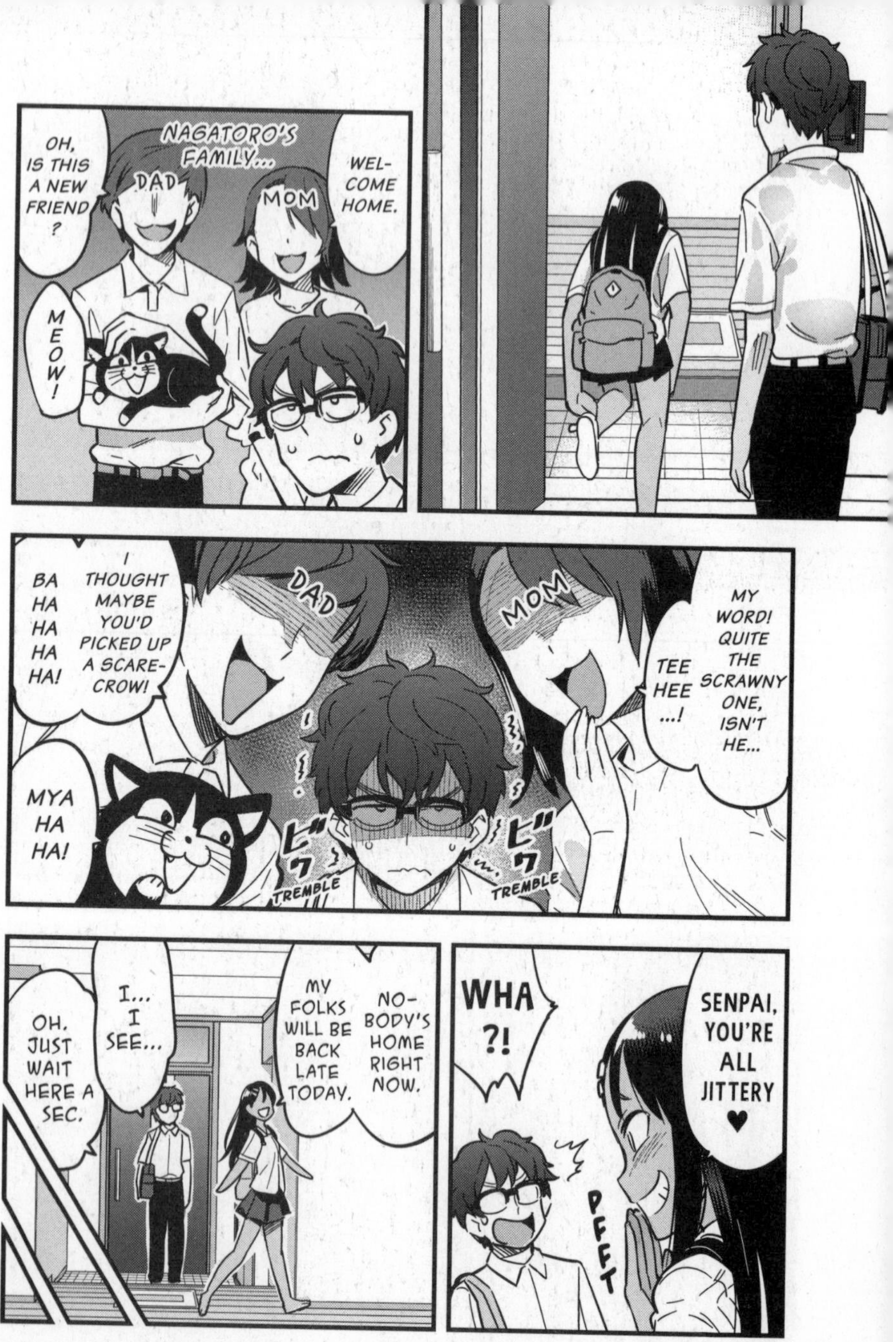
WEL-COME HOME.
NAGATORO'S FAMILY...
MOM
DAD
OH, IS THIS A NEW FRIEND?
MEOW!
MY WORD! QUITE THE SCRAWNY ONE, ISN'T HE...
TEE HEE ...!
MOM
DAD
I THOUGHT MAYBE YOU'D PICKED UP A SCARE-CROW!
BA HA HA HA HA!
TREMBLE
TREMBLE
MYA HA HA!
SENPAI, YOU'RE ALL JITTERY ♥
PFFT
WHA ?!
NO-BODY'S HOME RIGHT NOW.
MY FOLKS WILL BE BACK LATE TODAY.
I... I SEE...
OH. JUST WAIT HERE A SEC.

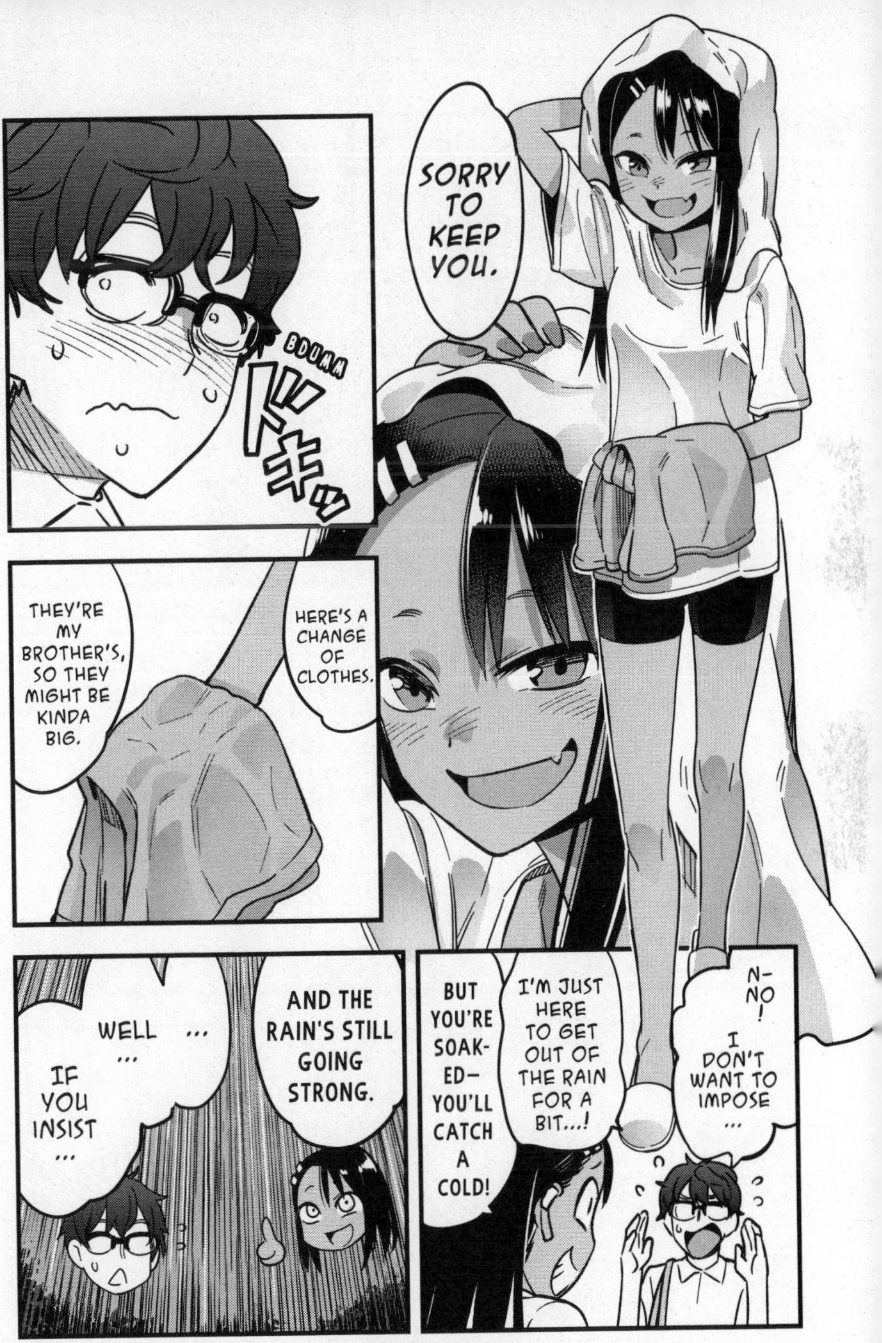
SORRY TO KEEP YOU.
BDUMM
ドキッ
HERE'S A CHANGE OF CLOTHES.
THEY'RE MY BROTHER'S, SO THEY MIGHT BE KINDA BIG.
N-NO! I DON'T WANT TO IMPOSE ...
I'M JUST HERE TO GET OUT OF THE RAIN FOR A BIT...!
BUT YOU'RE SOAK-ED—YOU'LL CATCH A COLD!
AND THE RAIN'S STILL GOING STRONG.
WELL ... ... IF YOU INSIST ...

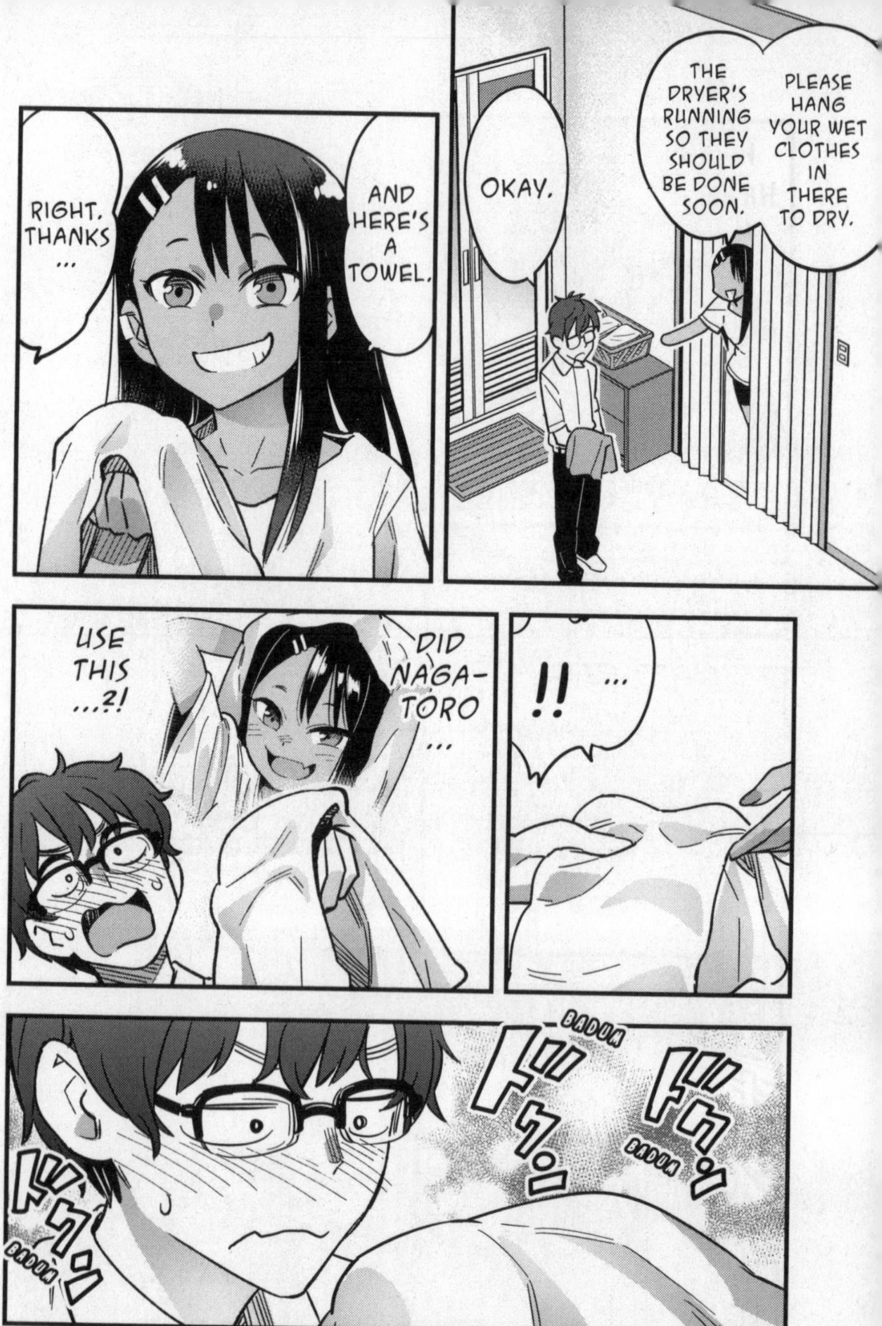
PLEASE HANG YOUR WET CLOTHES IN THERE TO DRY.
THE DRYER'S RUNNING SO THEY SHOULD BE DONE SOON.
OKAY.
AND HERE'S A TOWEL.
RIGHT. THANKS ...
...
!!
DID NAGATORO ...
USE THIS ...?!
BADUM
BADUM
BADUM

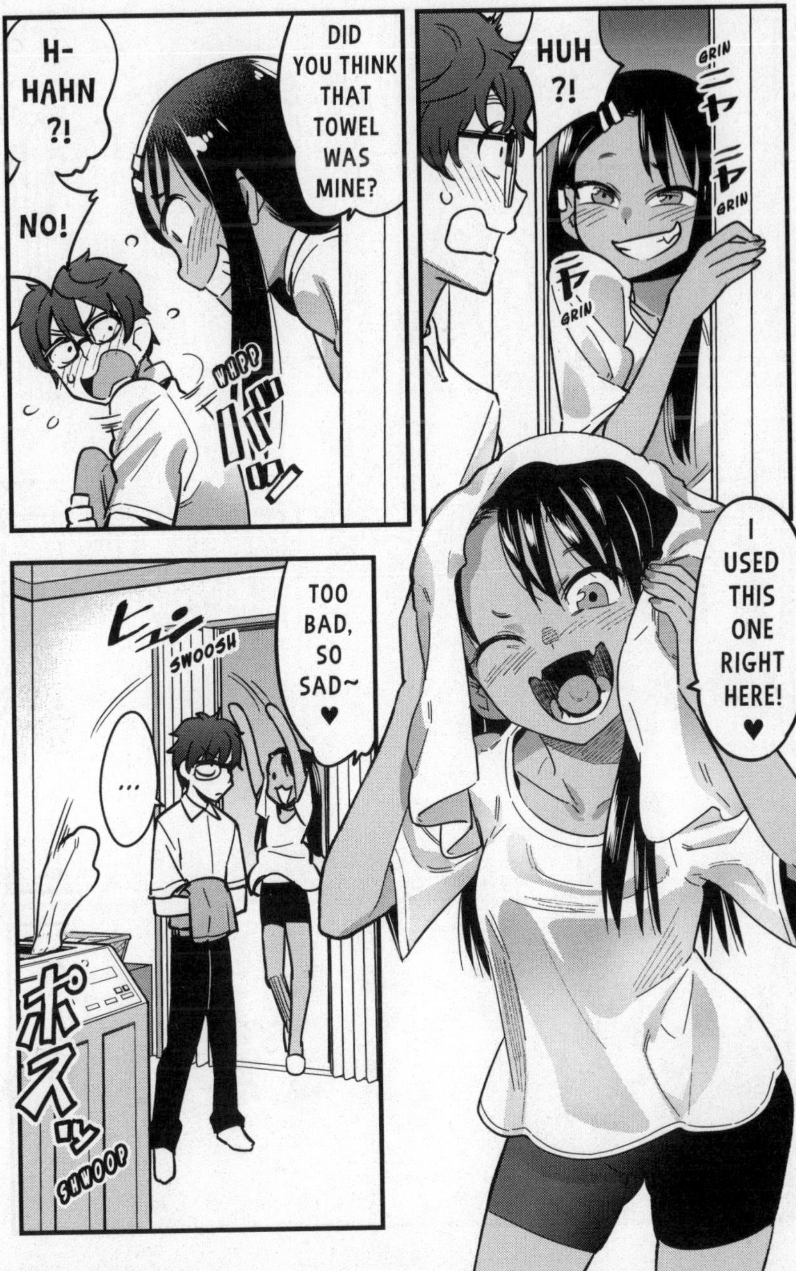
HUH ?!
GRIN
GRIN
GRIN
DID YOU THINK THAT TOWEL WAS MINE?
H- HAHN ?!
NO!
WHPP
I USED THIS ONE RIGHT HERE! ♥
TOO BAD, SO SAD~ ♥
SWOOSH
...
SHWOOP

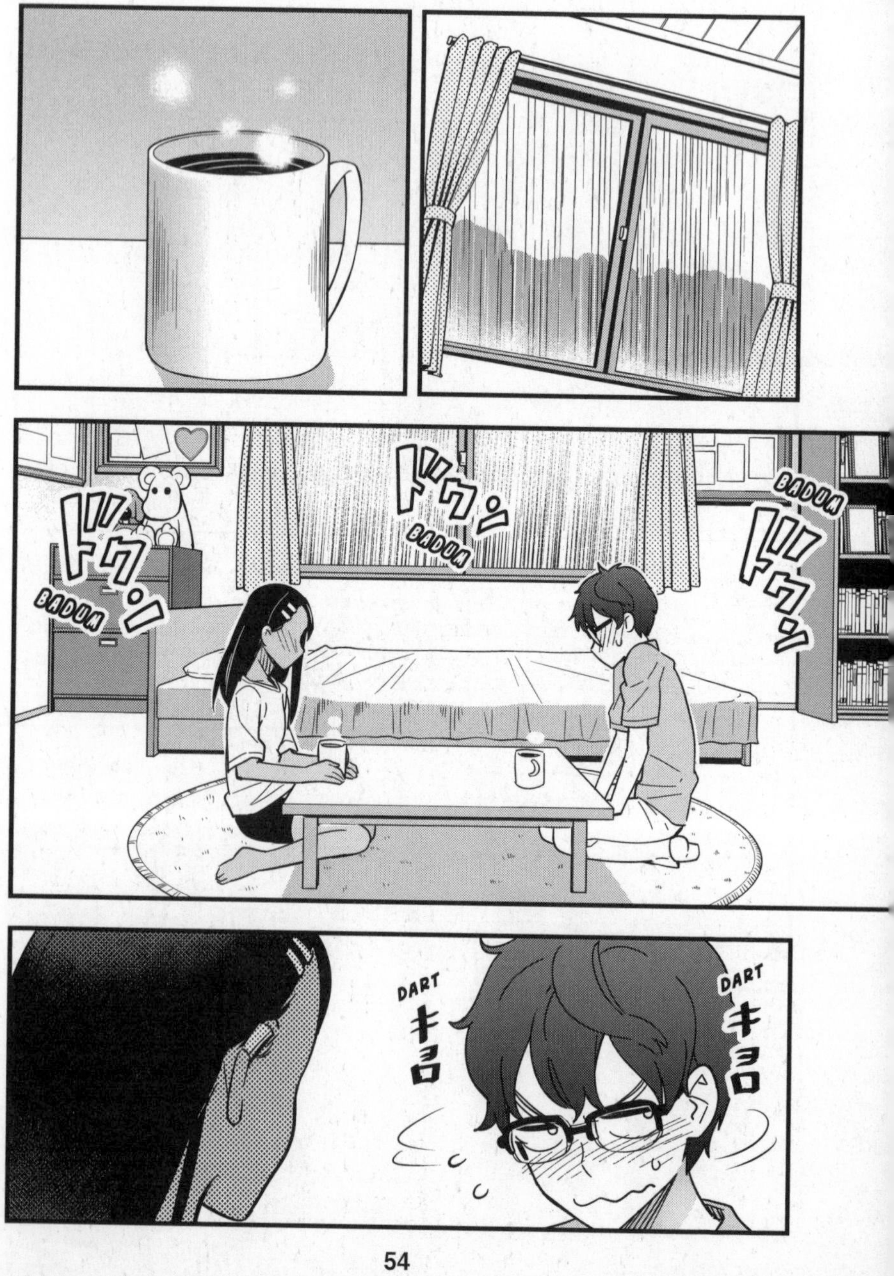
BADUM
ドクン
ドクン
BADUM
ドクン
BADUM
DART
キョロ
DART
キョロ

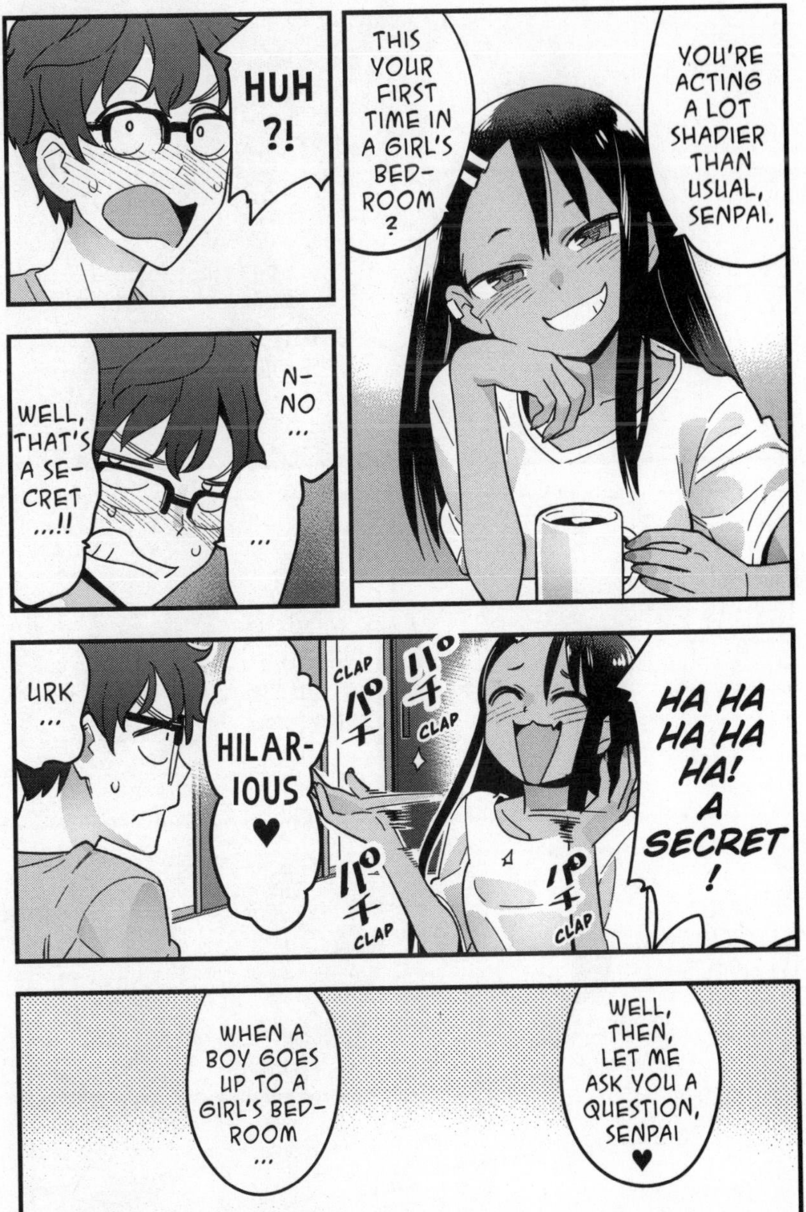
YOU'RE ACTING A LOT SHADIER THAN USUAL, SENPAI.
THIS YOUR FIRST TIME IN A GIRL'S BED-ROOM?
HUH ?!
N-NO ...
...
WELL, THAT'S A SE-CRET ....!!
HA HA HA HA HA! A SECRET!
パチ CLAP
パチ CLAP
パチ CLAP
パチ CLAP
HILAR-IOUS ♥
URK ...
WELL, THEN, LET ME ASK YOU A QUESTION, SENPAI ♥
WHEN A BOY GOES UP TO A GIRL'S BED-ROOM ...

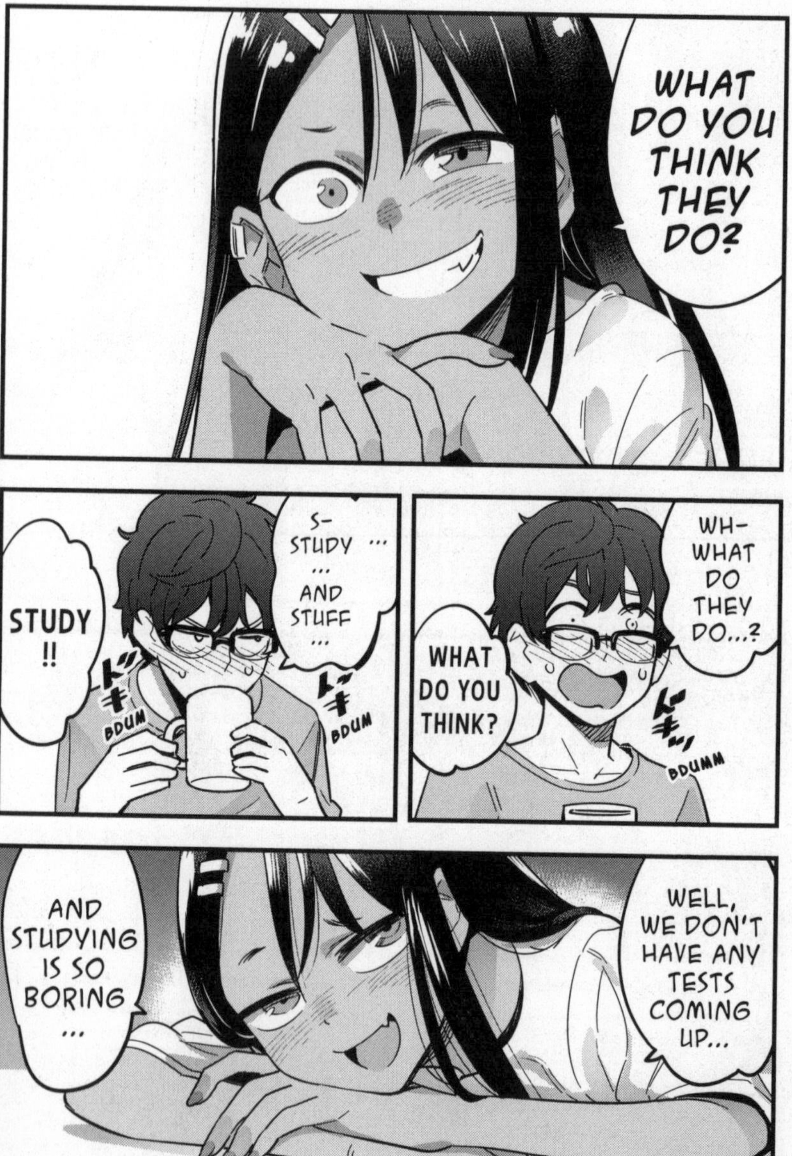
WHAT DO YOU THINK THEY DO?
WH- WHAT DO THEY DO...?
WHAT DO YOU THINK?
BDUMM
S- STUDY ... AND STUFF ...
...
STUDY !!
BDUM
BDUM
WELL, WE DON'T HAVE ANY TESTS COMING UP...
AND STUDYING IS SO BORING ...

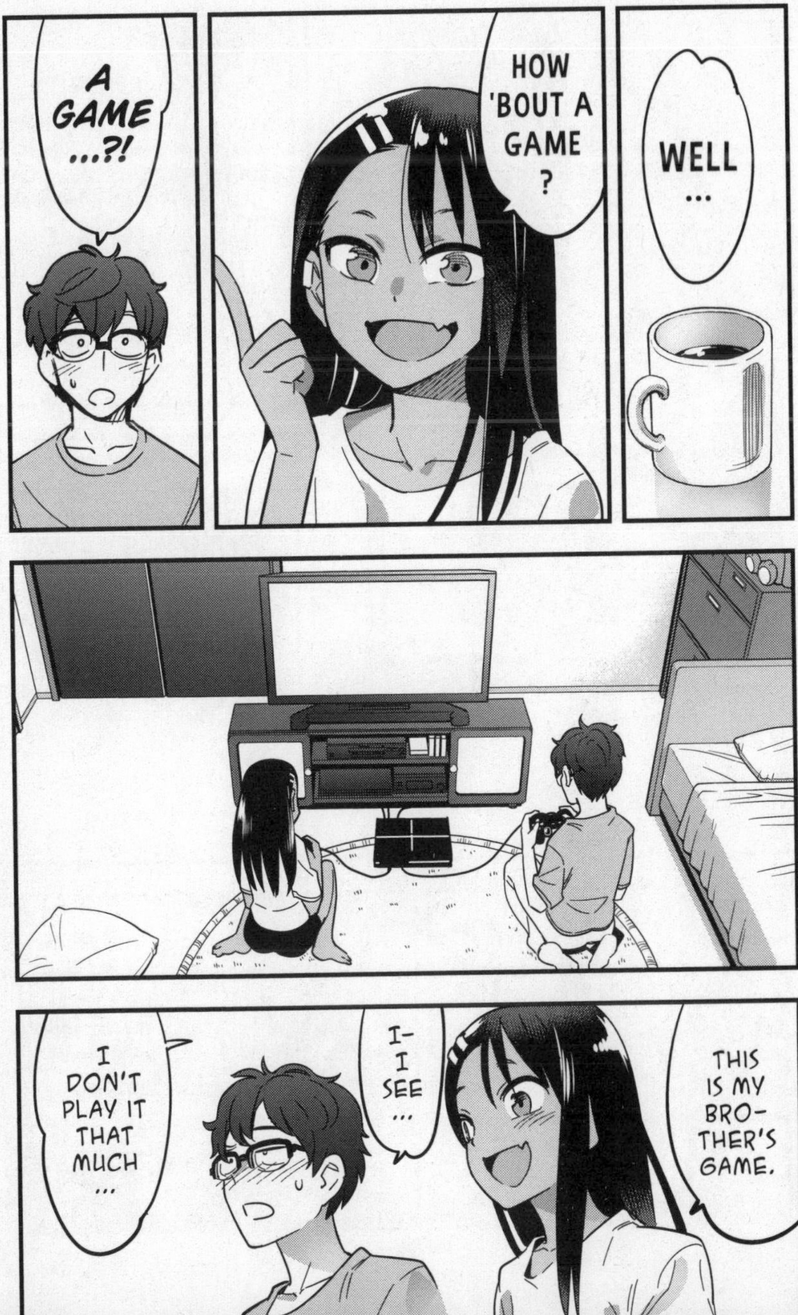
WELL ...
HOW 'BOUT A GAME ?
A GAME ...?!
THIS IS MY BRO-THER'S GAME.
I-I SEE ...
I DON'T PLAY IT THAT MUCH ...

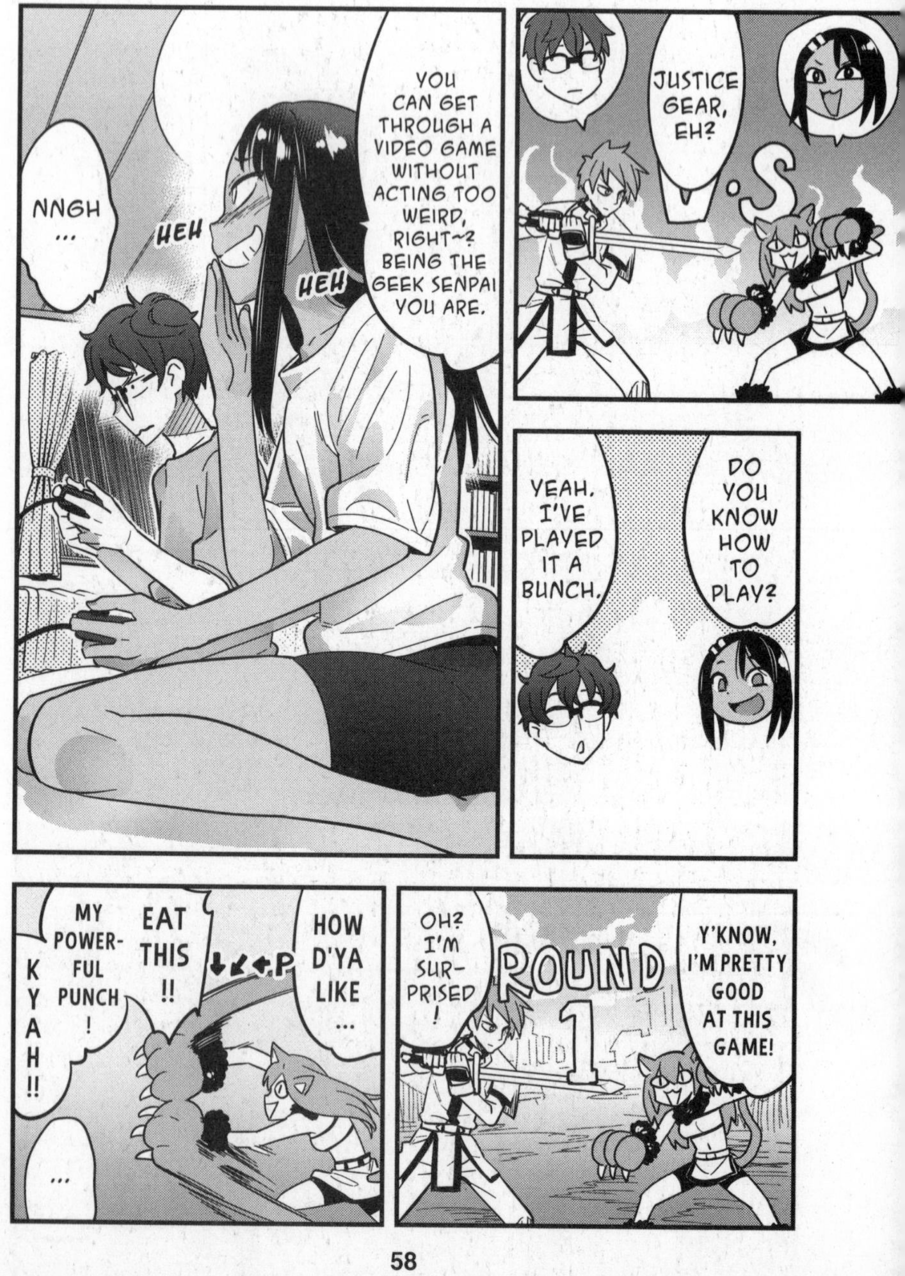
JUSTICE GEAR, EH?
DO YOU KNOW HOW TO PLAY?
YEAH. I'VE PLAYED IT A BUNCH.
YOU CAN GET THROUGH A VIDEO GAME WITHOUT ACTING TOO WEIRD, RIGHT~? BEING THE GEEK SENPAI YOU ARE.
HEH
HEH
NNGH ...
Y'KNOW, I'M PRETTY GOOD AT THIS GAME!
ROUND 1
OH? I'M SUR-PRISED!
HOW D'YA LIKE ...
↓↙←P
EAT THIS !!
MY POWER-FUL PUNCH !
KYAH!!
...

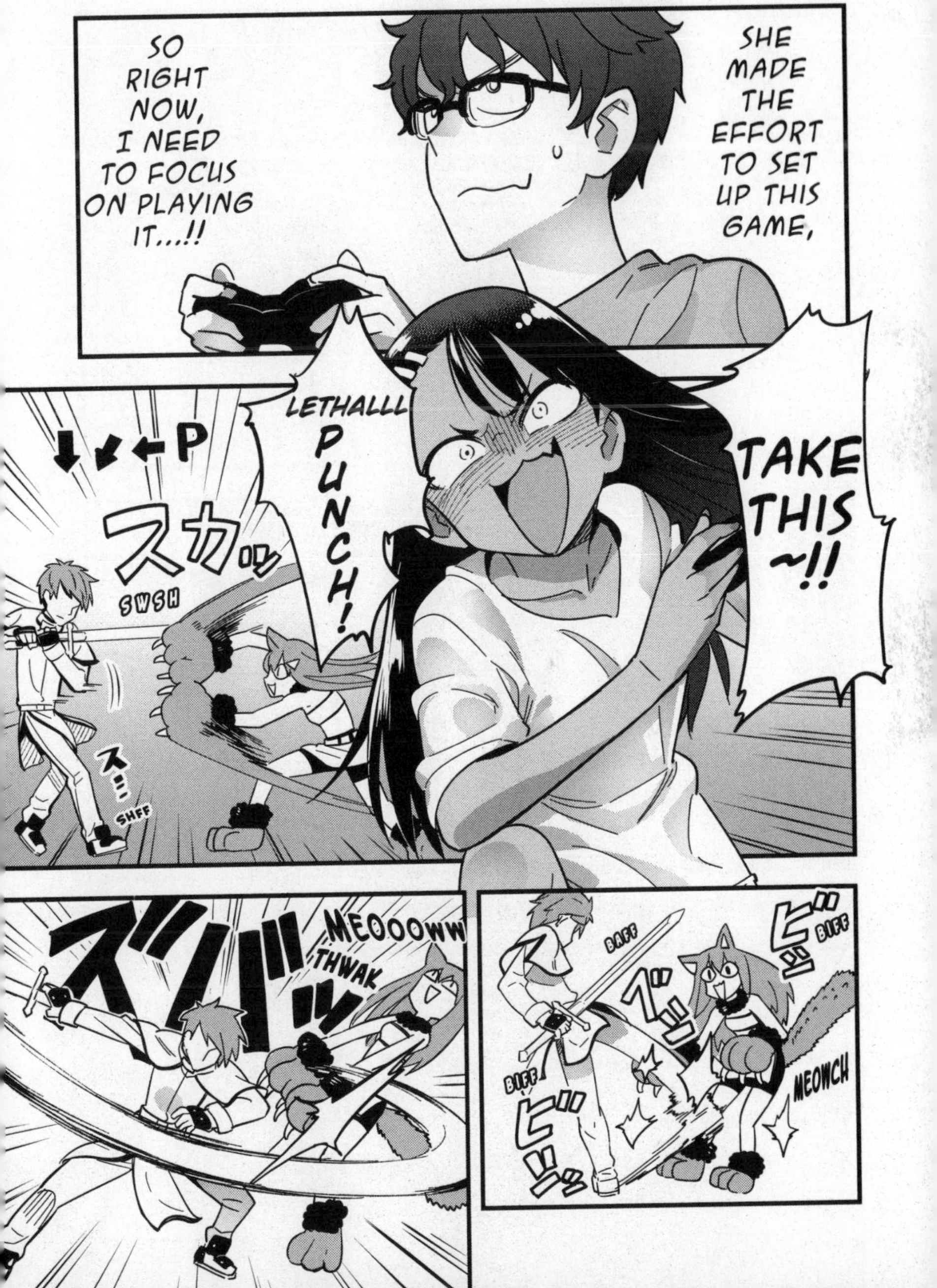
SHE MADE THE EFFORT TO SET UP THIS GAME,
SO RIGHT NOW, I NEED TO FOCUS ON PLAYING IT...!!
TAKE THIS ~!!
LETHALLL PUNCH!
↓↙←P
SWSH
SHFF
BIFF
BAFF
BIFF
MEOWCH
MEOOOWW
THWAK

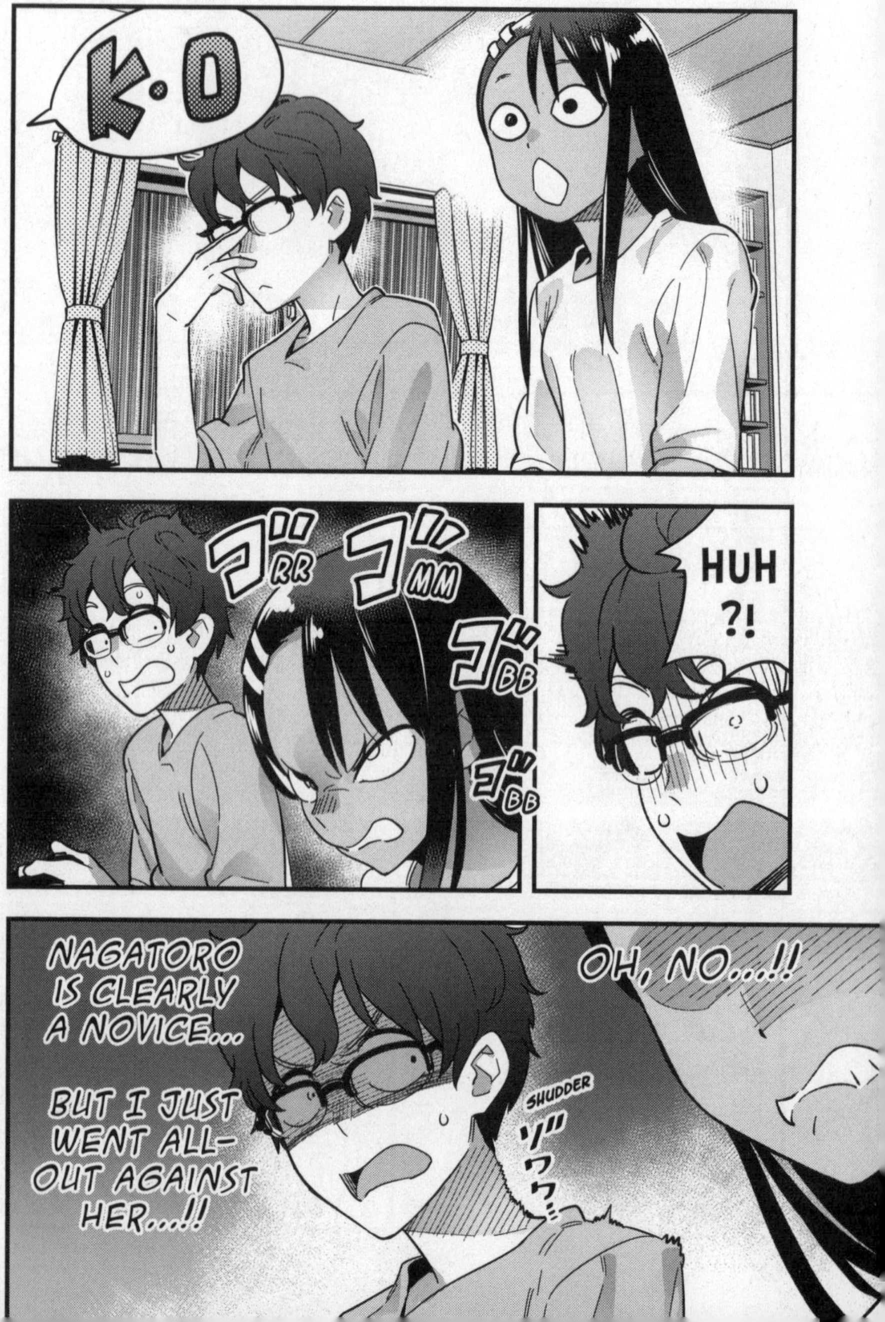
K.O
HUH ?!
ゴRR
ゴMM
ゴBB
ゴBB
OH, NO...!!
NAGATORO IS CLEARLY A NOVICE...
BUT I JUST WENT ALL-OUT AGAINST HER...!!
SHUDDER
ゾワワ...

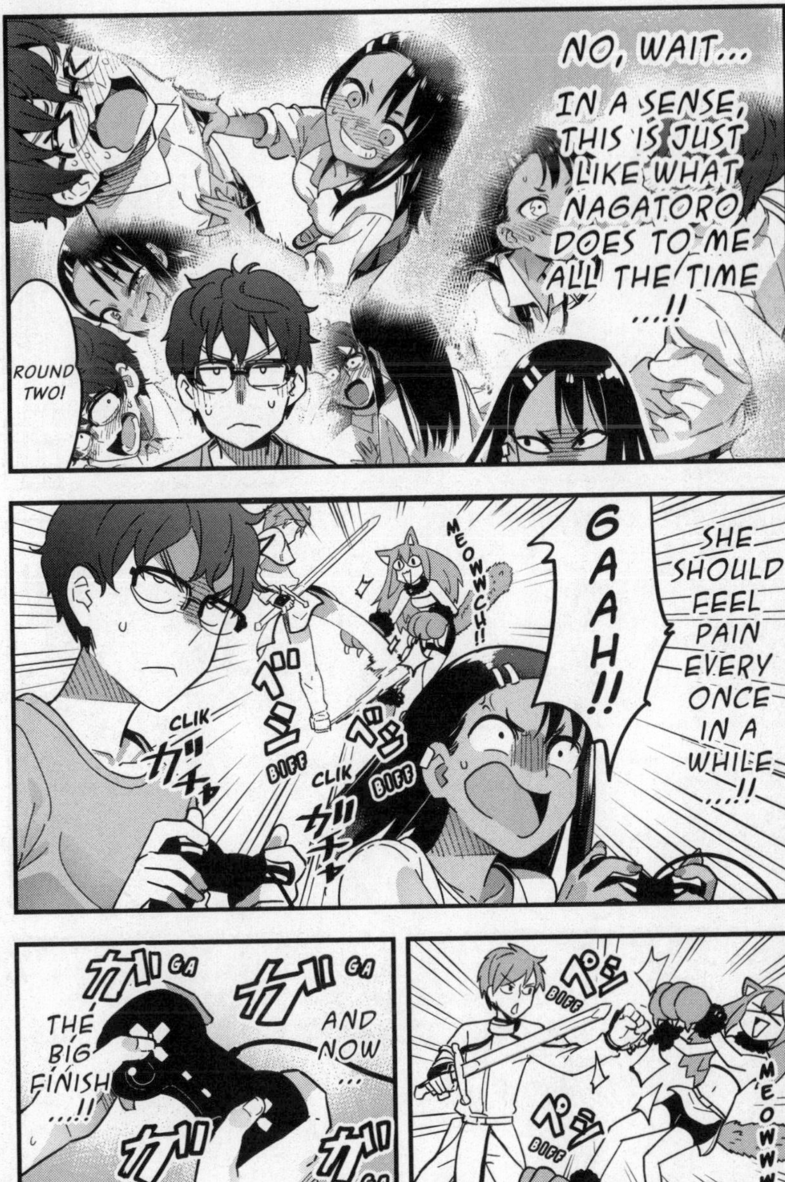
NO, WAIT...
IN A SENSE, THIS IS JUST LIKE WHAT NAGATORO DOES TO ME ALL THE TIME ...!!
ROUND TWO!
SHE SHOULD FEEL PAIN EVERY ONCE IN A WHILE ...!!
GAAAH!!
MEOWWCH!!
BIFF
BIFF
CLIK
CLIK
BIFF
MEOWWW
BIFF
GA
AND NOW ...
GA
THE BIG FINISH ...!!
GA
GA

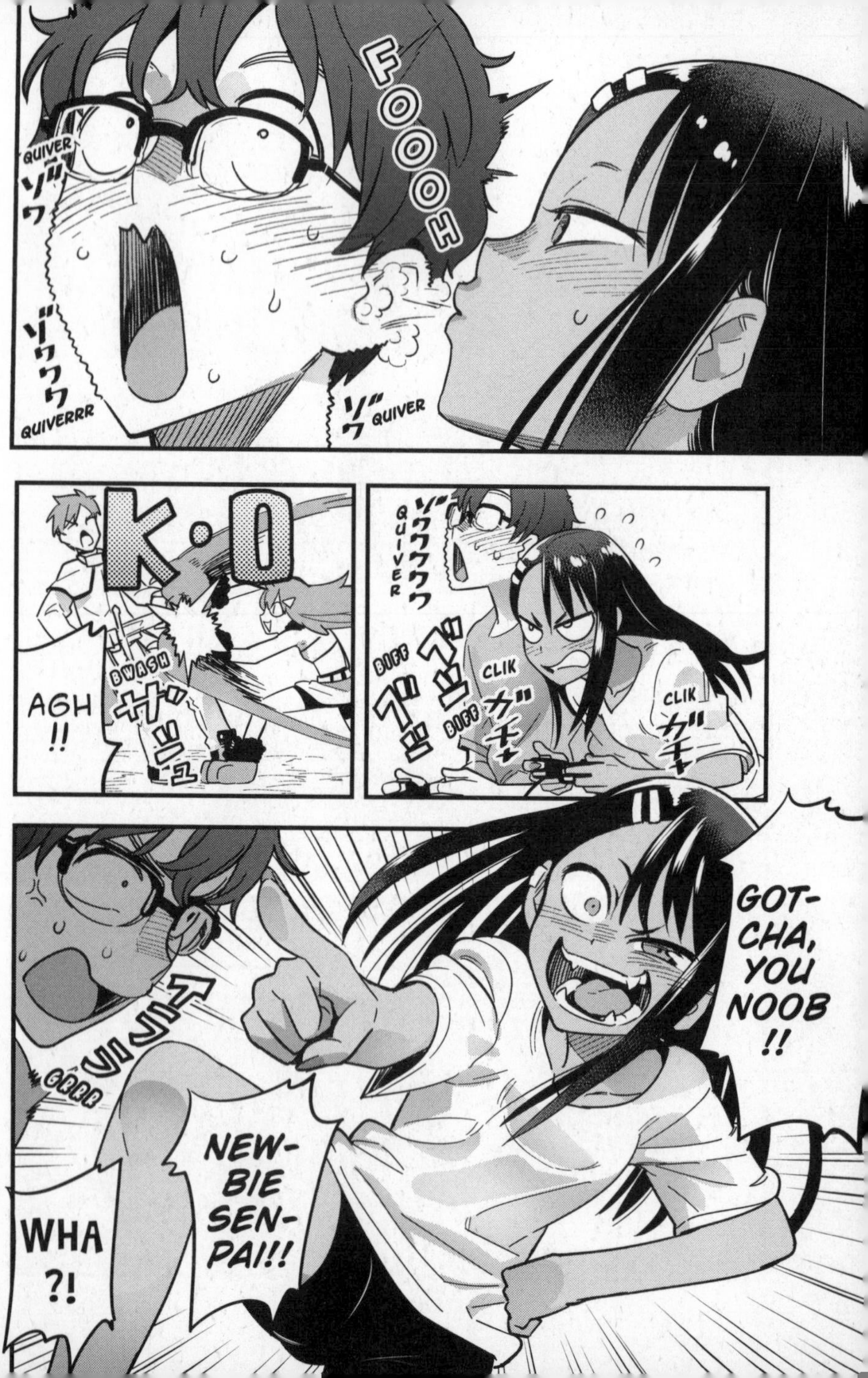
FOOOOH
QUIVER
ゾワ
QUIVER
ゾワ
ゾワワワ
QUIVERRR
QUIVER
BIFF
BIFF
CLIK
CLIK
K.O
BWASH
AGH!!
GOT-CHA, YOU NOOB!!
NEW-BIE SEN-PAI!!
GRRR
WHA?!

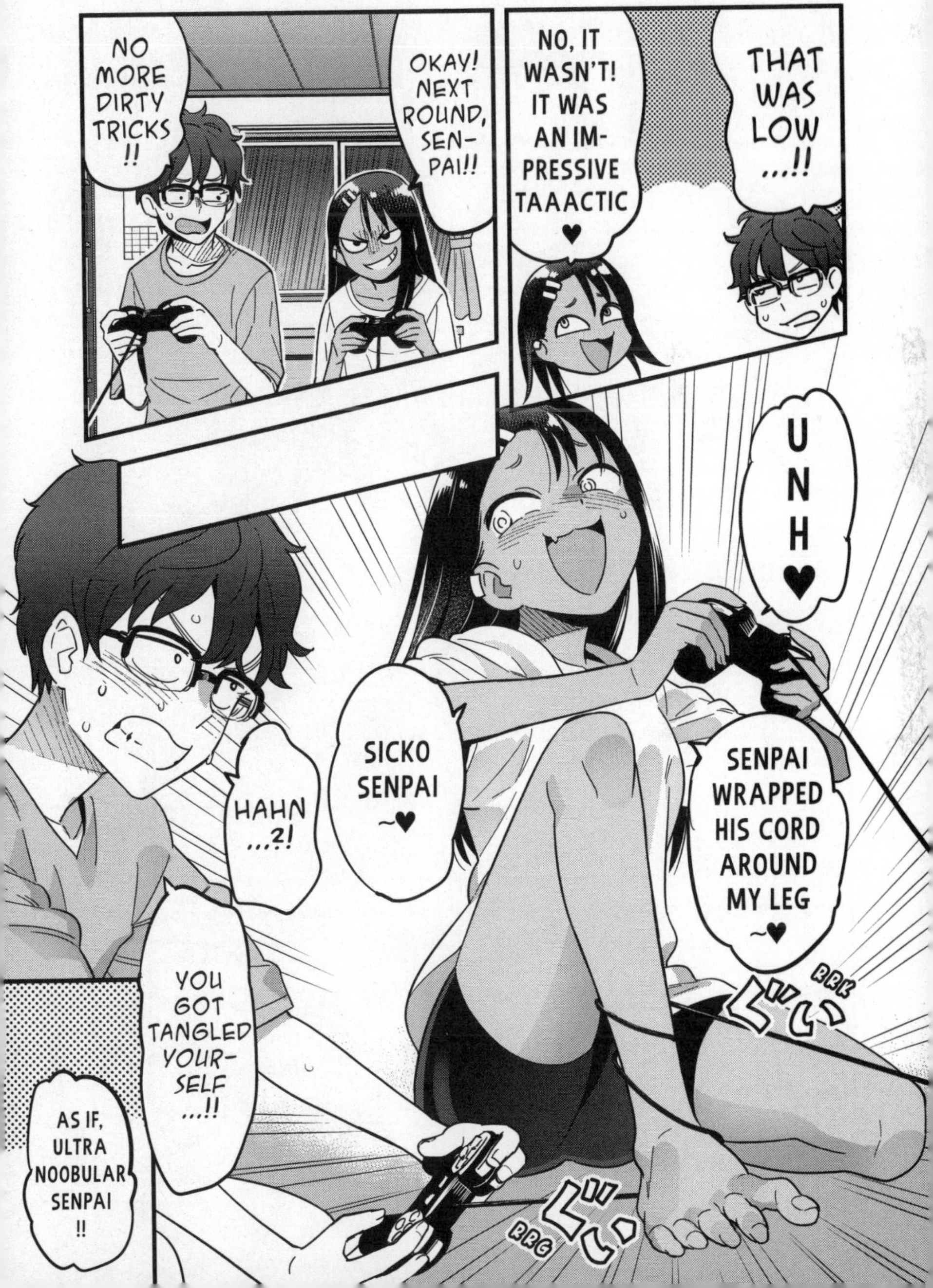
THAT WAS LOW ...!!
NO, IT WASN'T! IT WAS AN IM-PRESSIVE TAAACTIC ♥
OKAY! NEXT ROUND, SEN-PAI!!
NO MORE DIRTY TRICKS !!
UNH ♥
SENPAI WRAPPED HIS CORD AROUND MY LEG ~♥
RBK
SICKO SENPAI ~♥
HAHN ...?!
YOU GOT TANGLED YOUR-SELF ...!!
AS IF, ULTRA NOOBULAR SENPAI !!
RRG

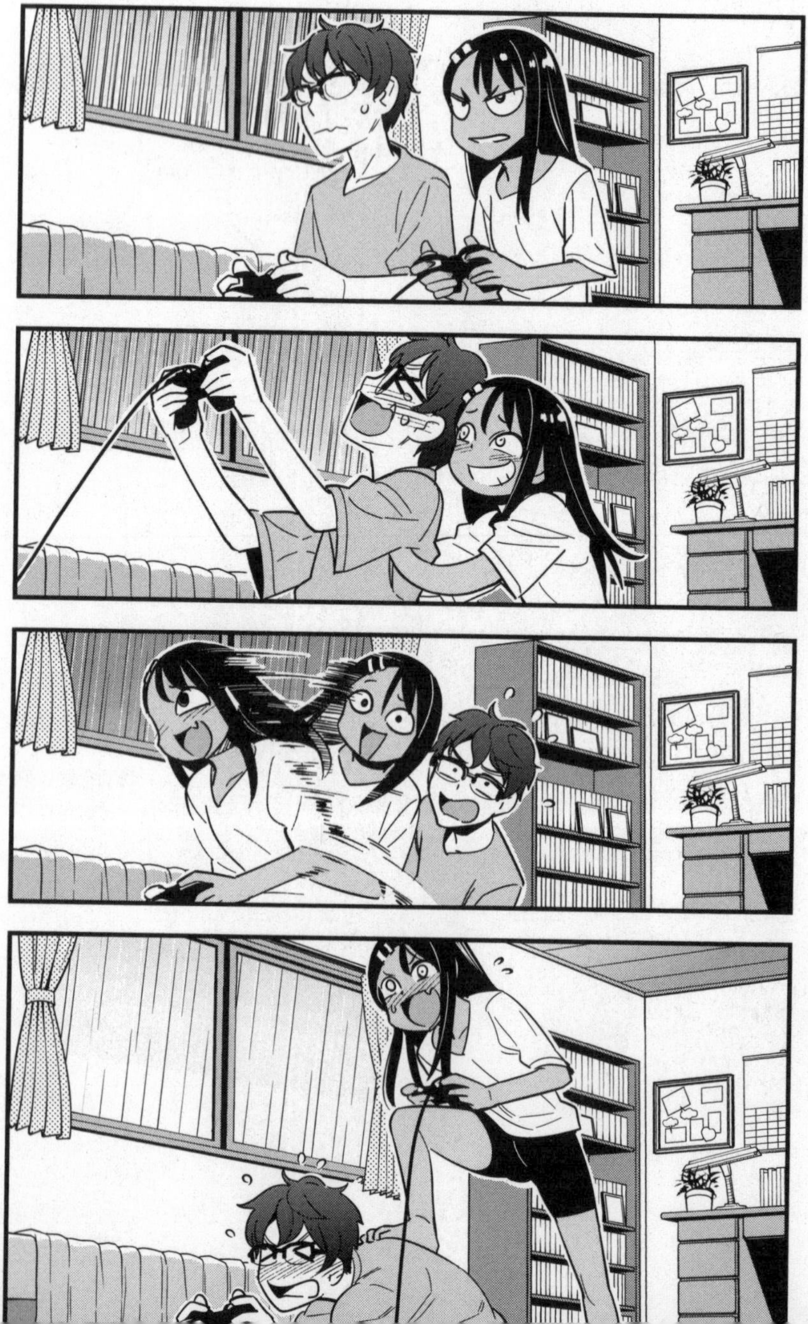

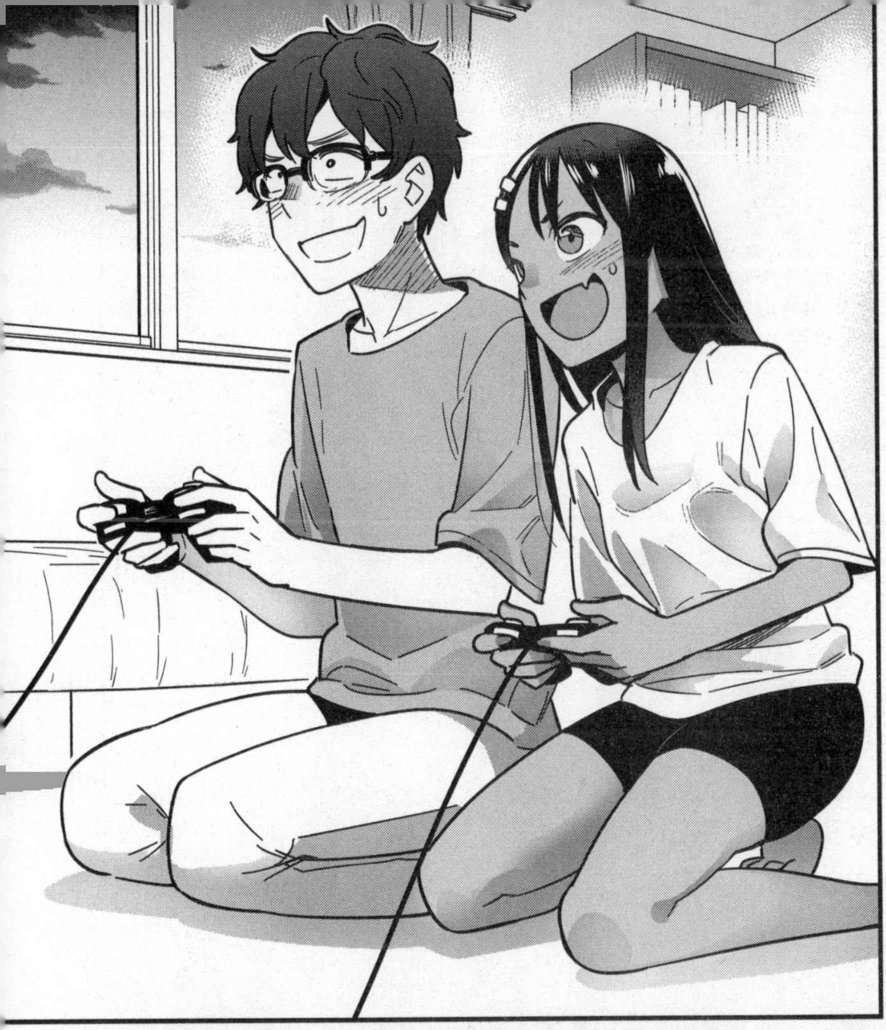

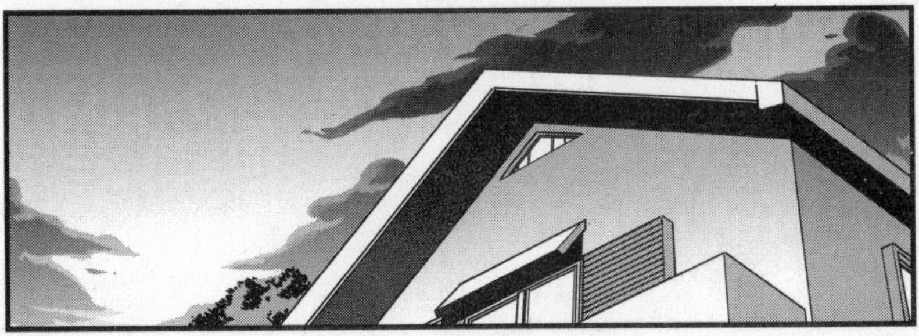

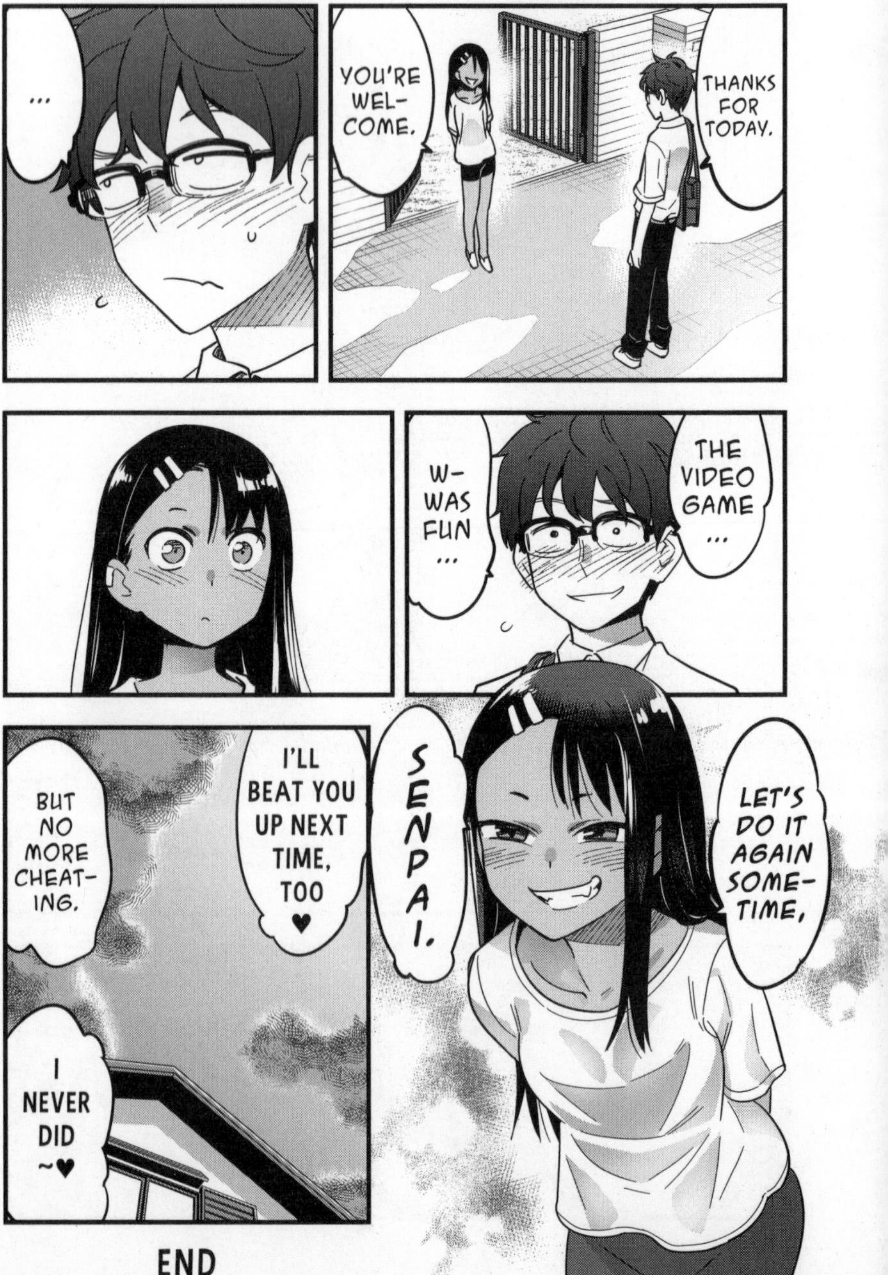
THANKS FOR TODAY.
YOU'RE WELCOME.
...
THE VIDEO GAME ...
W-WAS FUN ...
LET'S DO IT AGAIN SOMETIME,
SENPAI.
I'LL BEAT YOU UP NEXT TIME, TOO ♥
BUT NO MORE CHEATING.
I NEVER DID ~♥
END

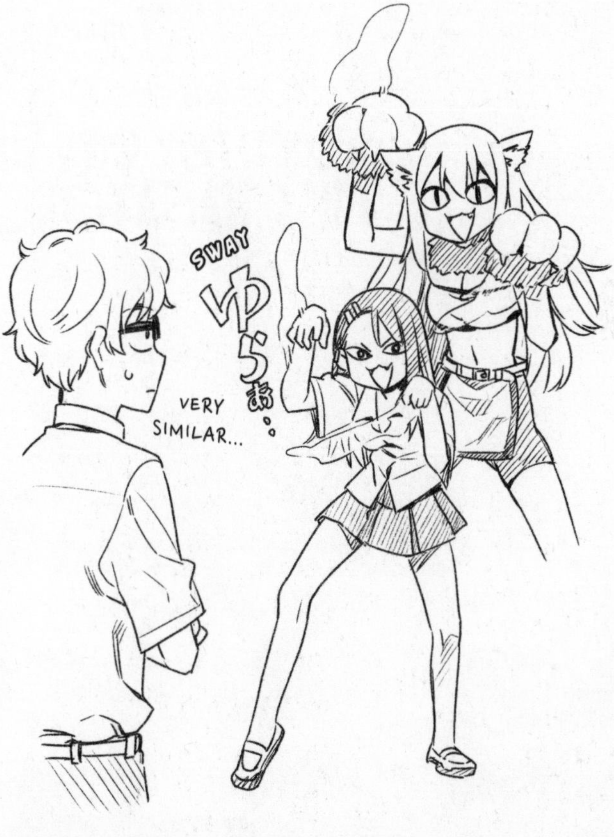
SWAY
ゆらぁ…
VERY SIMILAR...

DON'T TOY WITH ME,
MISS NAGATORO

CHAPTER 19: SENPAI, YOU CREEEP! ♥

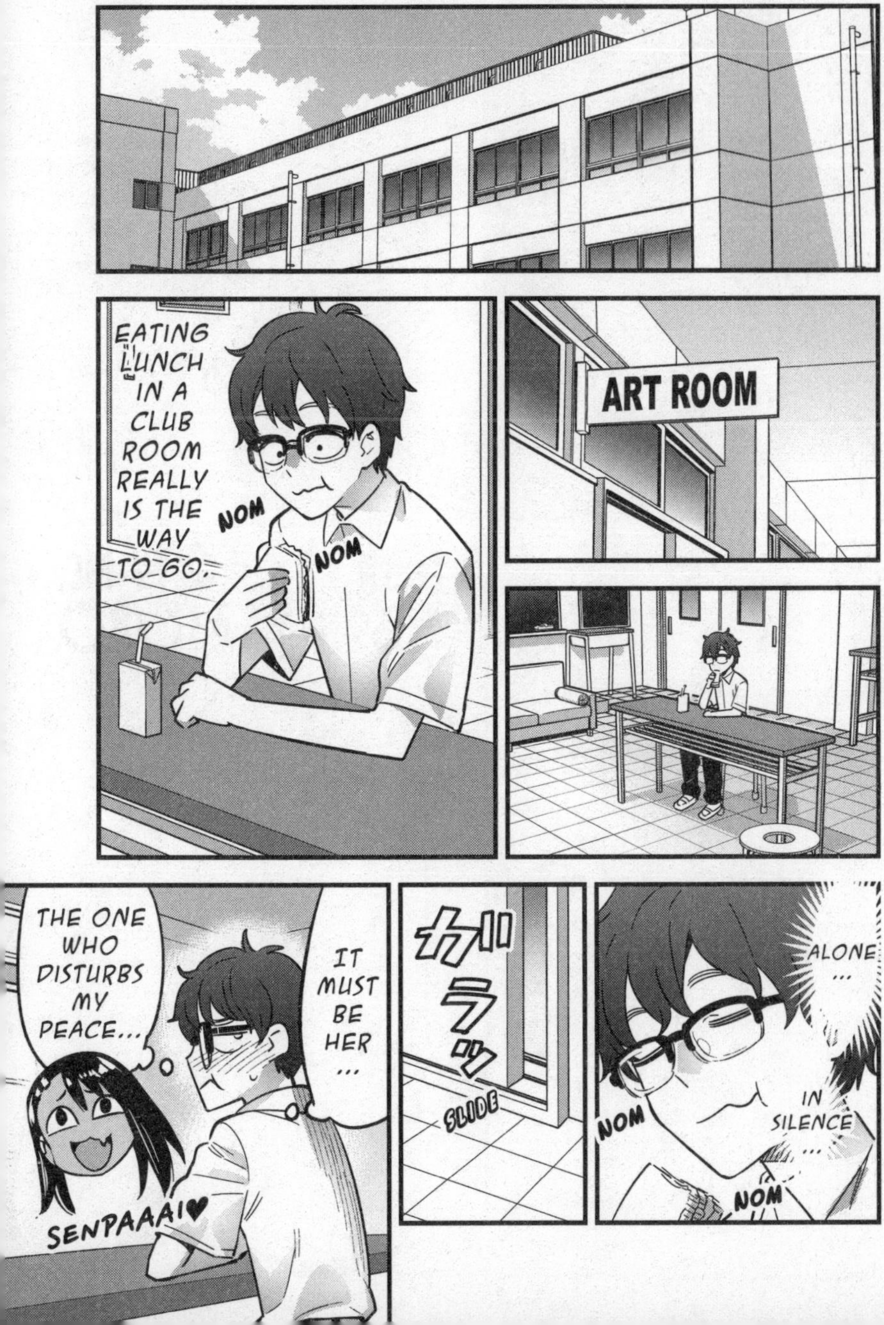
ART ROOM
EATING LUNCH IN A CLUB ROOM REALLY IS THE WAY TO GO.
NOM
NOM
ALONE...
IN SILENCE...
NOM
NOM
カラッ
SLIDE
THE ONE WHO DISTURBS MY PEACE...
IT MUST BE HER...
SENPAAAI♥

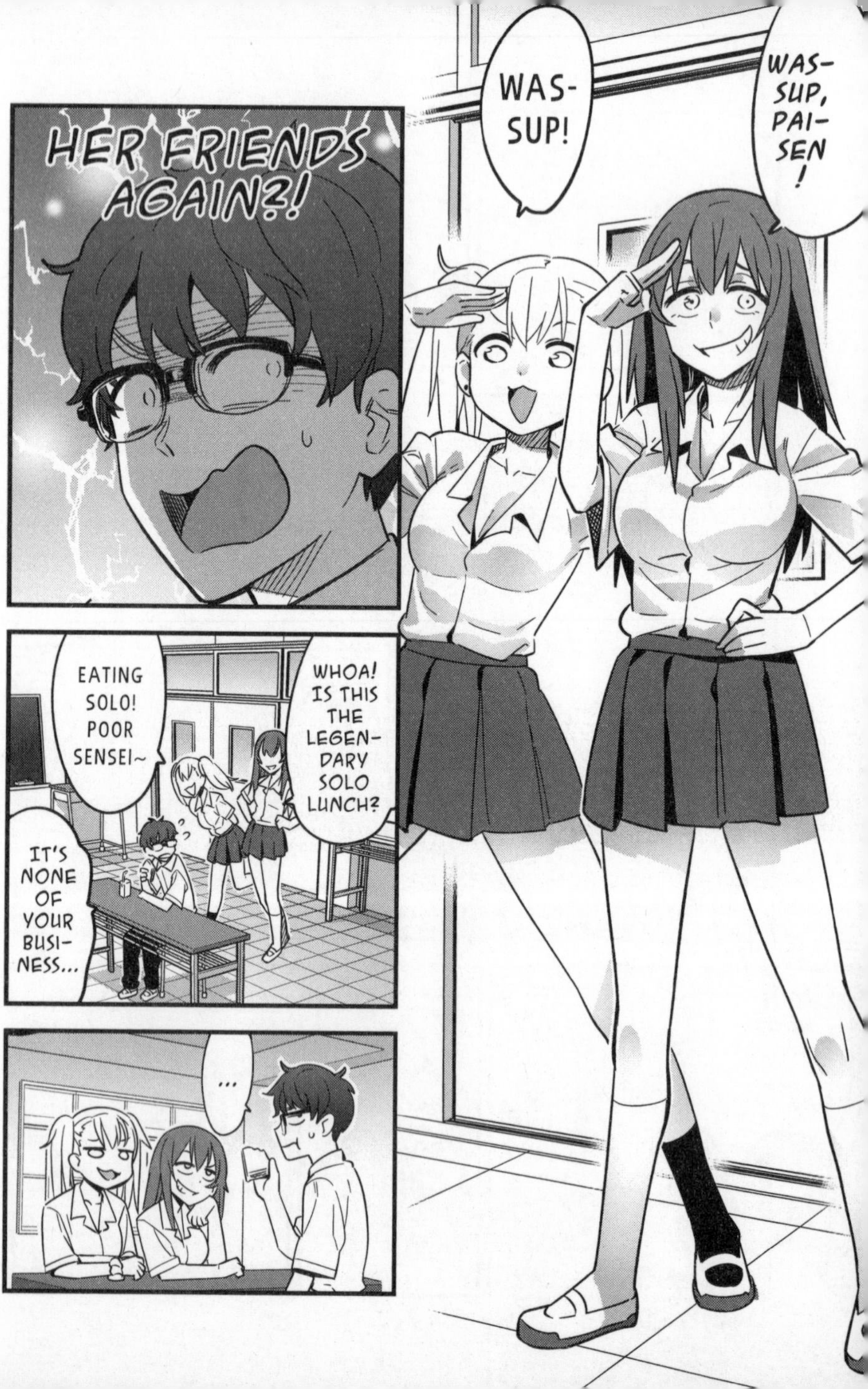
WAS-SUP, PAI-SEN!
WAS-SUP!
HER FRIENDS AGAIN?!
WHOA! IS THIS THE LEGEN-DARY SOLO LUNCH?
EATING SOLO! POOR SENSEI~
IT'S NONE OF YOUR BUSI-NESS...
...

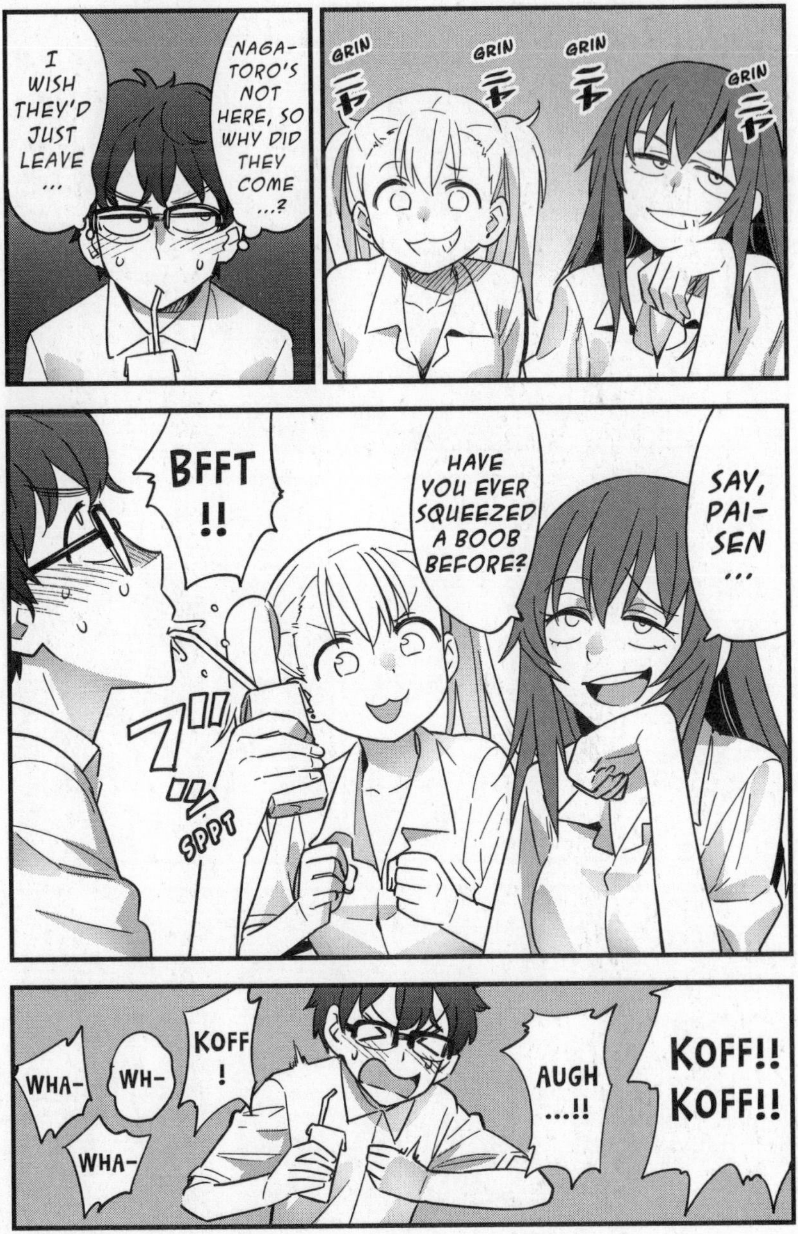
GRIN
GRIN
GRIN
GRIN
NAGA-TORO'S NOT HERE, SO WHY DID THEY COME ...?
I WISH THEY'D JUST LEAVE ...
SAY, PAI-SEN ...
HAVE YOU EVER SQUEEZED A BOOB BEFORE?
BFFT !!
SPPT
KOFF!! KOFF!!
AUGH ...!!
KOFF !
WH-
WHA-
WHA-

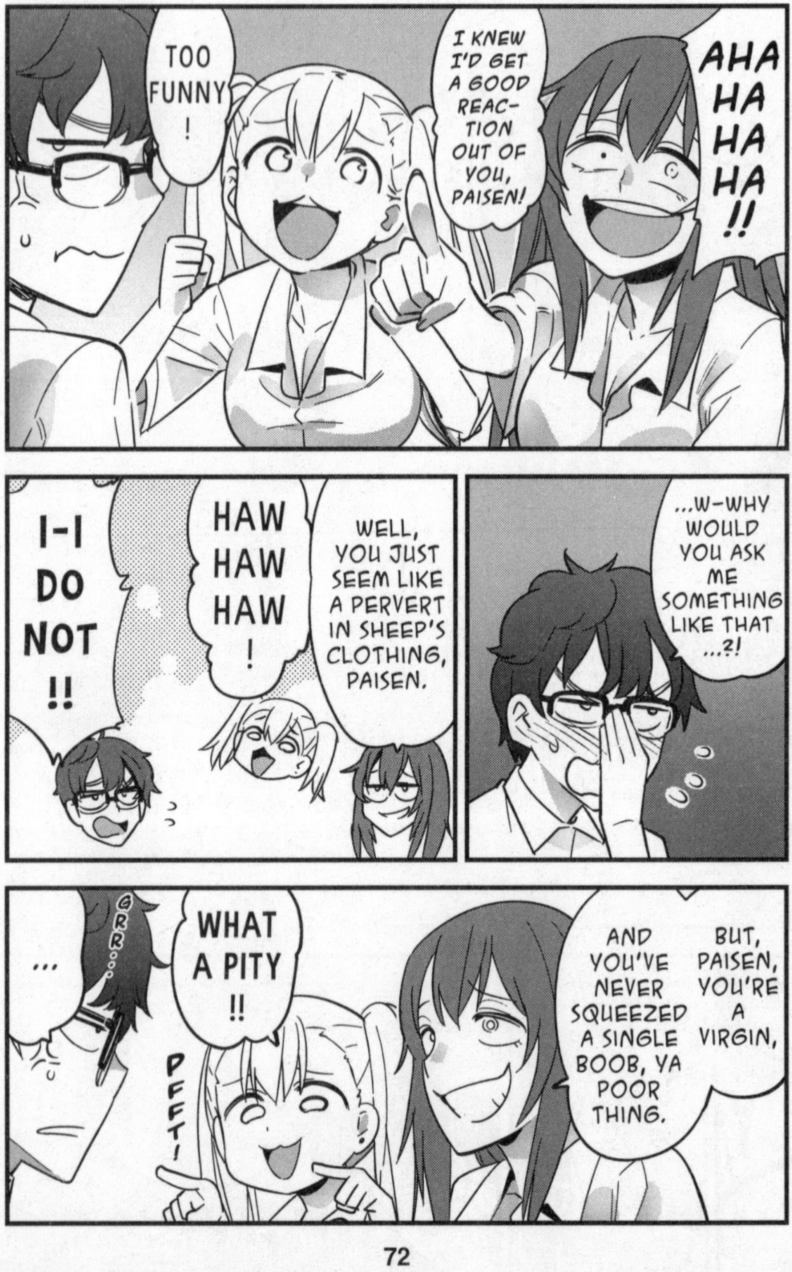
AHA HA HA HA!!
I KNEW I'D GET A GOOD REACTION OUT OF YOU, PAISEN!
TOO FUNNY!
...W-WHY WOULD YOU ASK ME SOMETHING LIKE THAT...?!
WELL, YOU JUST SEEM LIKE A PERVERT IN SHEEP'S CLOTHING, PAISEN.
HAW HAW HAW!
I-I DO NOT!!
BUT, PAISEN, YOU'RE A VIRGIN,
AND YOU'VE NEVER SQUEEZED A SINGLE BOOB, YA POOR THING.
WHAT A PITY!!
PFFT!
GRR...
...

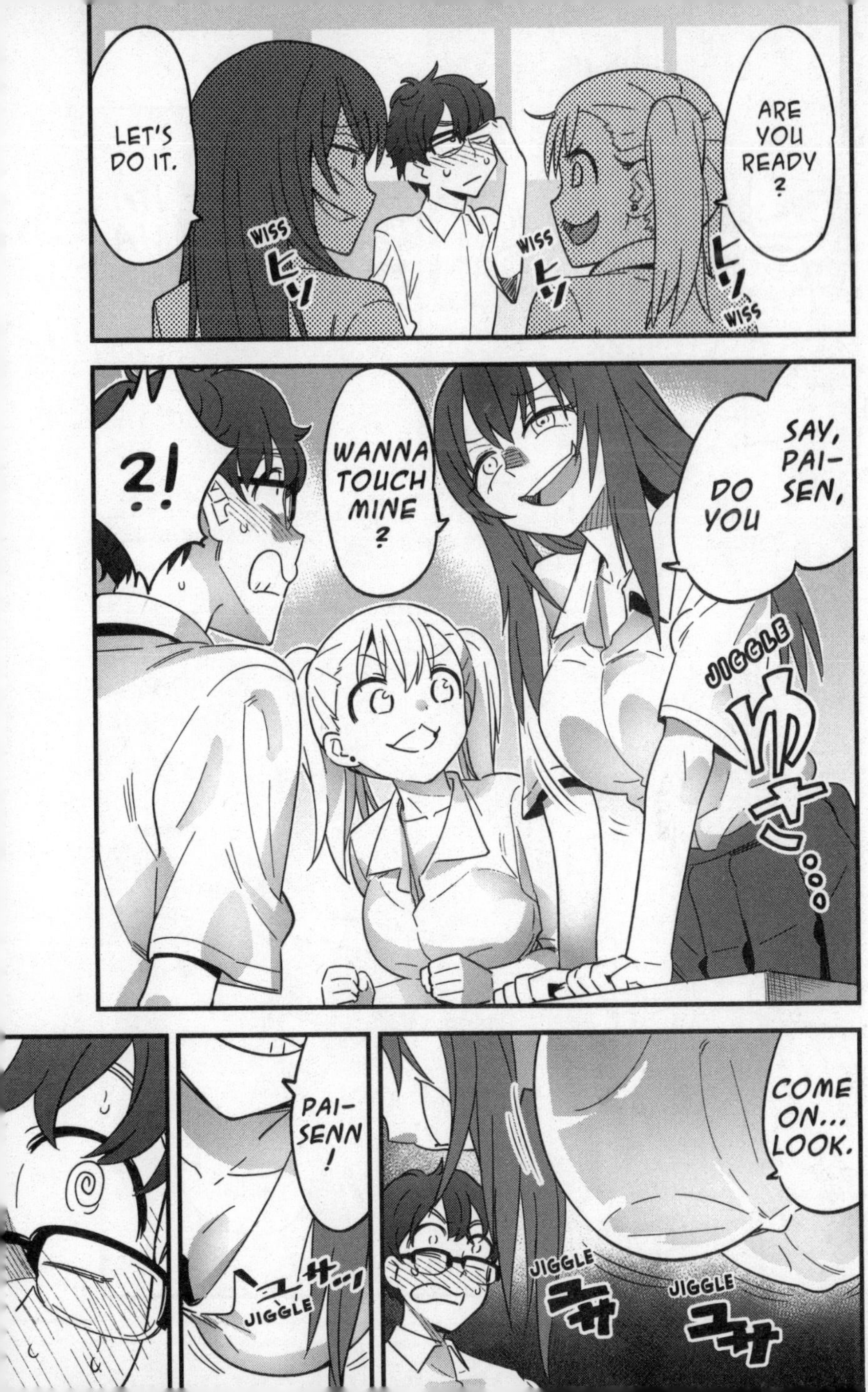
ARE YOU READY?
WISS
WISS
LET'S DO IT.
WISS
SAY, PAI-SEN, DO YOU
WANNA TOUCH MINE?
?!
JIGGLE
COME ON... LOOK.
JIGGLE
JIGGLE
PAI-SENN!
JIGGLE

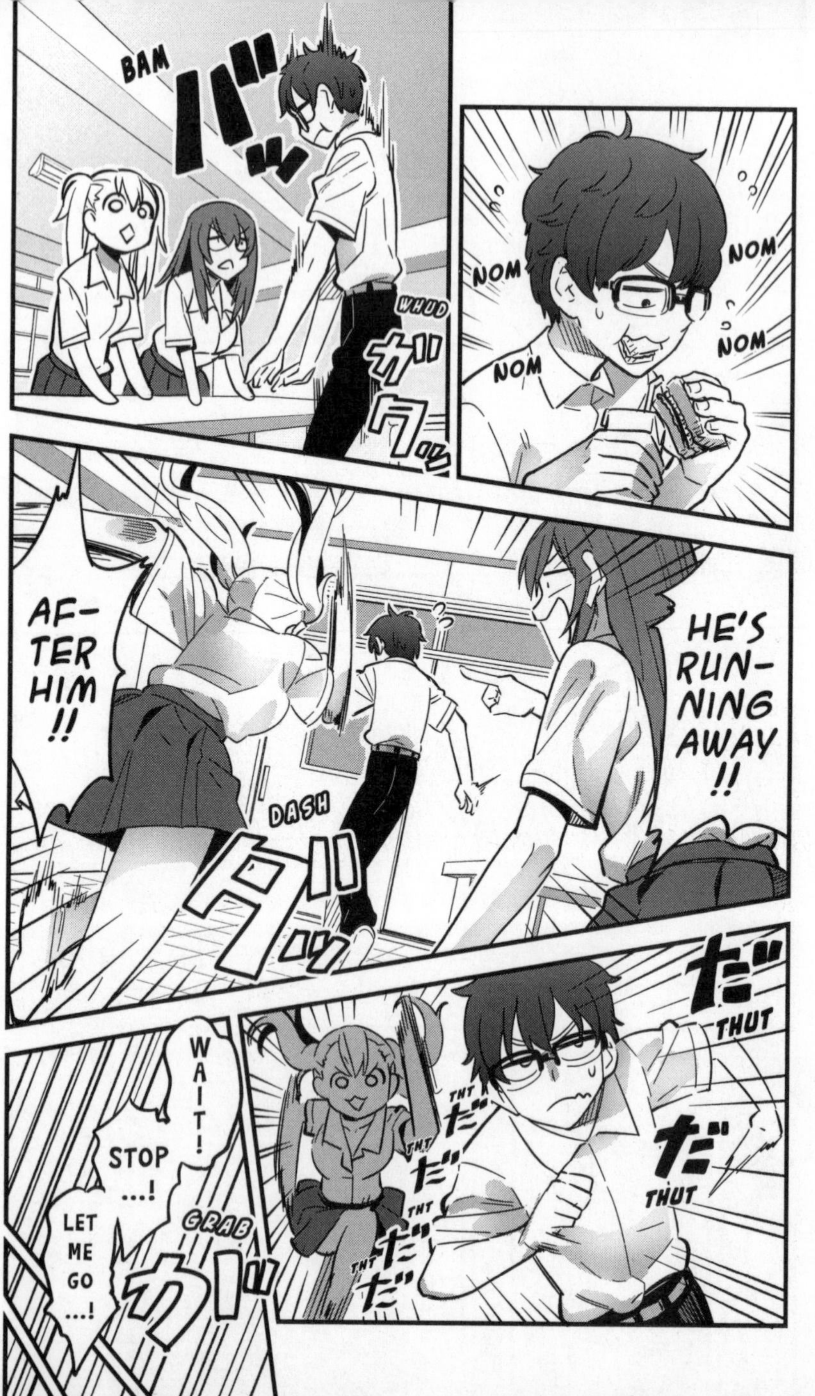
NOM
NOM
NOM
NOM
BAM
WHUD
HE'S RUN-NING AWAY!!
AF-TER HIM!!
DASH
THUT
THT
THT
THT
THT
THUT
WAIT!
STOP ...!
GRAB
LET ME GO ...!

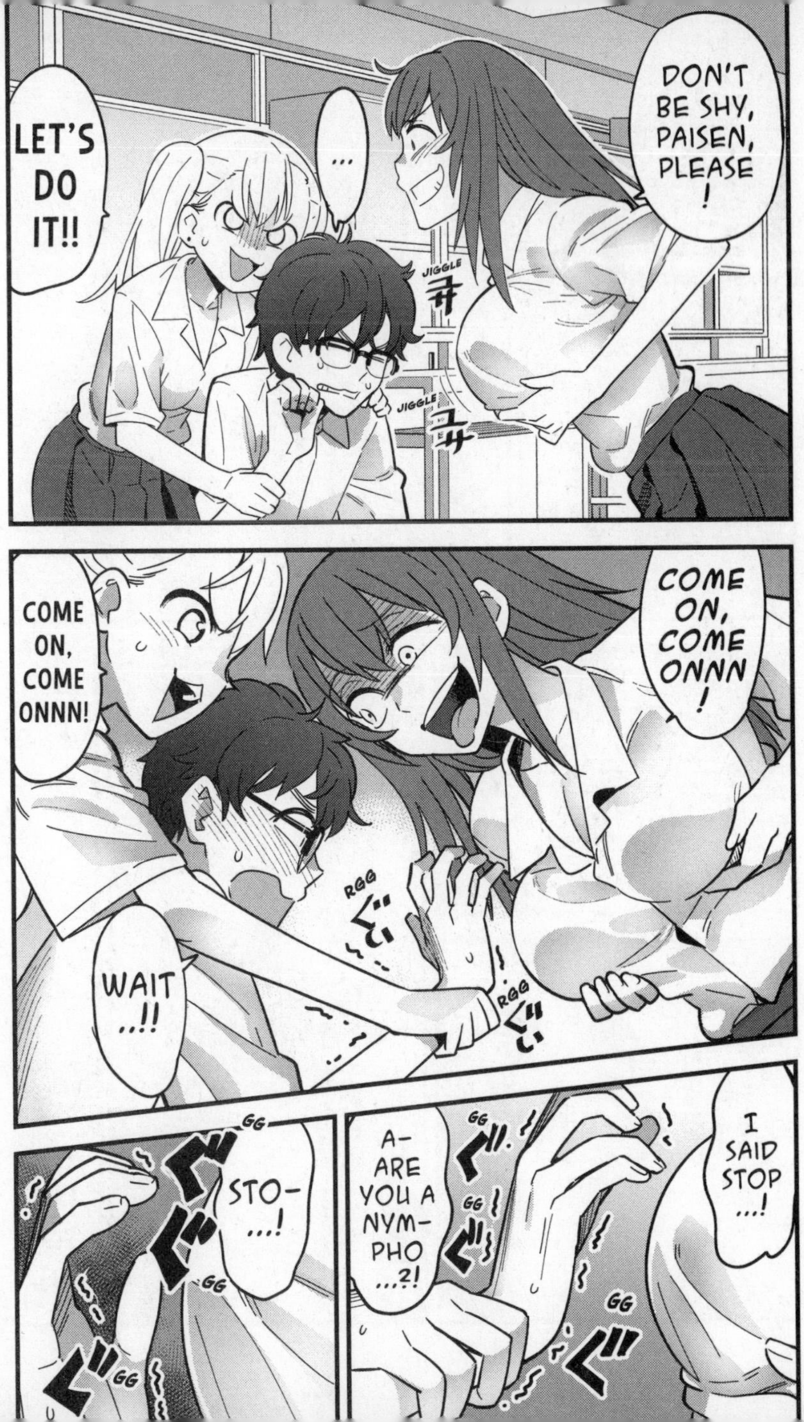
DON'T BE SHY, PAISEN, PLEASE!
...
LET'S DO IT!!
JIGGLE
JIGGLE
COME ON, COME ONNN!
COME ON, COME ONNN!
RGG
WAIT ..!!
RGG
I SAID STOP ...!
GG
A- ARE YOU A NYMPHO ...?!
GG
GG
GG
STO- ...!
GG
GG

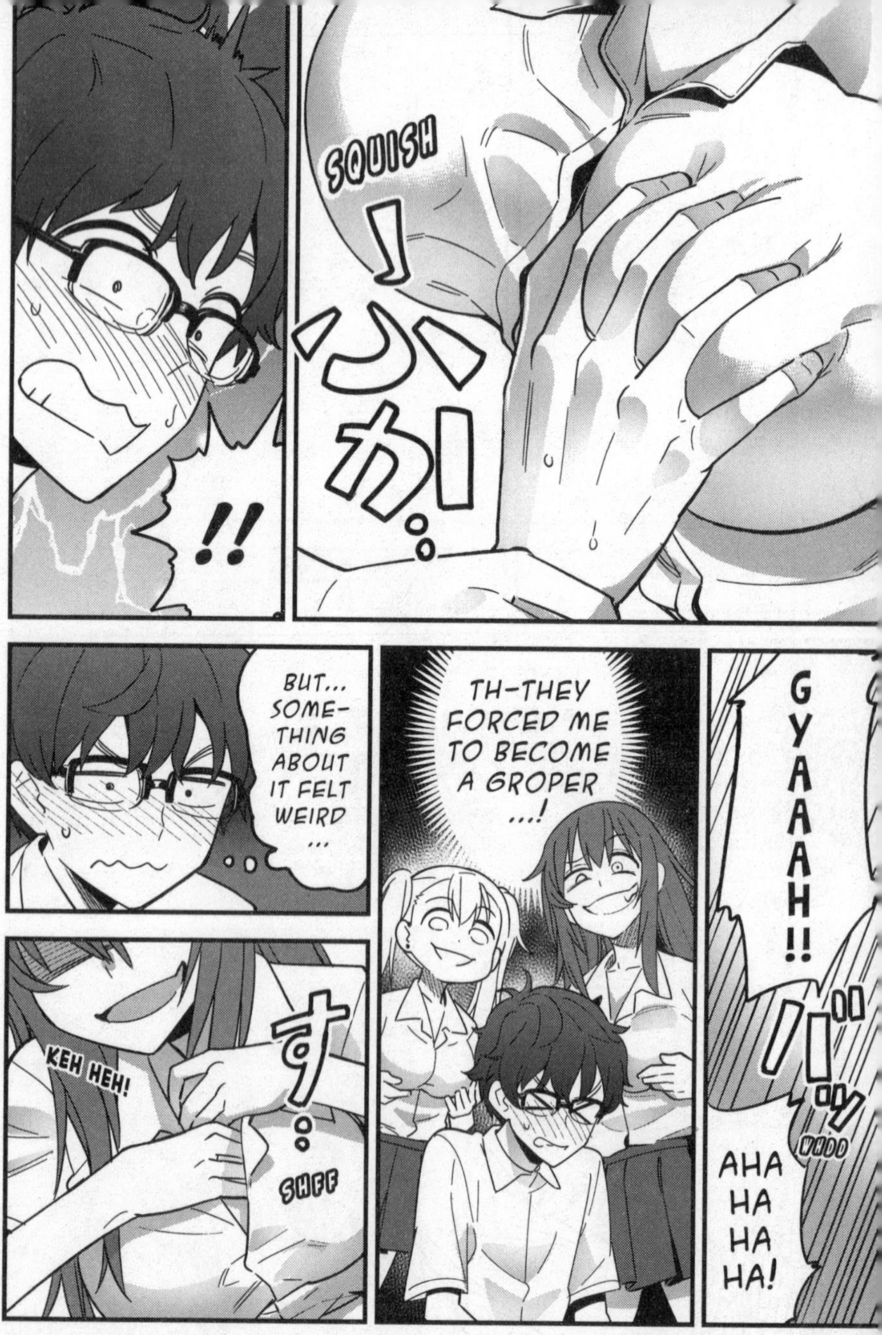

SQUISH
!!
GYAAAH!!
バッ
WHOO
AHA HA HA HA!
TH-THEY FORCED ME TO BECOME A GROPER ...!
BUT... SOMETHING ABOUT IT FELT WEIRD ...
KEH HEH!
す。
SHFF

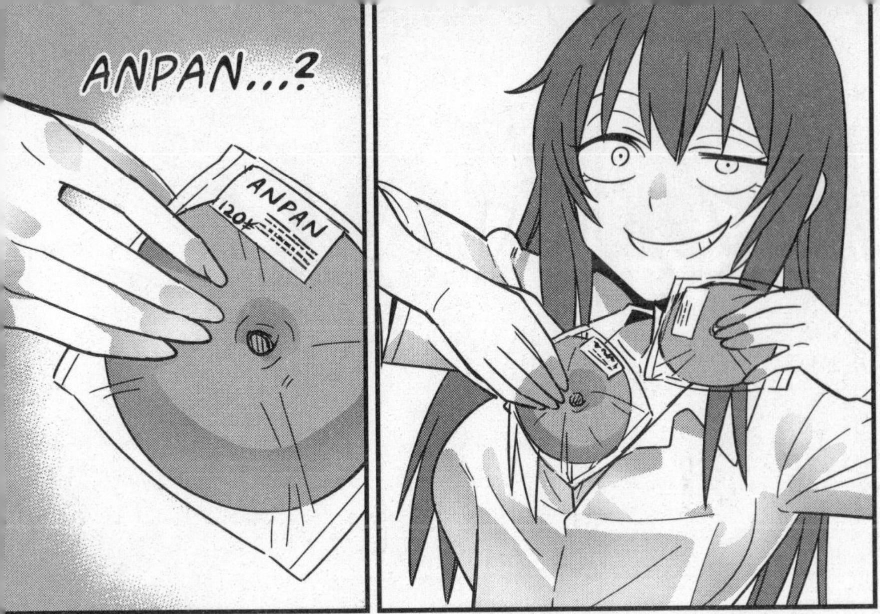
ANPAN...?
ANPAN
120¥

*pastry filled with sweet red bean paste

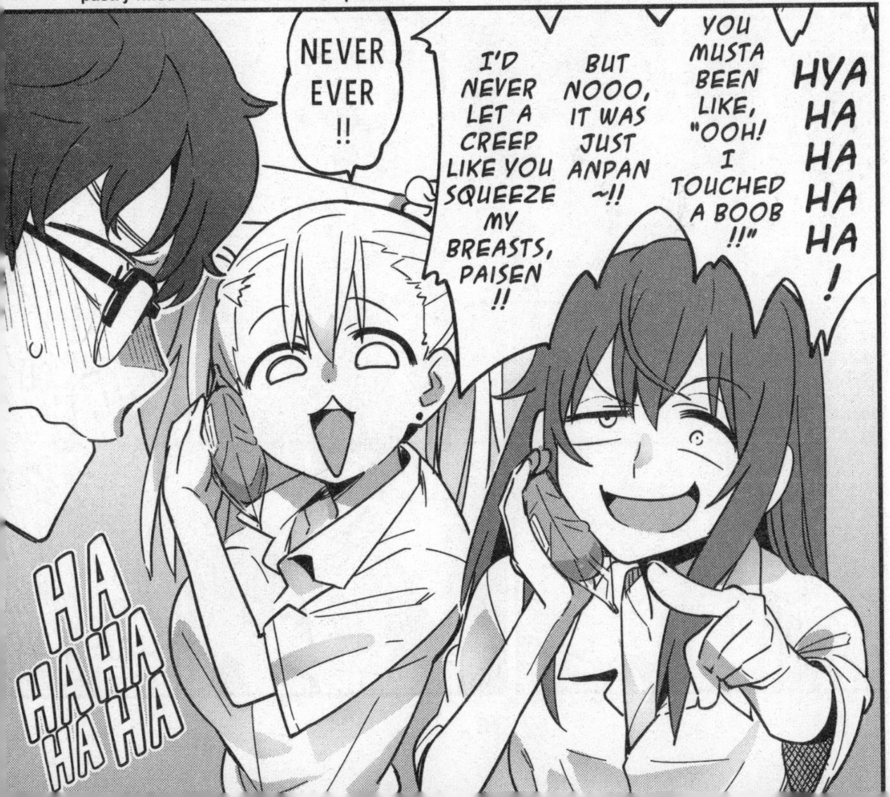
HYA HA HA HA HA HA!
YOU MUSTA BEEN LIKE, "OOH! I TOUCHED A BOOB!!"
BUT NOOO, IT WAS JUST ANPAN~!!
I'D NEVER LET A CREEP LIKE YOU SQUEEZE MY BREASTS, PAISEN!!
NEVER EVER!!
HA HAHA HAHA HA HA

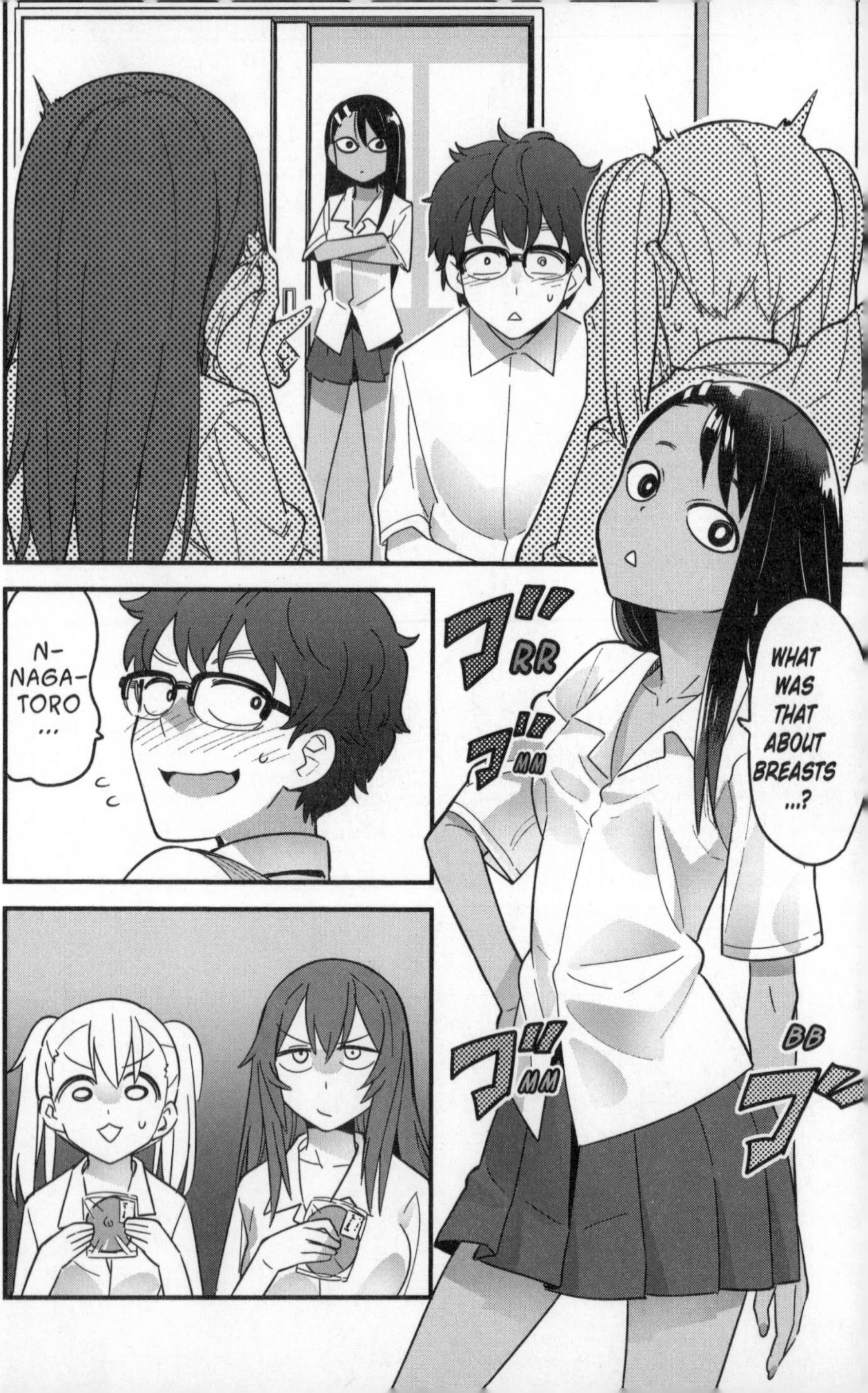
WHAT WAS THAT ABOUT BREASTS ...?
ゴRR
ゴMM
ゴMM
BB ゴ
N-NAGATORO ...

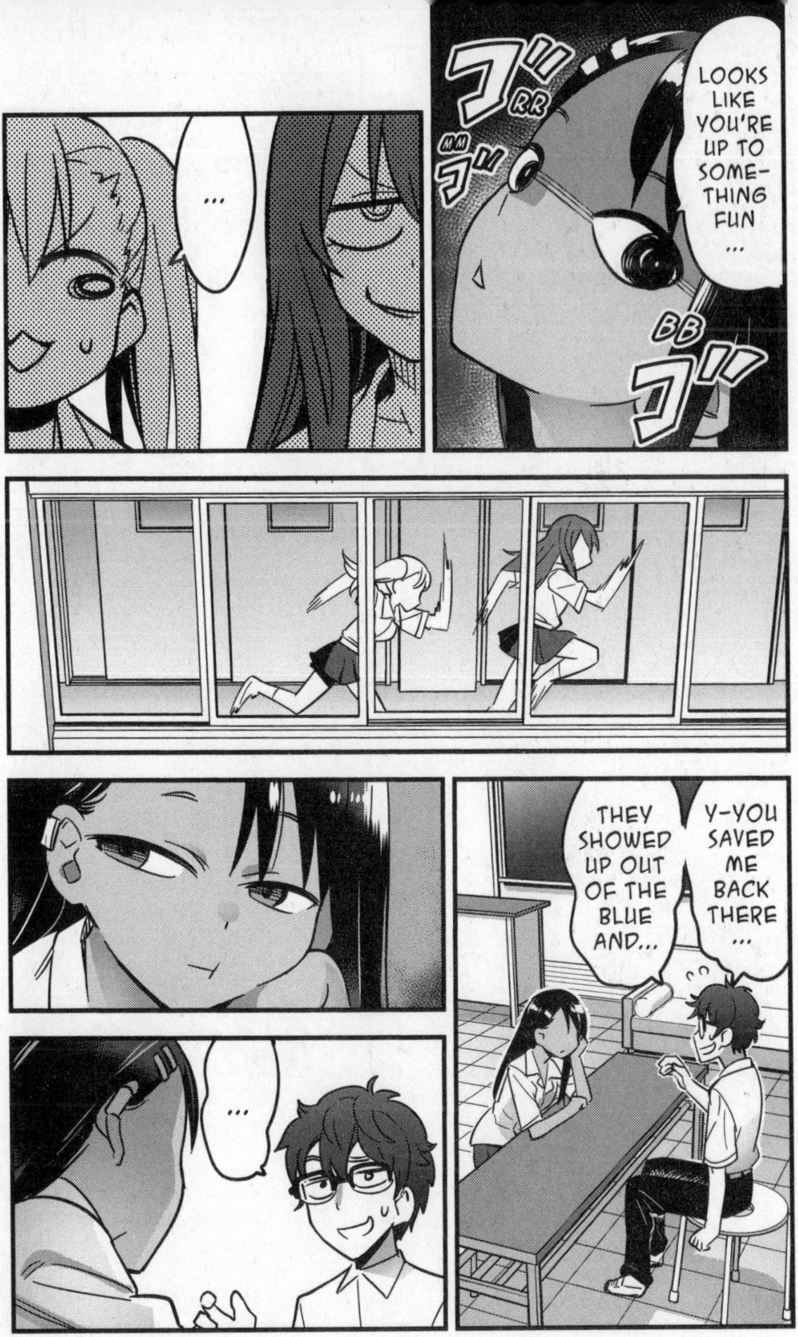
LOOKS LIKE YOU'RE UP TO SOME-THING FUN ...
RR
MM
BB
...
Y-YOU SAVED ME BACK THERE ...
THEY SHOWED UP OUT OF THE BLUE AND...
...

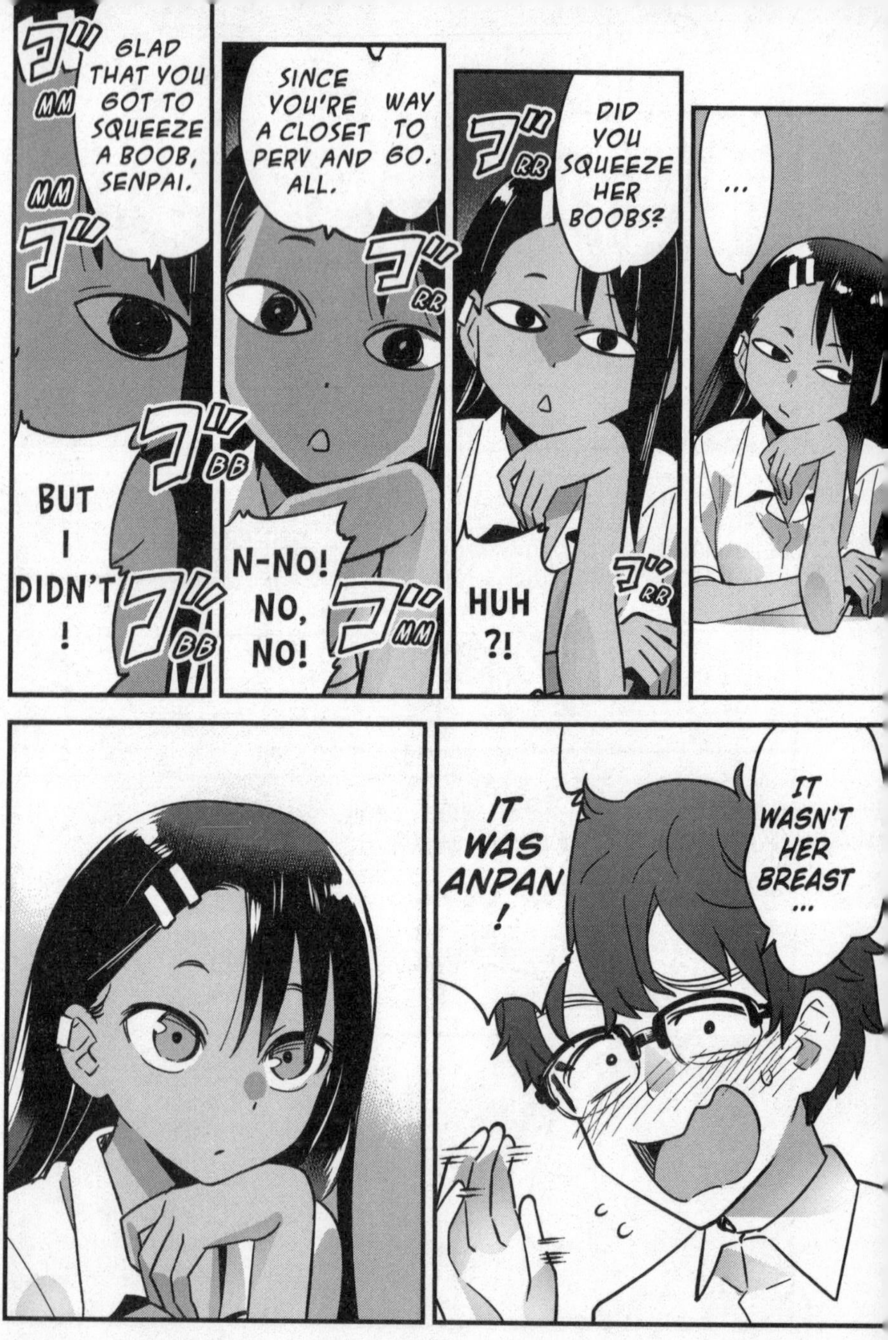
...
DID YOU SQUEEZE HER BOOBS?
RR
RR
HUH ?!
WAY TO GO.
SINCE YOU'RE A CLOSET PERV AND ALL.
RR
MM
N-NO! NO, NO!
GLAD THAT YOU GOT TO SQUEEZE A BOOB, SENPAI.
MM
MM
BB
BB
BUT I DIDN'T!
IT WASN'T HER BREAST...
IT WAS ANPAN!

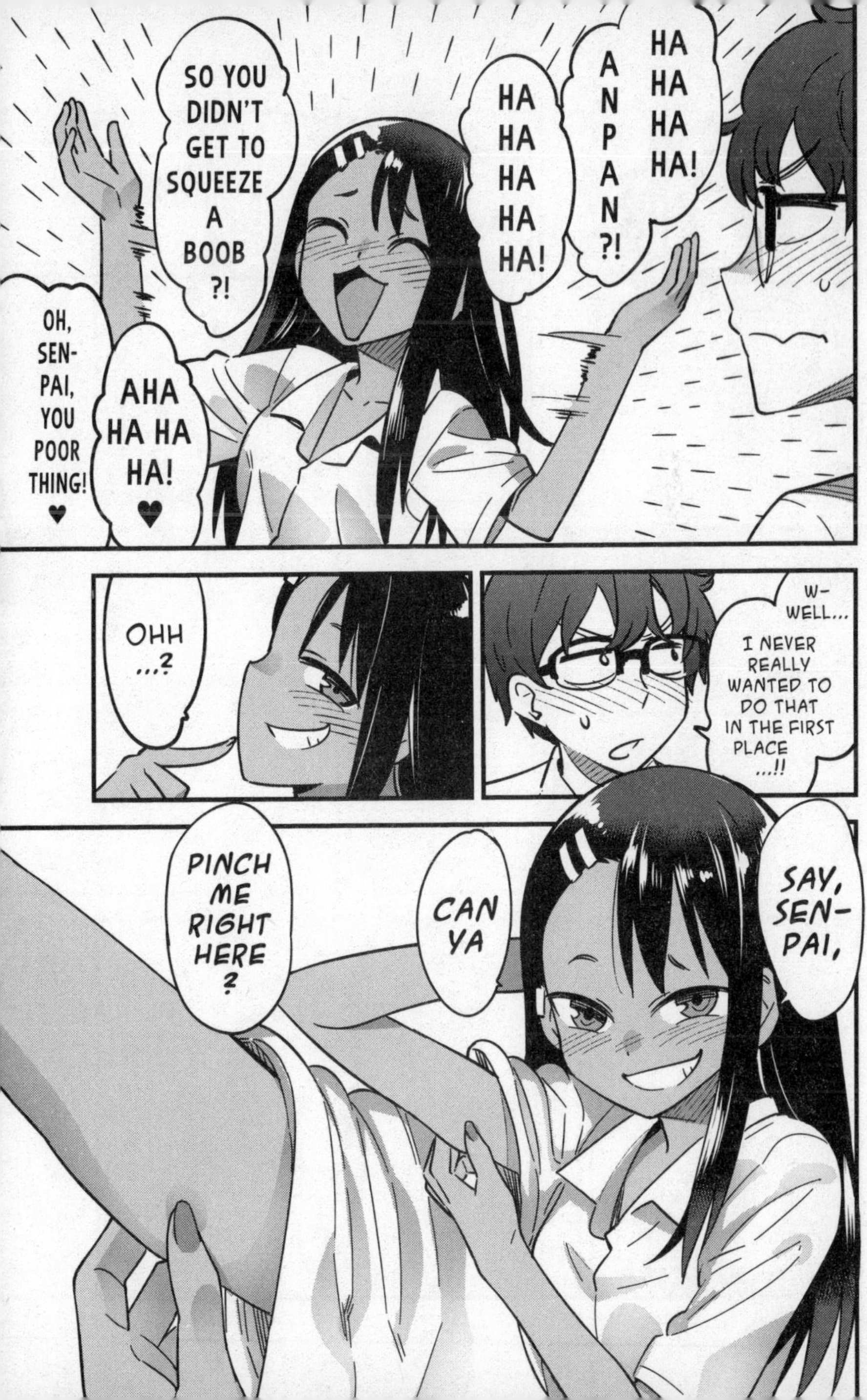
HA HA HA HA!
ANPAN?!
HA HA HA HA HA!
SO YOU DIDN'T GET TO SQUEEZE A BOOB ?!
AHA HA HA HA! ♥
OH, SEN-PAI, YOU POOR THING! ♥
W-WELL... I NEVER REALLY WANTED TO DO THAT IN THE FIRST PLACE ...!!
OHH ...?
SAY, SEN-PAI,
CAN YA
PINCH ME RIGHT HERE?

 I-IF IT'S JUST YOUR ARM, THEN OKAY...

 JUST DO IT!

W-WHY...?

 SOSH

 BADUM BADUM

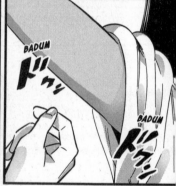 BADUM

BADUM

 HEH...

SENPAI, DONTCHA KNOW...?

 HOW IS IT?

...V-VERY SOFT...

82

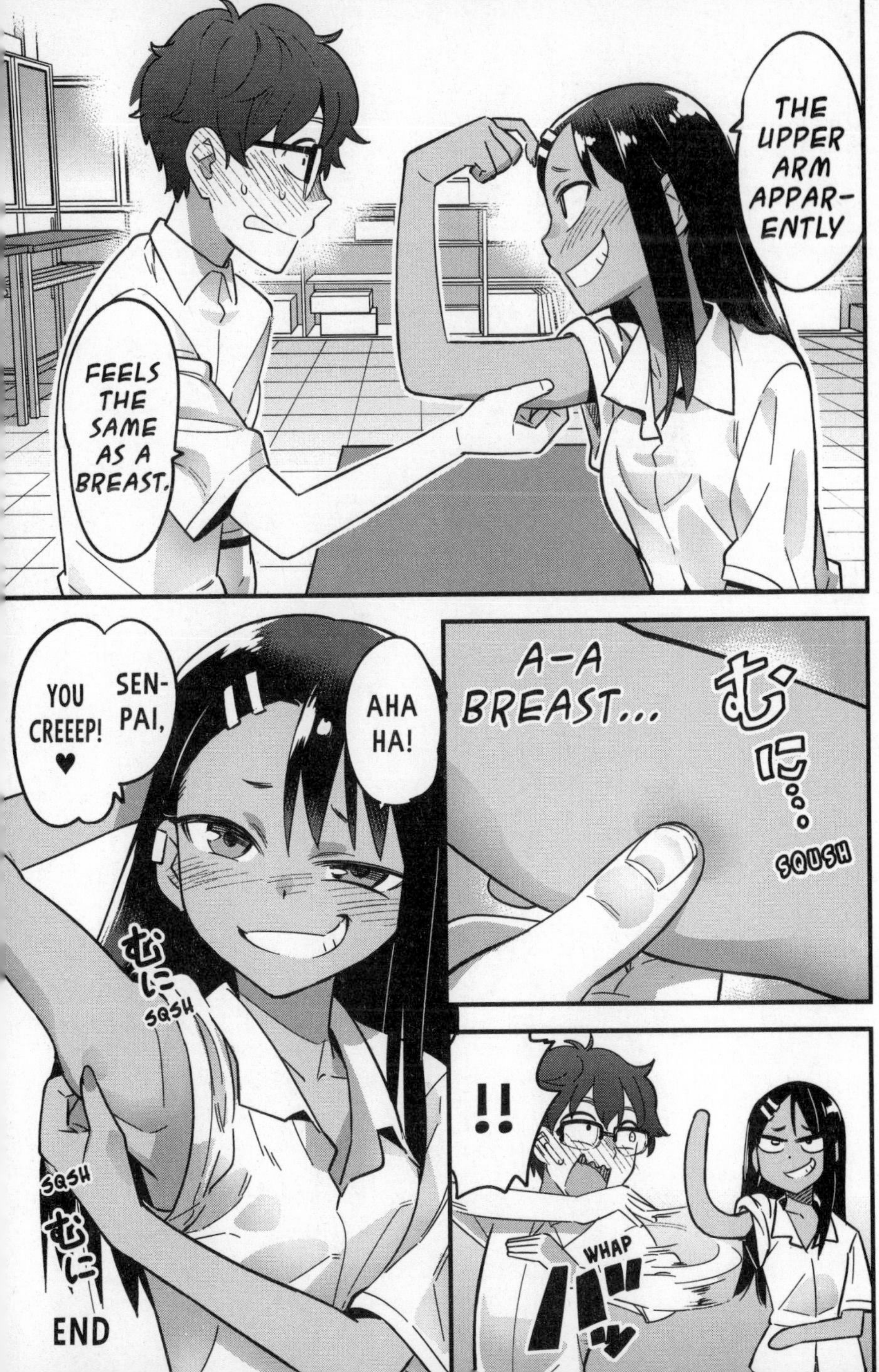
THE UPPER ARM APPARENTLY
FEELS THE SAME AS A BREAST.
A-A BREAST...
むに。。。
SQUSH
!!
WHAP
AHA HA!
SEN-PAI,
YOU CREEEP! ♥
むに
SQSH
SQSH
むに
END

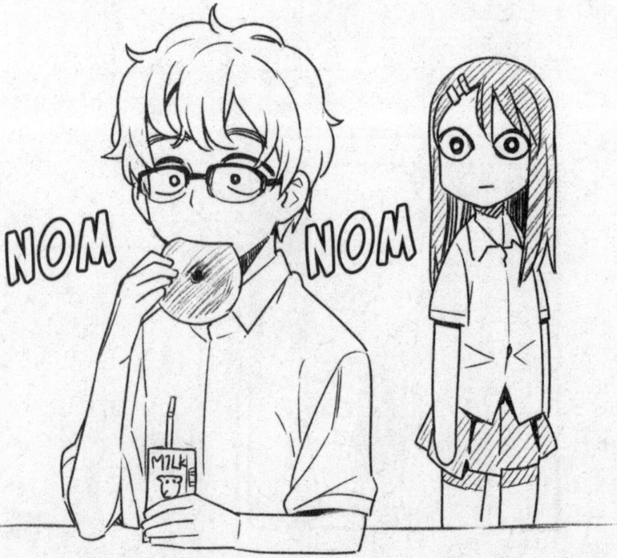
NOM
NOM
MILK

CHAPTER 20: THANKS, SENPAI...

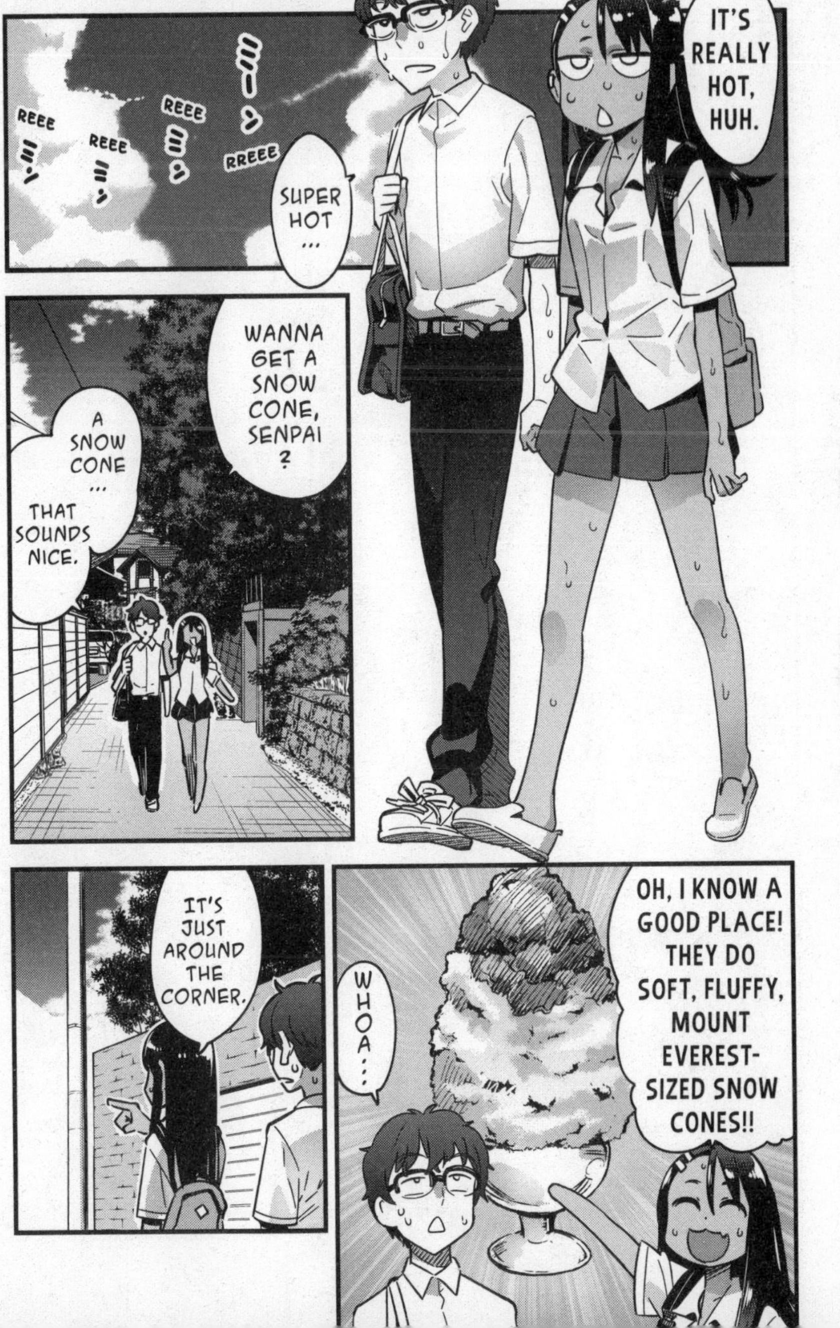
IT'S REALLY HOT, HUH.
RREEE
REEE
REEE
REEE
SUPER HOT ...
WANNA GET A SNOW CONE, SENPAI?
A SNOW CONE ... THAT SOUNDS NICE.
OH, I KNOW A GOOD PLACE! THEY DO SOFT, FLUFFY, MOUNT EVEREST-SIZED SNOW CONES!!
WHOA...
IT'S JUST AROUND THE CORNER.

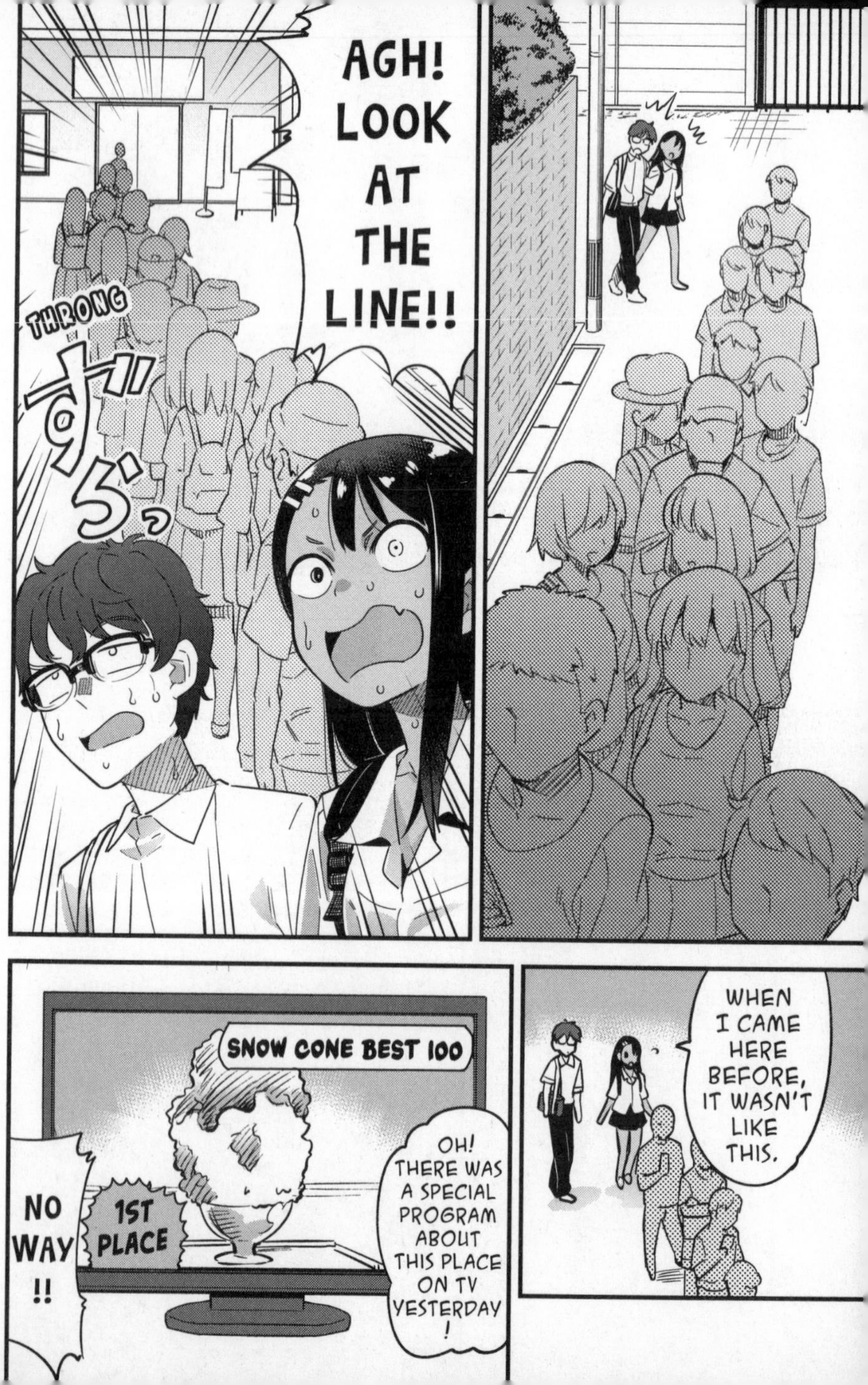
AGH! LOOK AT THE LINE!!
THRONG
ずらっ
WHEN I CAME HERE BEFORE, IT WASN'T LIKE THIS.
OH! THERE WAS A SPECIAL PROGRAM ABOUT THIS PLACE ON TV YESTERDAY!
SNOW CONE BEST 100
1ST PLACE
NO WAY!!

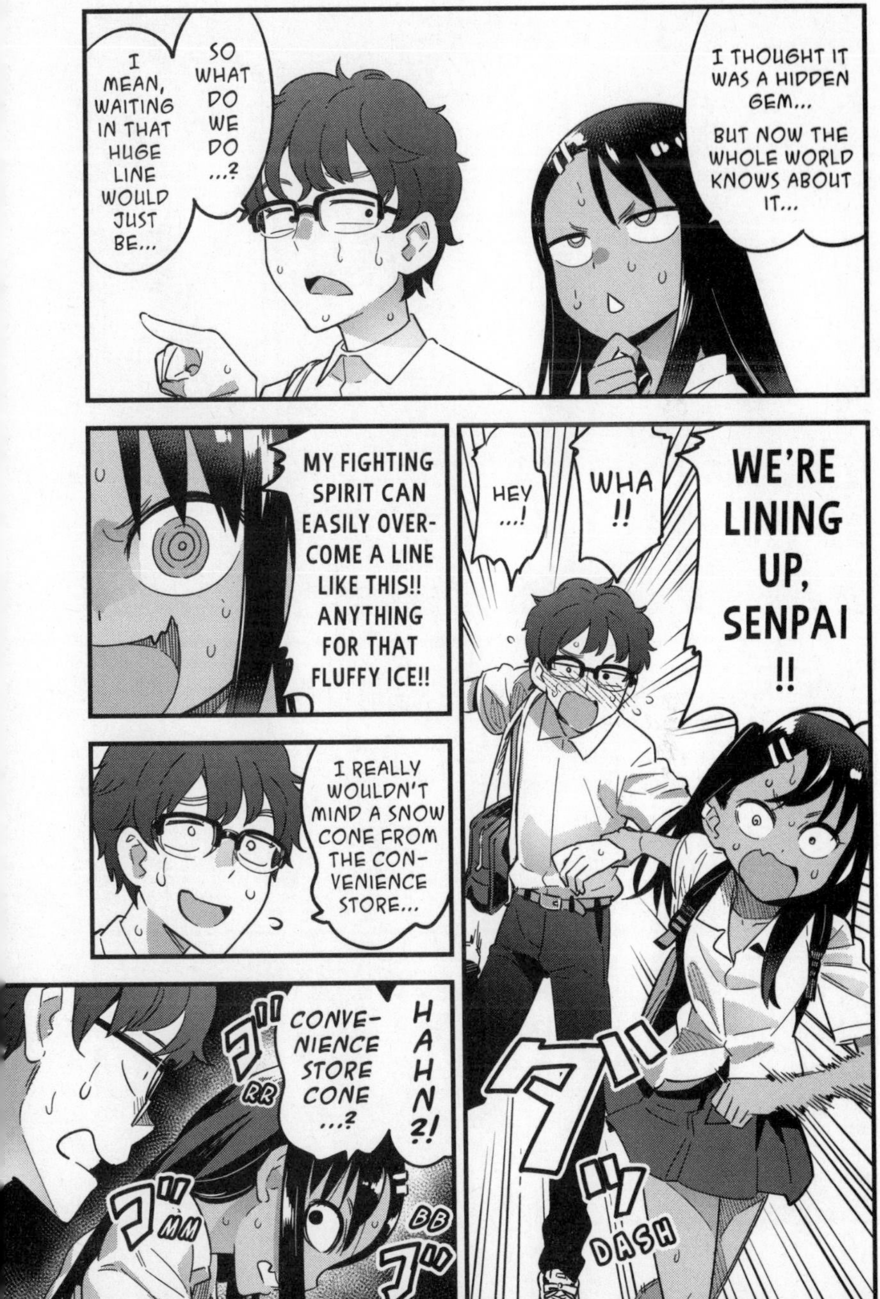

I THOUGHT IT WAS A HIDDEN GEM...
BUT NOW THE WHOLE WORLD KNOWS ABOUT IT...
SO WHAT DO WE DO...?
I MEAN, WAITING IN THAT HUGE LINE WOULD JUST BE...
WE'RE LINING UP, SENPAI!!
WHA!!
HEY...!
DASH
MY FIGHTING SPIRIT CAN EASILY OVER-COME A LINE LIKE THIS!! ANYTHING FOR THAT FLUFFY ICE!!
I REALLY WOULDN'T MIND A SNOW CONE FROM THE CON-VENIENCE STORE...
HAHN?!
CONVE-NIENCE STORE CONE...?
RR
MM
BB

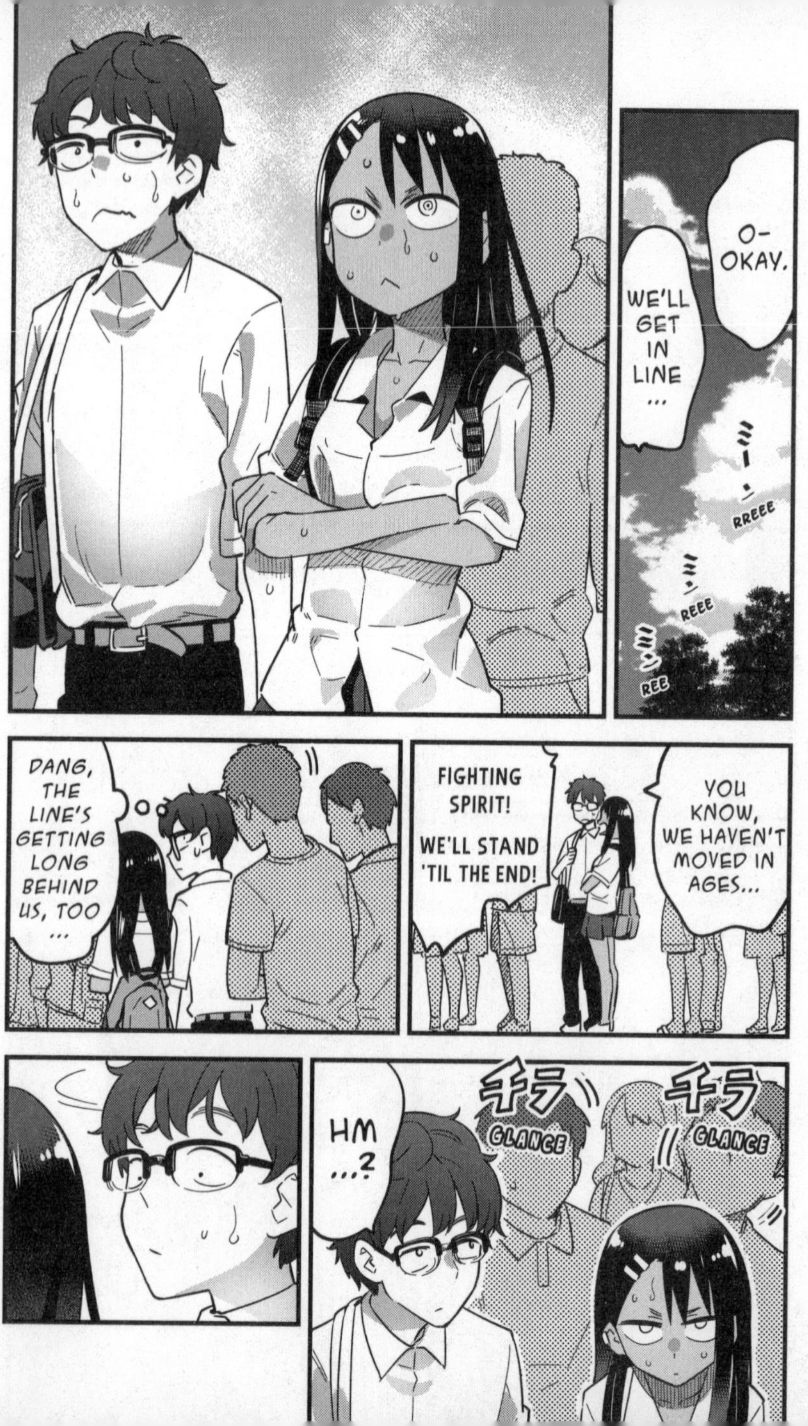

O-OKAY.
WE'LL GET IN LINE...
RREEE
REEE
REE
YOU KNOW, WE HAVEN'T MOVED IN AGES...
FIGHTING SPIRIT!
WE'LL STAND 'TIL THE END!
DANG, THE LINE'S GETTING LONG BEHIND US, TOO...
HM...?
チラ
GLANCE
チラ
GLANCE

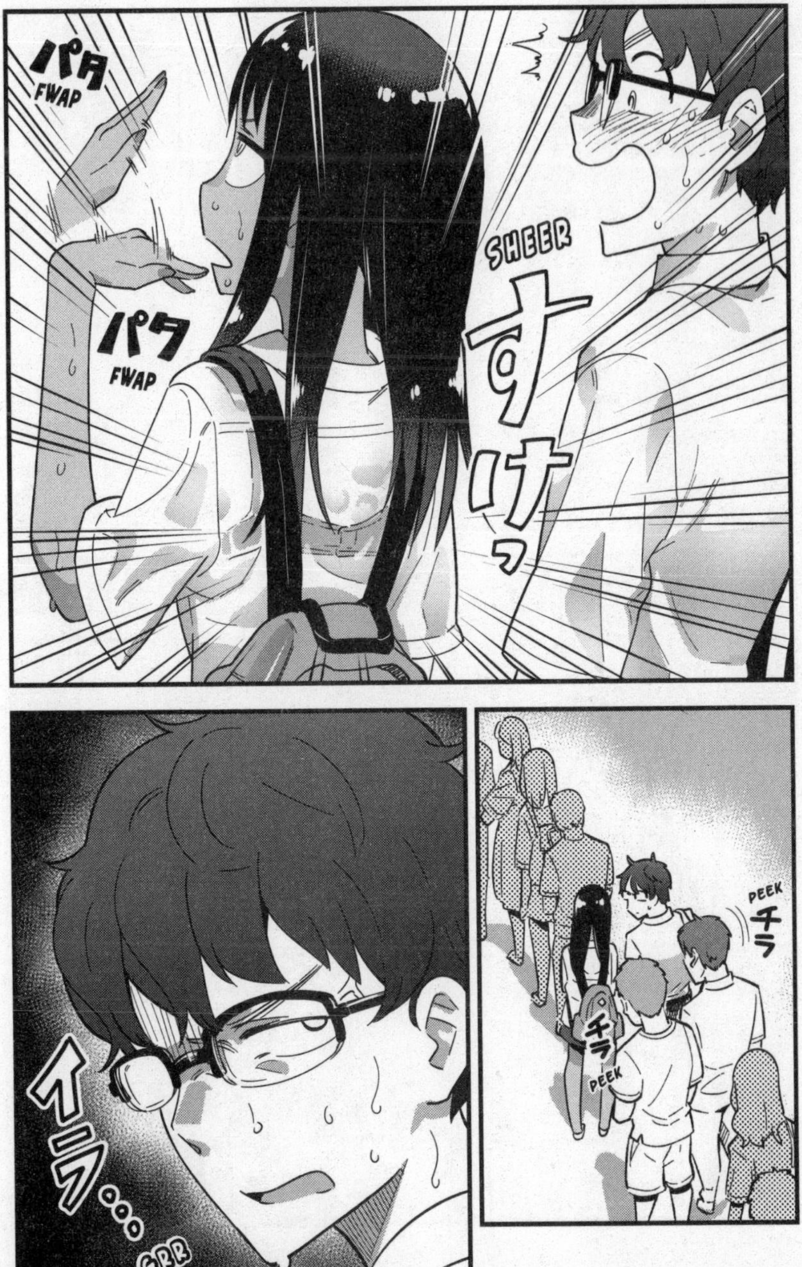
すけっ
SHEER
パタ
FWAP
パタ
FWAP
チラ
PEEK
チラ
PEEK
イラ…
GRR

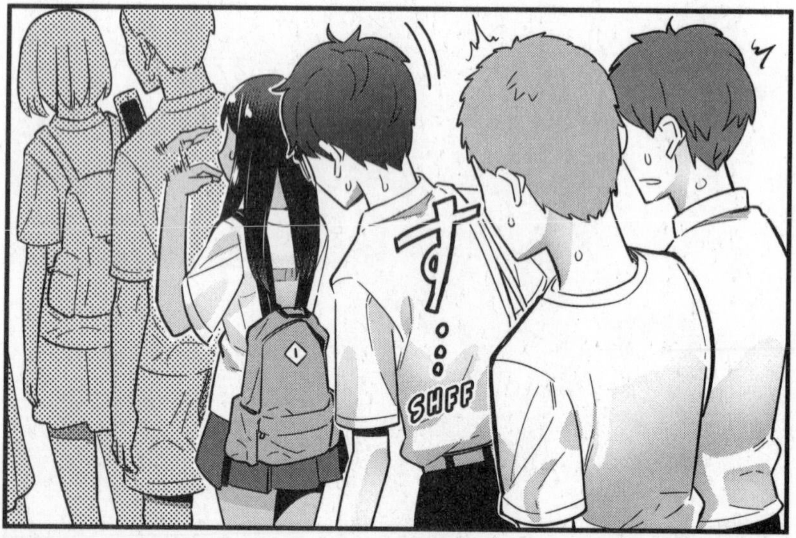
す
SHFF
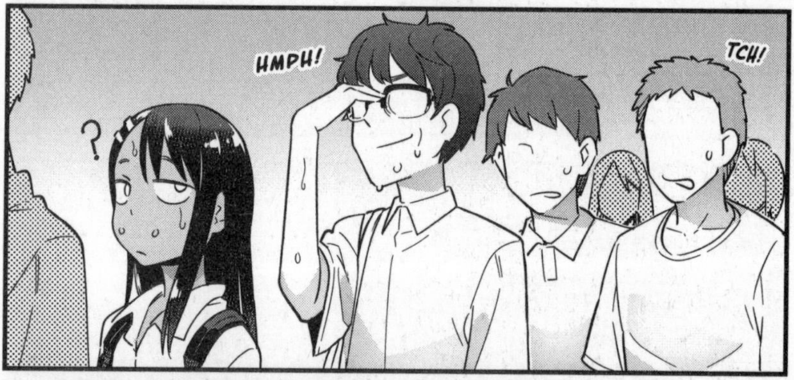
TCH!
HMPH!
?
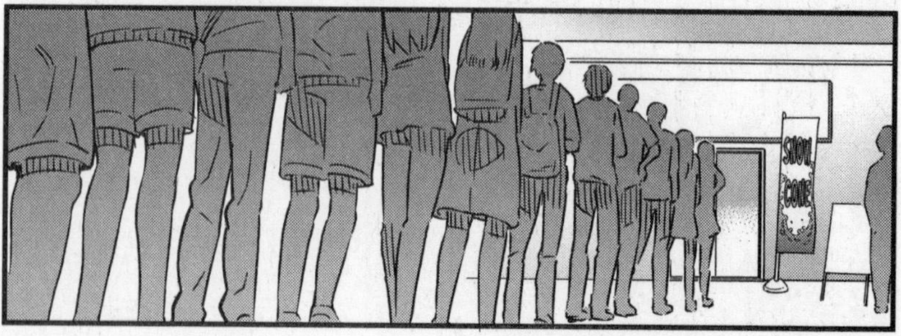

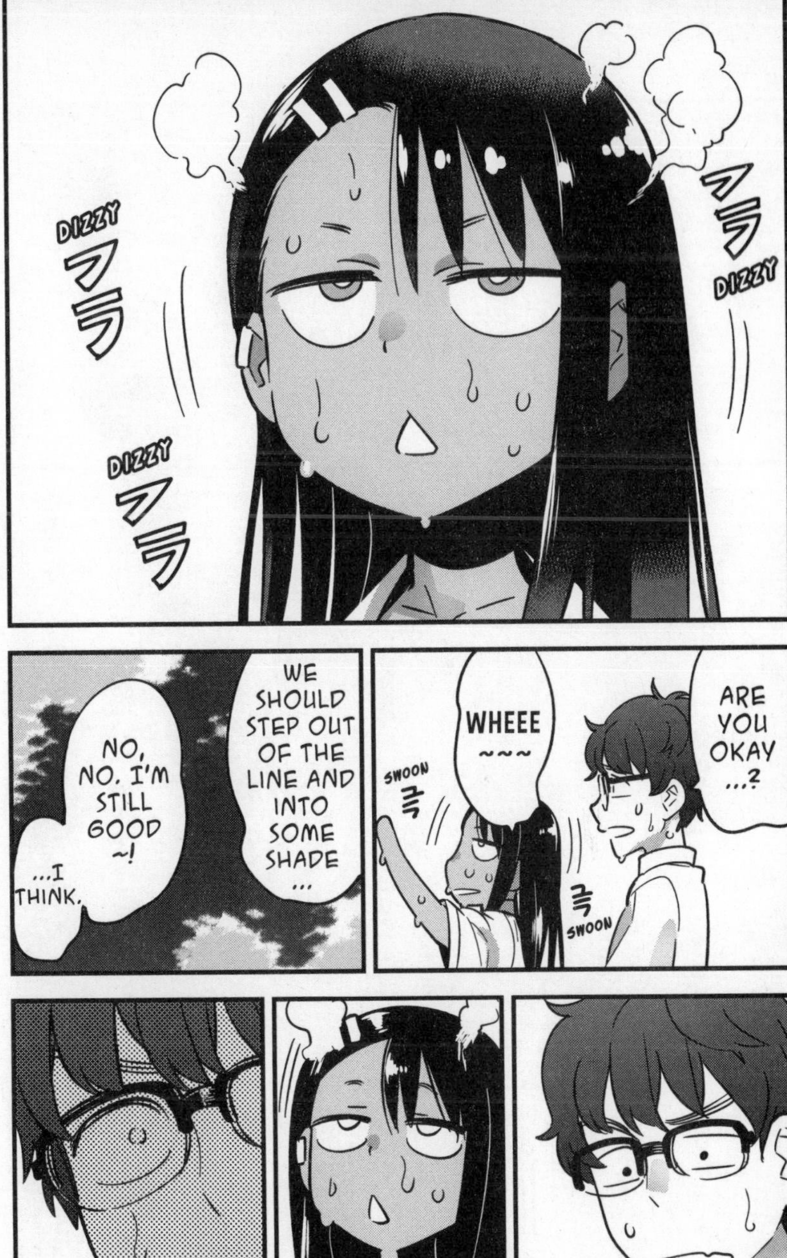
フラ
DIZZY
DIZZY
フラ
DIZZY
フラ
ARE YOU OKAY ...?
WHEEE ~~~
SWOON
SWOON
WE SHOULD STEP OUT OF THE LINE AND INTO SOME SHADE ...
NO, NO. I'M STILL GOOD ~!
...I THINK.

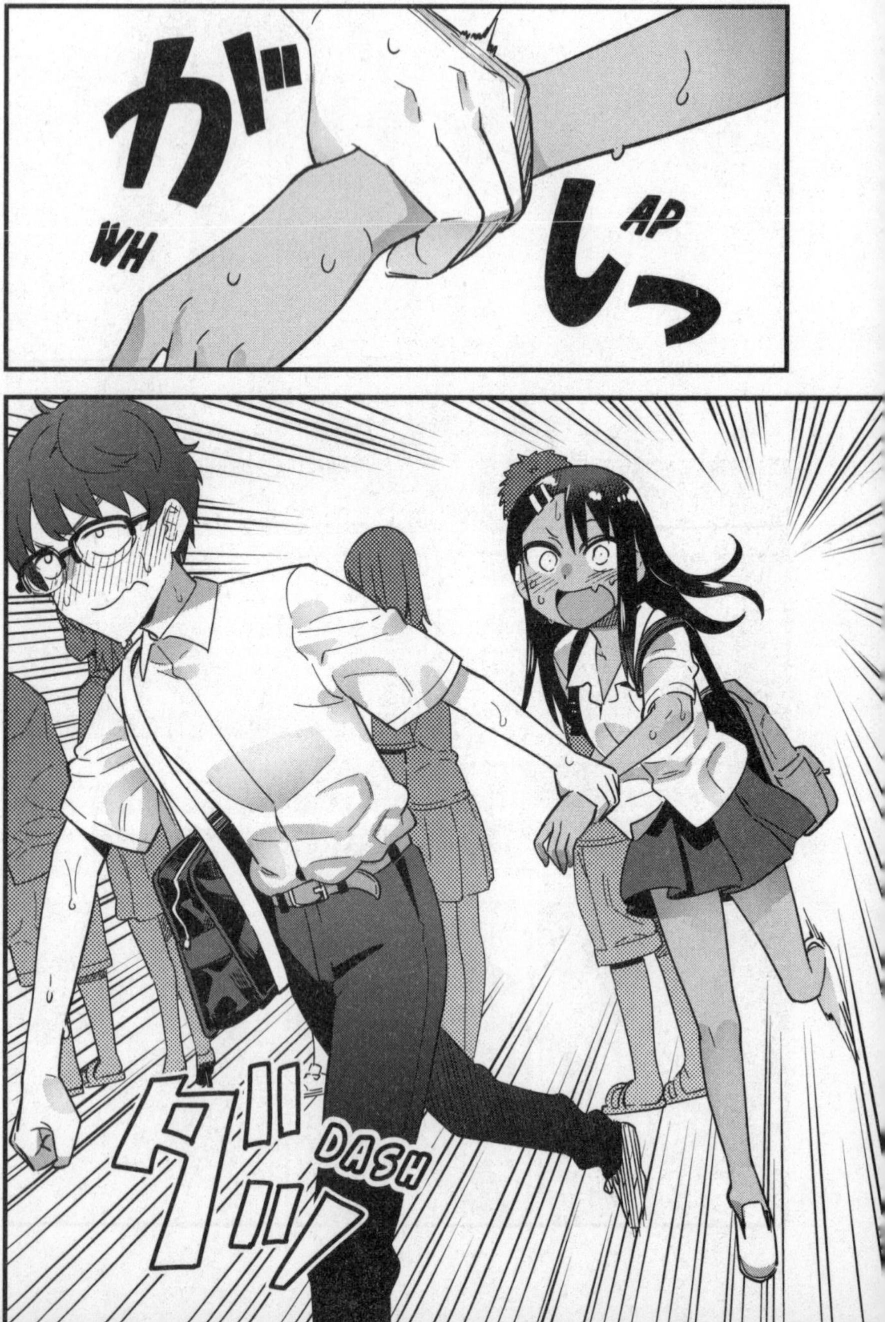
がしっ
WHAP
ダッ
DASH

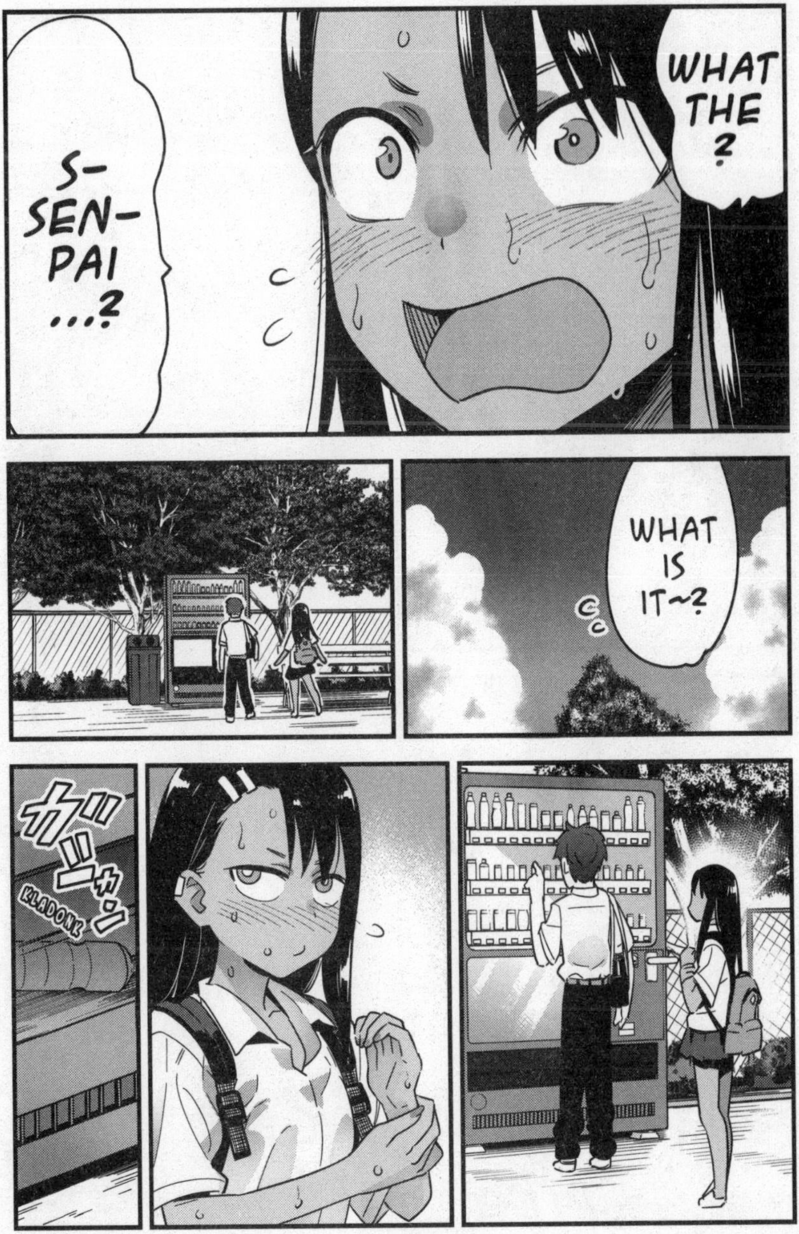
WHAT THE?
S-SEN-PAI...?
WHAT IS IT~?
KLADONK

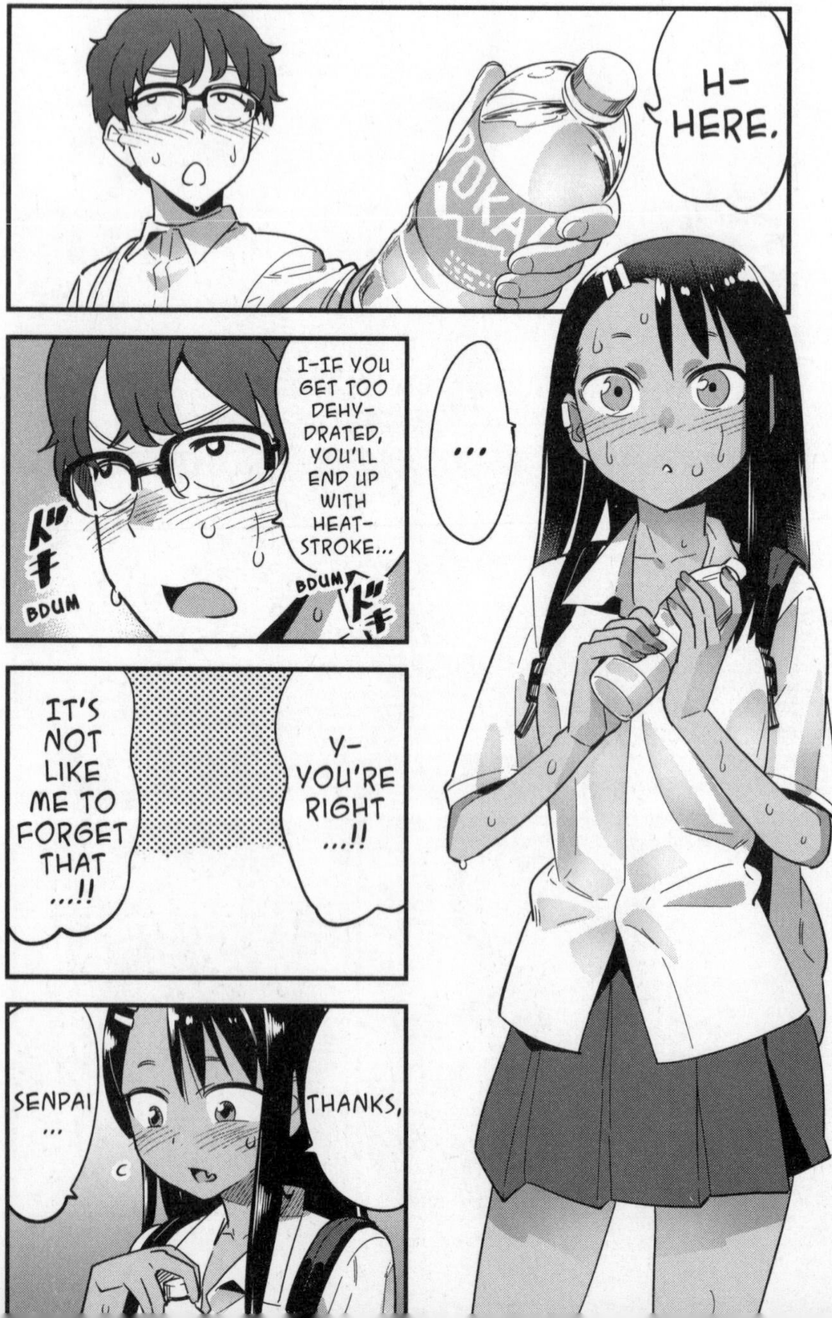
H-
HERE.
...
I-IF YOU GET TOO DEHYDRATED, YOU'LL END UP WITH HEAT-STROKE...
BDUM ドキ
ドキ BDUM
Y- YOU'RE RIGHT ...!!
IT'S NOT LIKE ME TO FORGET THAT ...!!
THANKS,
SENPAI ...

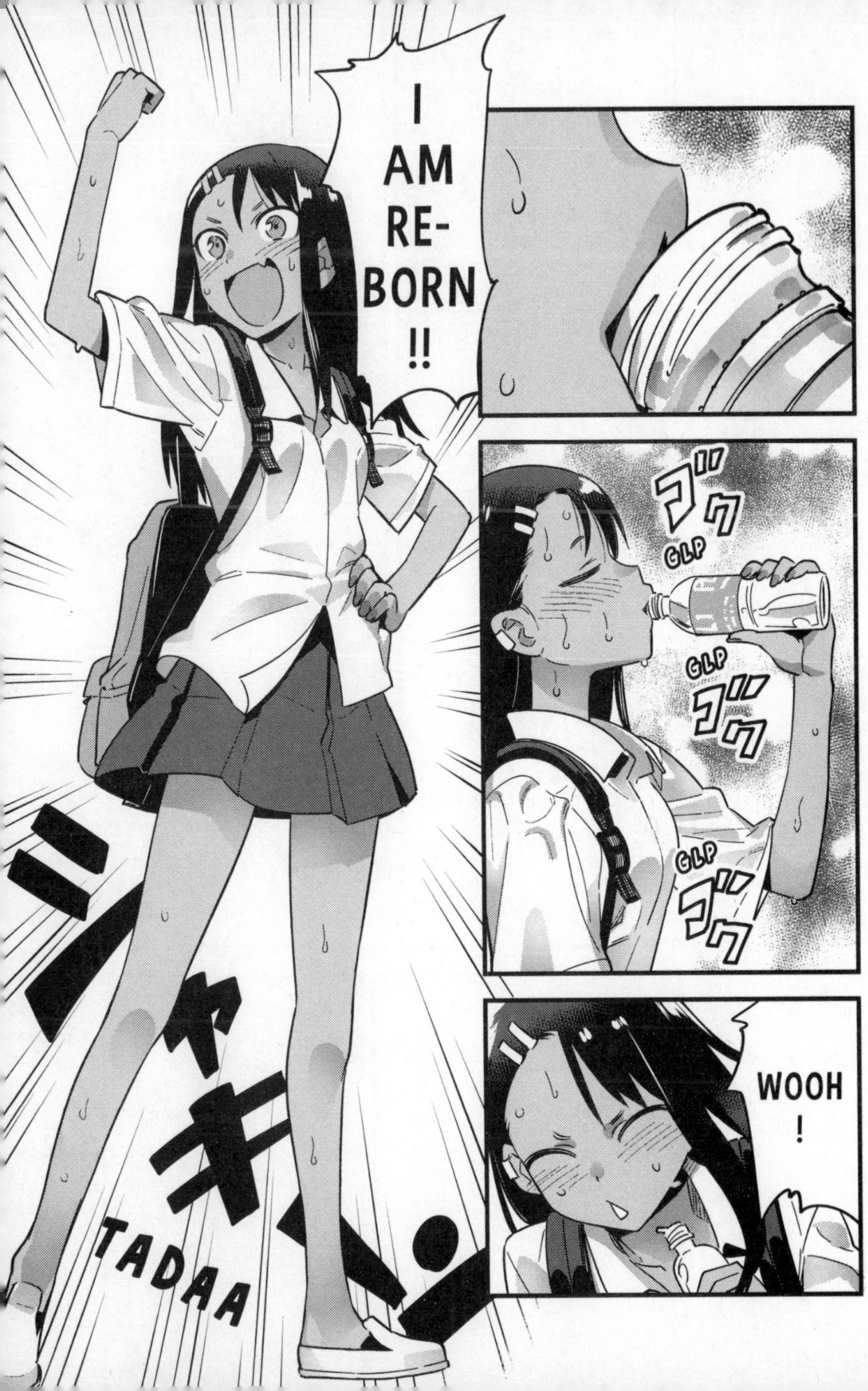
ゴク
GLP
GLP
ゴク
GLP
ゴク
WOOH !
I AM RE-BORN !!
TADAA

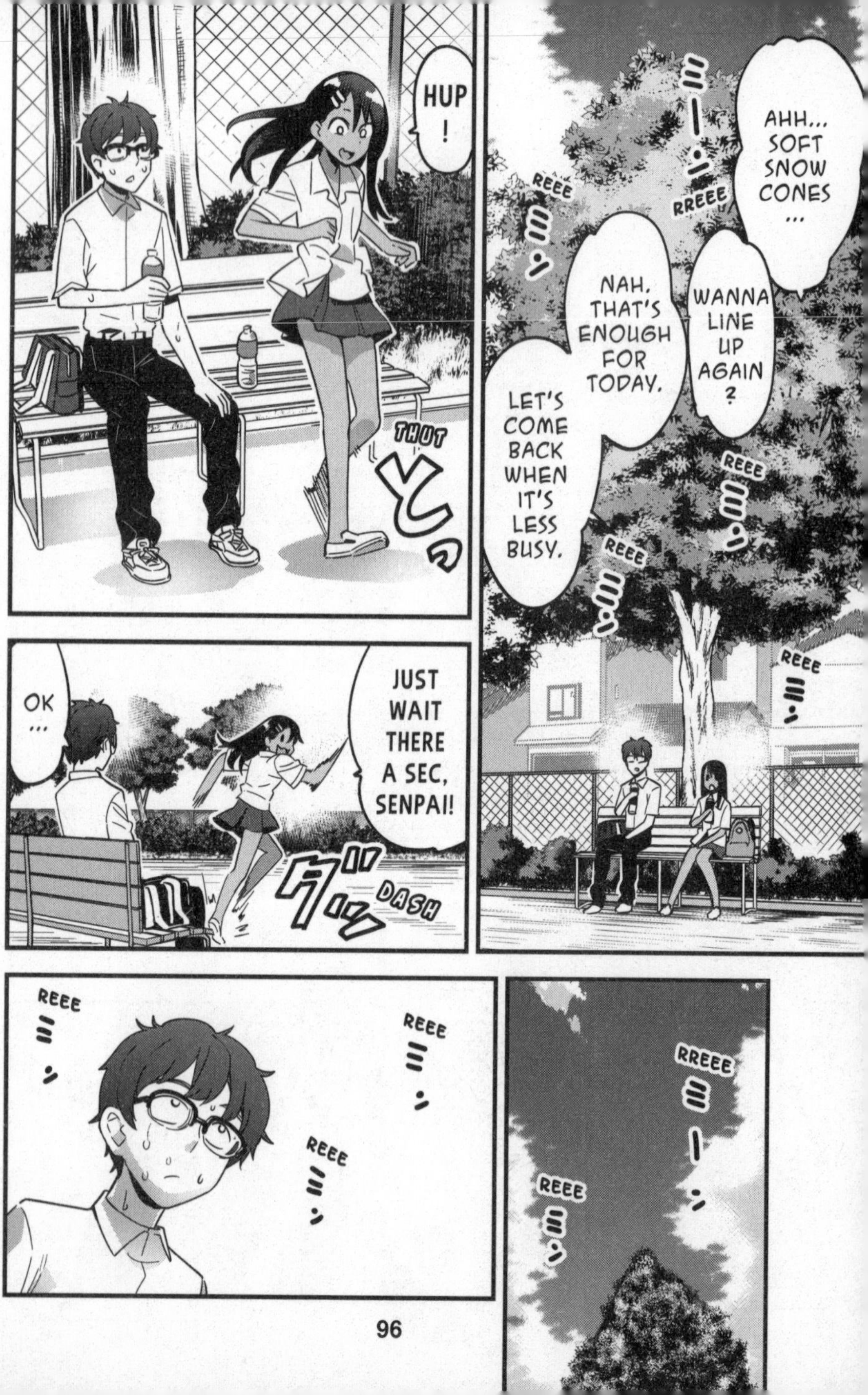

AHH... SOFT SNOW CONES ...
RREEE
REEE
WANNA LINE UP AGAIN ?
NAH. THAT'S ENOUGH FOR TODAY.
LET'S COME BACK WHEN IT'S LESS BUSY.
REEE
REEE
REEE
HUP !
THUT
JUST WAIT THERE A SEC, SENPAI!
OK ...
DASH
RREEE
REEE
REEE
REEE
REEE

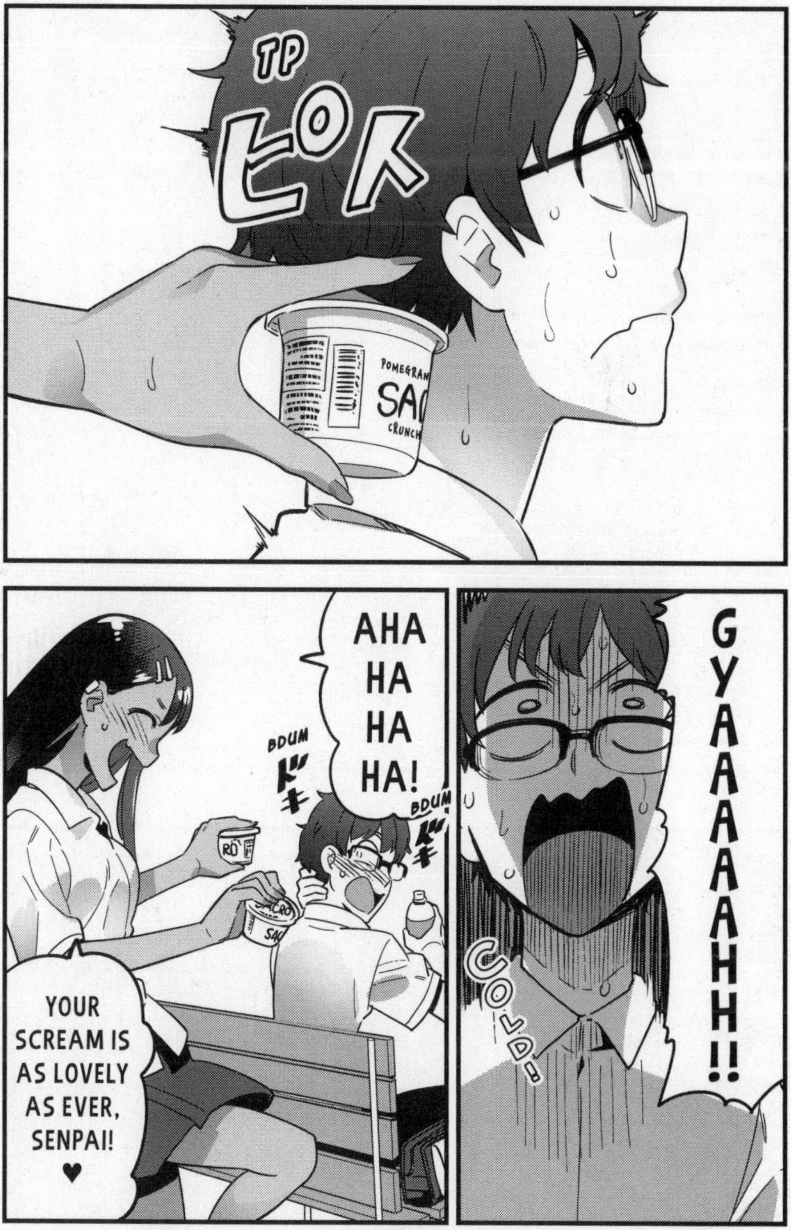
TP
GYAAAAAAAHH!!
COLD!
AHA HA HA HA!
BDUM
BDUM
YOUR SCREAM IS AS LOVELY AS EVER, SENPAI! ♥

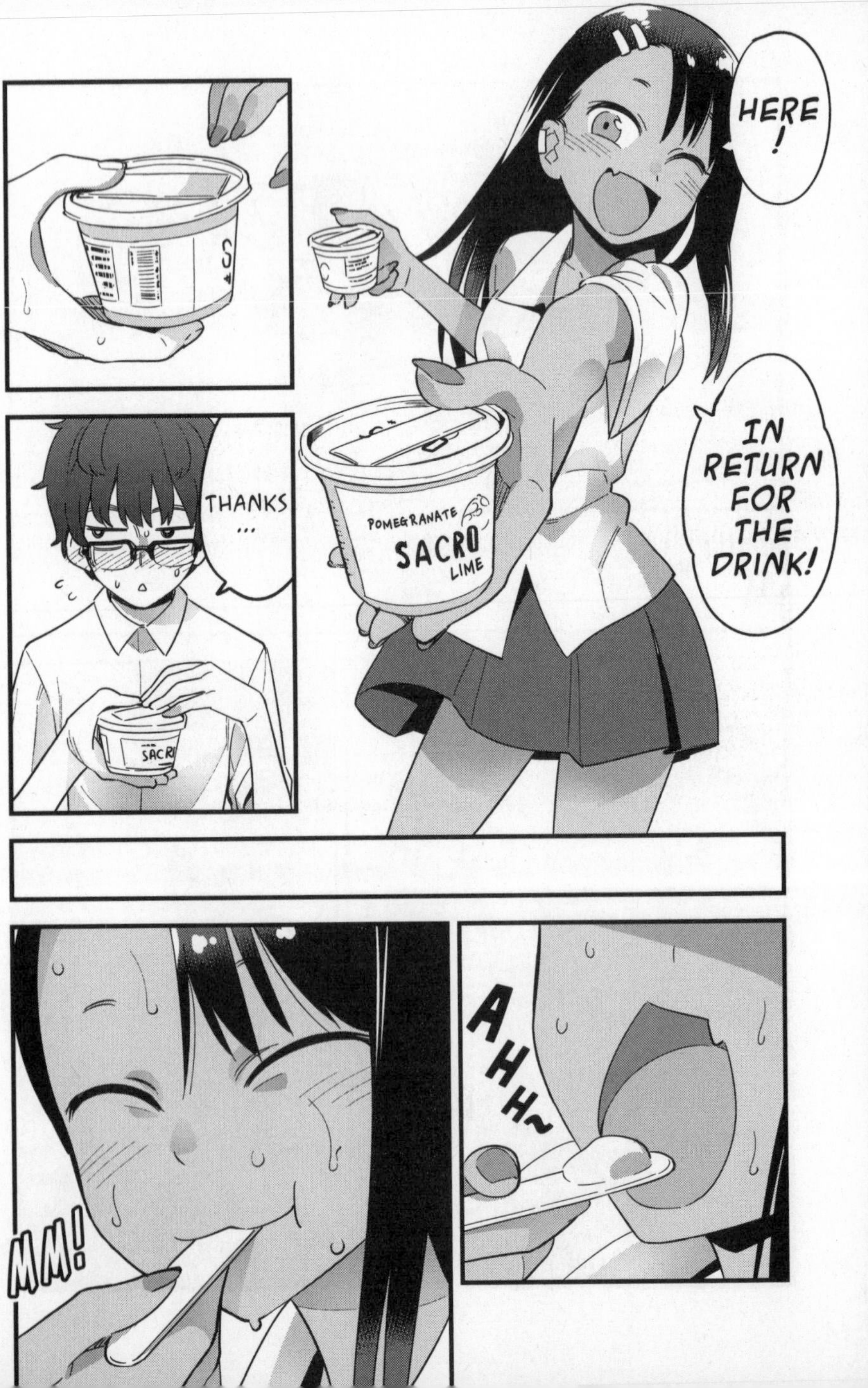
HERE!
IN RETURN FOR THE DRINK!
POMEGRANATE SACRO LIME
THANKS ...
AHH~
MM!

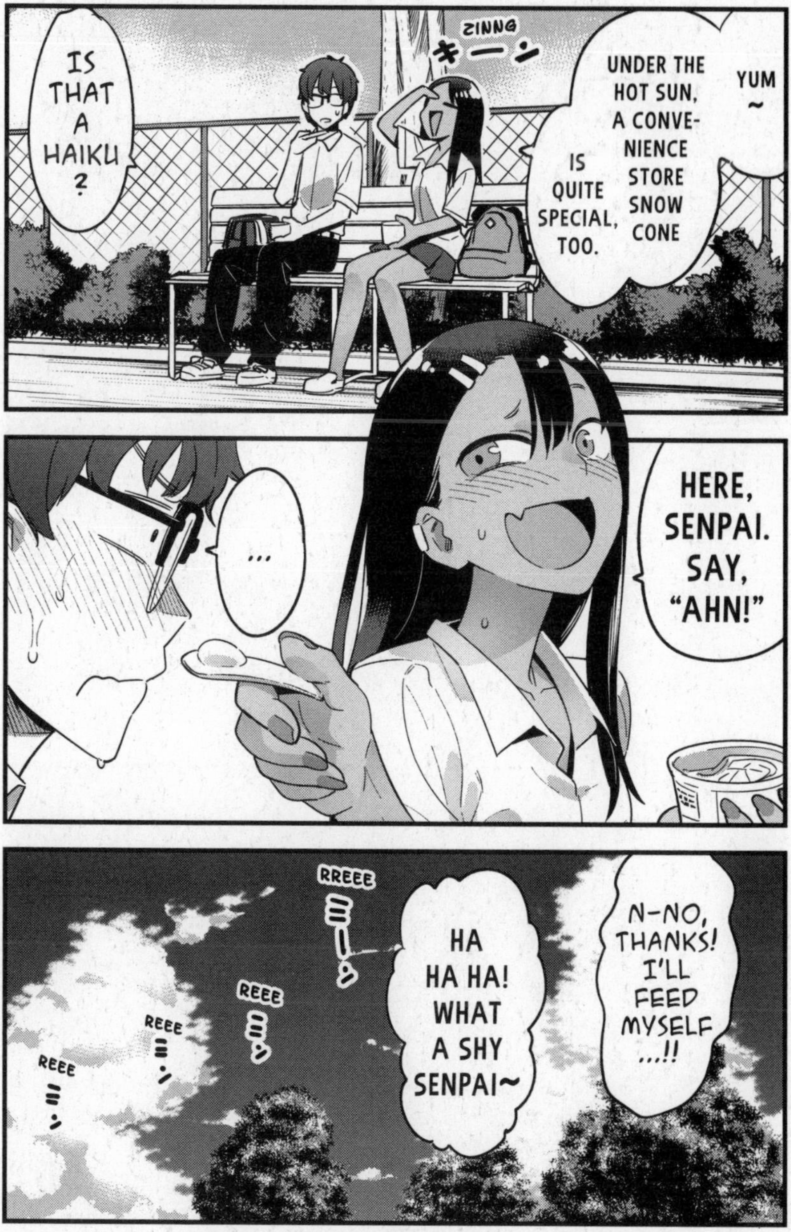
YUM ~
UNDER THE HOT SUN, A CONVENIENCE STORE SNOW CONE IS QUITE SPECIAL, TOO.
ZINNG キーン
IS THAT A HAIKU?
HERE, SENPAI. SAY, "AHN!"
...
N-NO, THANKS! I'LL FEED MYSELF ...!!
HA HA HA! WHAT A SHY SENPAI~
RREEE ミーン
REEE ミーン
REEE ミーン
REEE ミーン

END

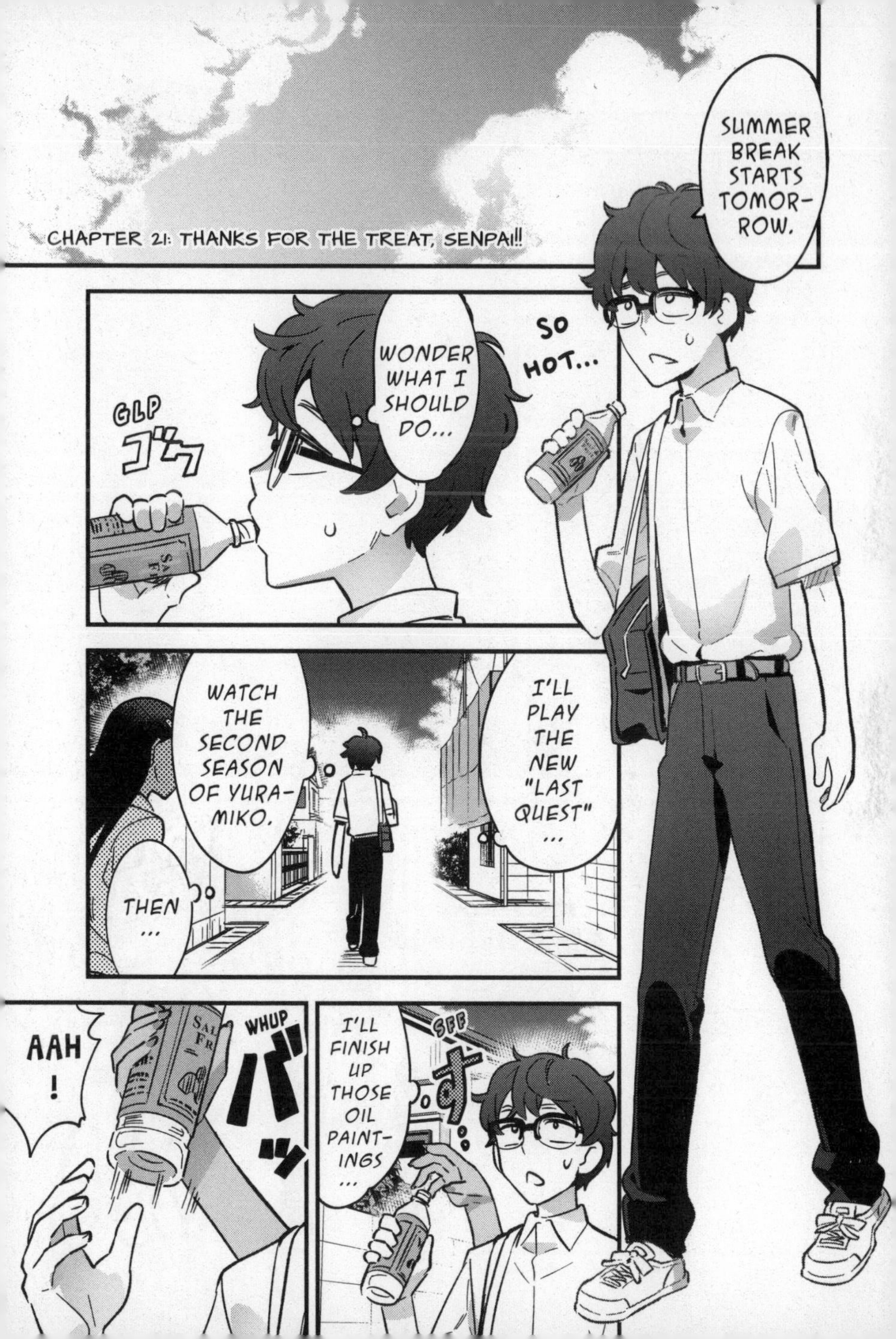
CHAPTER 21: THANKS FOR THE TREAT, SENPAI!!
SUMMER BREAK STARTS TOMOR-ROW.
SO HOT...
GLP
ゴク
WONDER WHAT I SHOULD DO...
I'LL PLAY THE NEW "LAST QUEST" ...
WATCH THE SECOND SEASON OF YURA-MIKO.
THEN ...
SFF
す
I'LL FINISH UP THOSE OIL PAINT-INGS ...
WHUP
バッ
AAH !

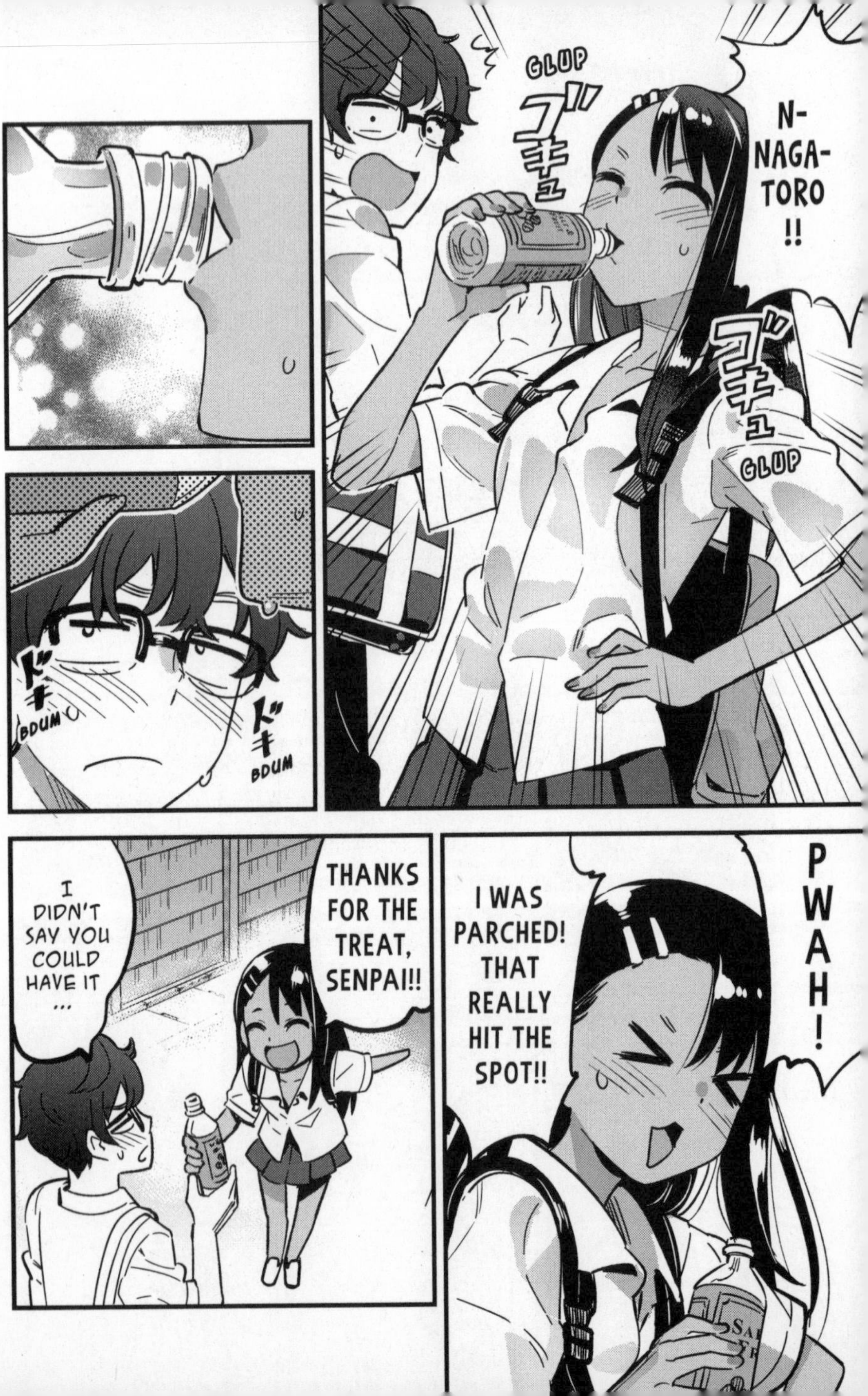
N-NAGA-TORO!!
GLUP
ゴキュ
ゴキュ
GLUP
ドキ
BDUM
ドキ
BDUM
PWAH!
I WAS PARCHED! THAT REALLY HIT THE SPOT!!
THANKS FOR THE TREAT, SENPAI!!
I DIDN'T SAY YOU COULD HAVE IT ...

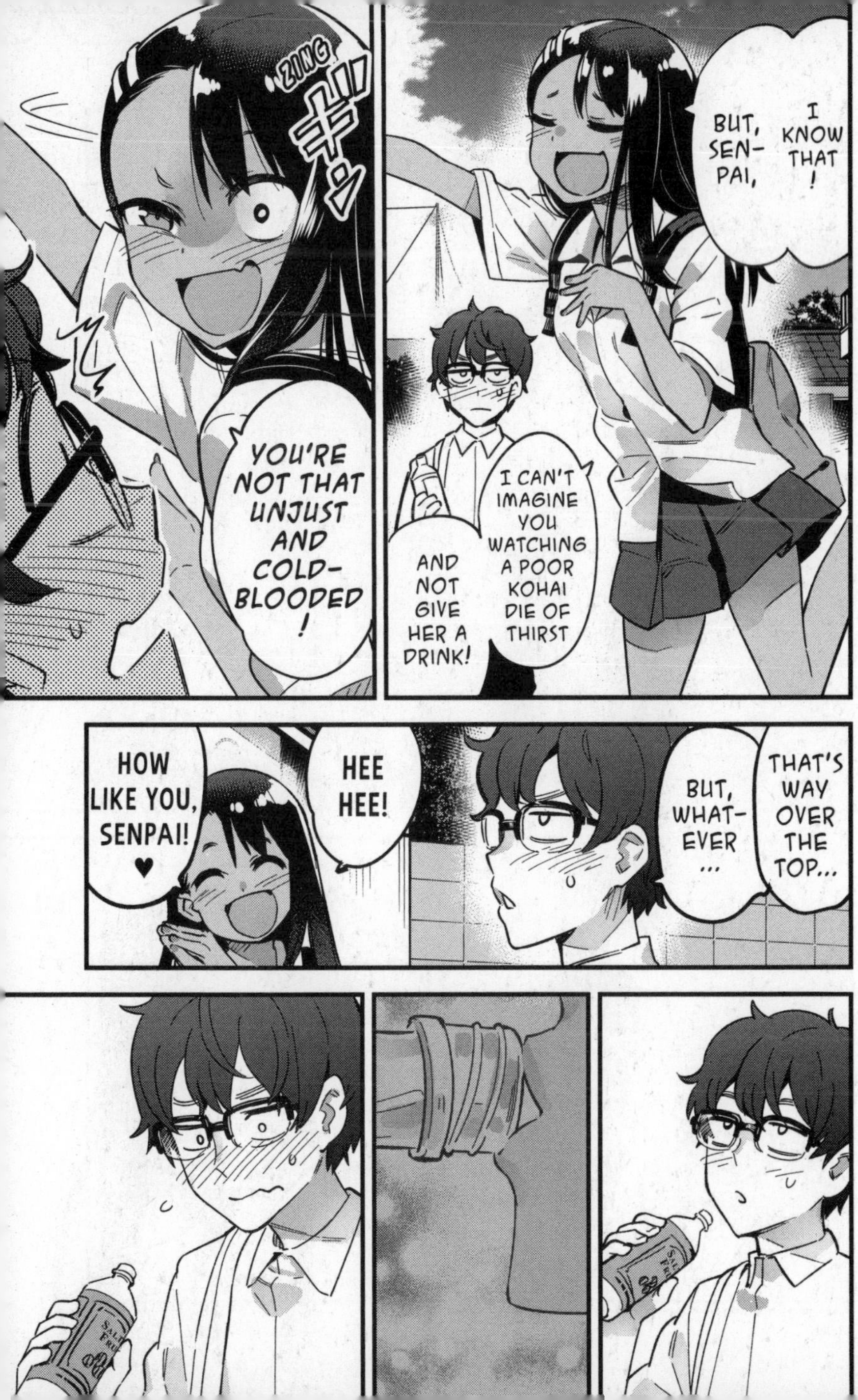
I KNOW THAT!
BUT, SENPAI,
I CAN'T IMAGINE YOU WATCHING A POOR KOHAI DIE OF THIRST
AND NOT GIVE HER A DRINK!
ZING
YOU'RE NOT THAT UNJUST AND COLD-BLOODED!
THAT'S WAY OVER THE TOP...
BUT, WHATEVER...
HEE HEE!
HOW LIKE YOU, SENPAI! ♥

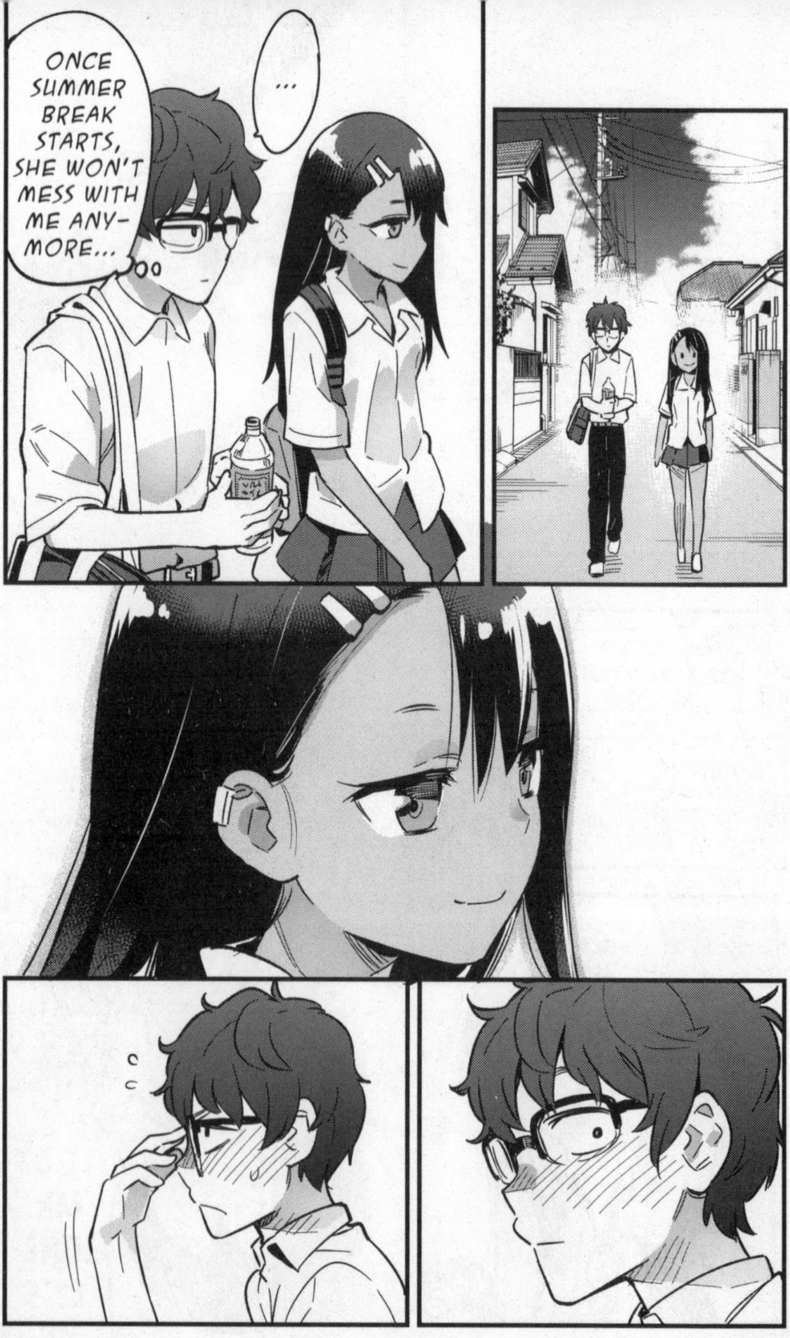
...
ONCE SUMMER BREAK STARTS, SHE WON'T MESS WITH ME ANY-MORE...

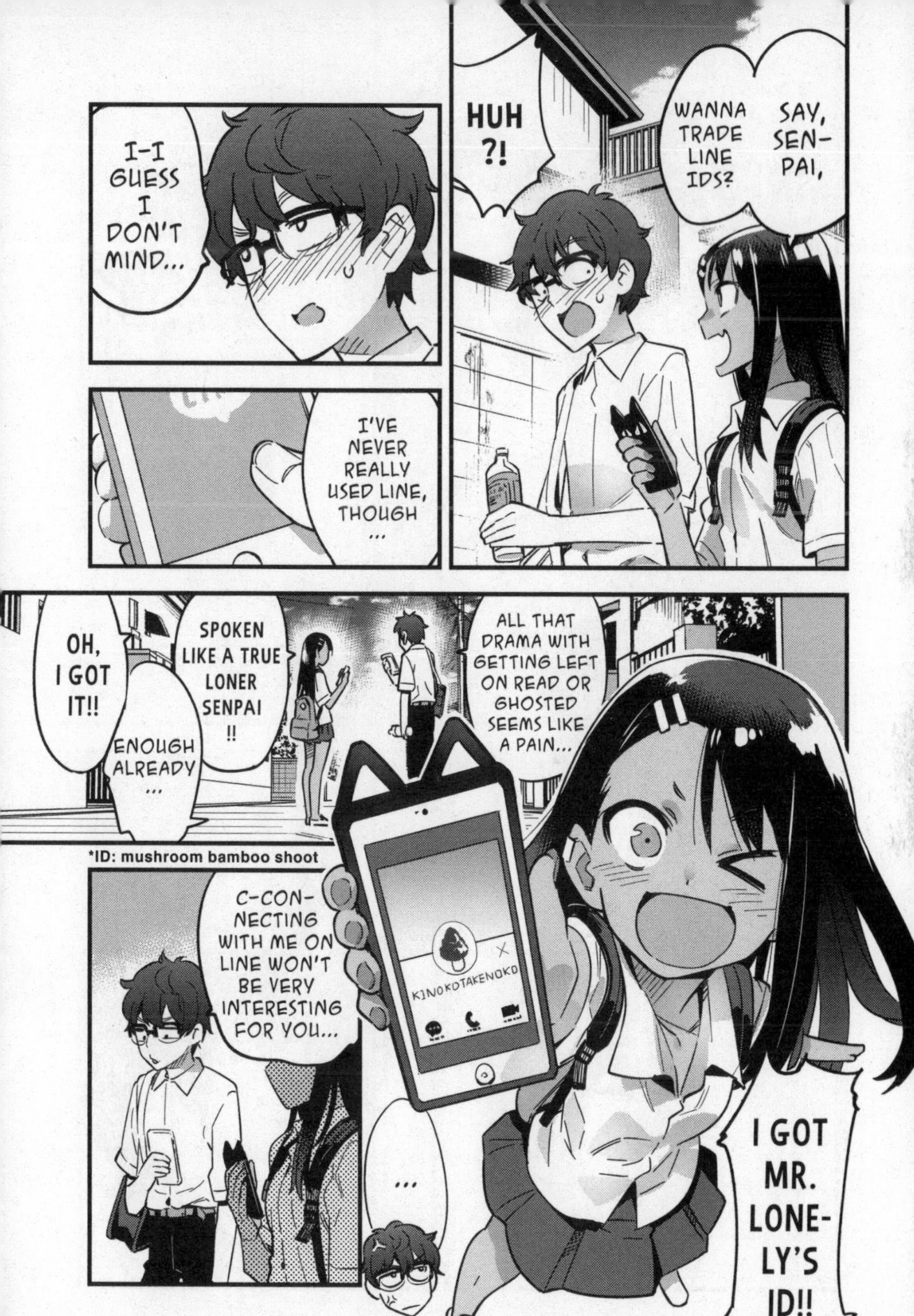
SAY, SENPAI,
WANNA TRADE LINE IDS?
HUH?!
I-I GUESS I DON'T MIND...
I'VE NEVER REALLY USED LINE, THOUGH...
ALL THAT DRAMA WITH GETTING LEFT ON READ OR GHOSTED SEEMS LIKE A PAIN...
SPOKEN LIKE A TRUE LONER SENPAI!!
OH, I GOT IT!!
ENOUGH ALREADY...
I GOT MR. LONELY'S ID!!
KINOKOTAKENOKO
C-CONNECTING WITH ME ON LINE WON'T BE VERY INTERESTING FOR YOU...
...

*ID: mushroom bamboo shoot

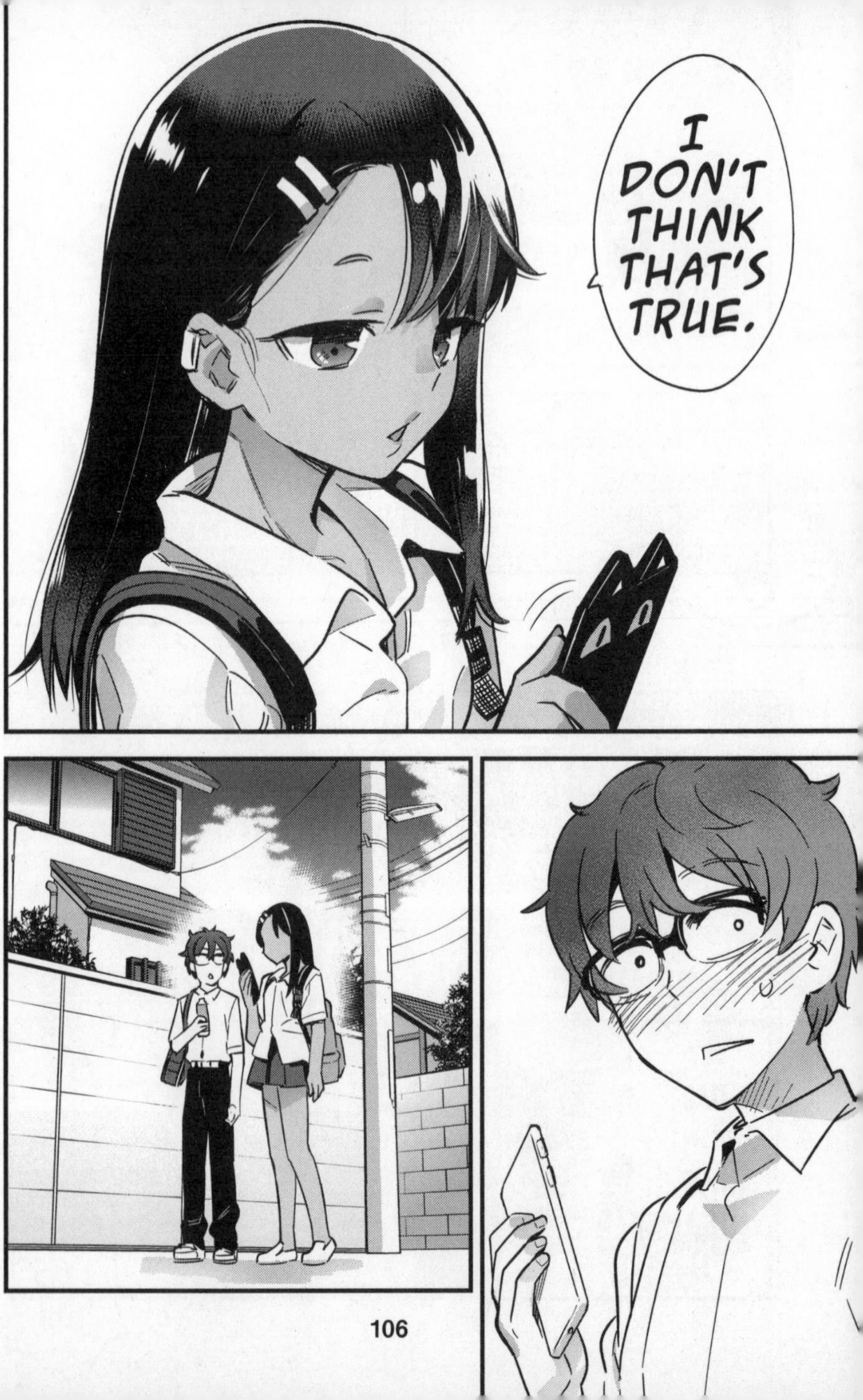
I DON'T THINK THAT'S TRUE.

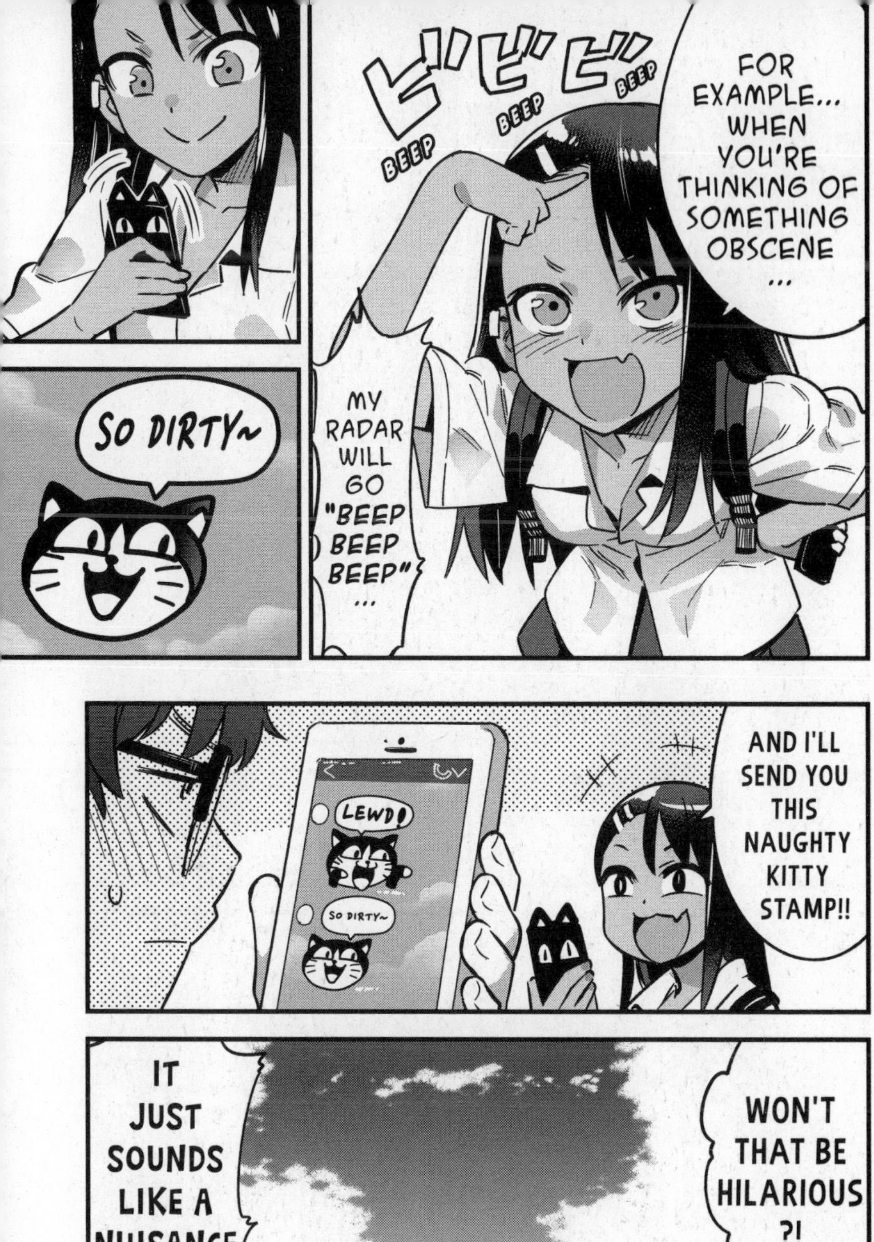
FOR EXAMPLE... WHEN YOU'RE THINKING OF SOMETHING OBSCENE ...
ビ ビ ビ
BEEP BEEP BEEP
MY RADAR WILL GO "BEEP BEEP BEEP" ...
SO DIRTY~
AND I'LL SEND YOU THIS NAUGHTY KITTY STAMP!!
LEWD!
SO DIRTY~
WON'T THAT BE HILARIOUS ?!
IT JUST SOUNDS LIKE A NUISANCE !!

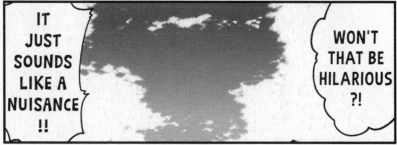

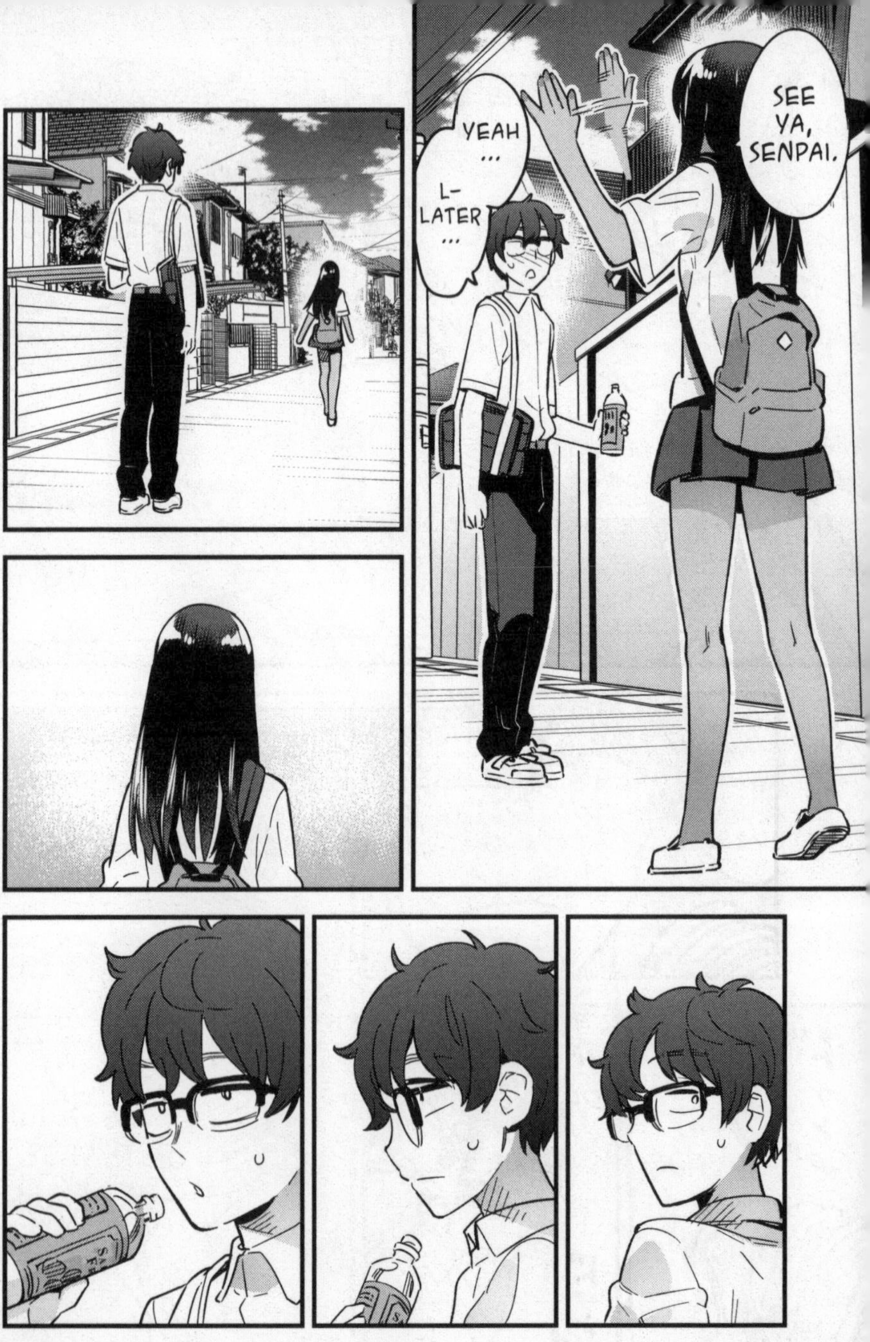
SEE YA, SENPAI.
YEAH ... L- LATER ...

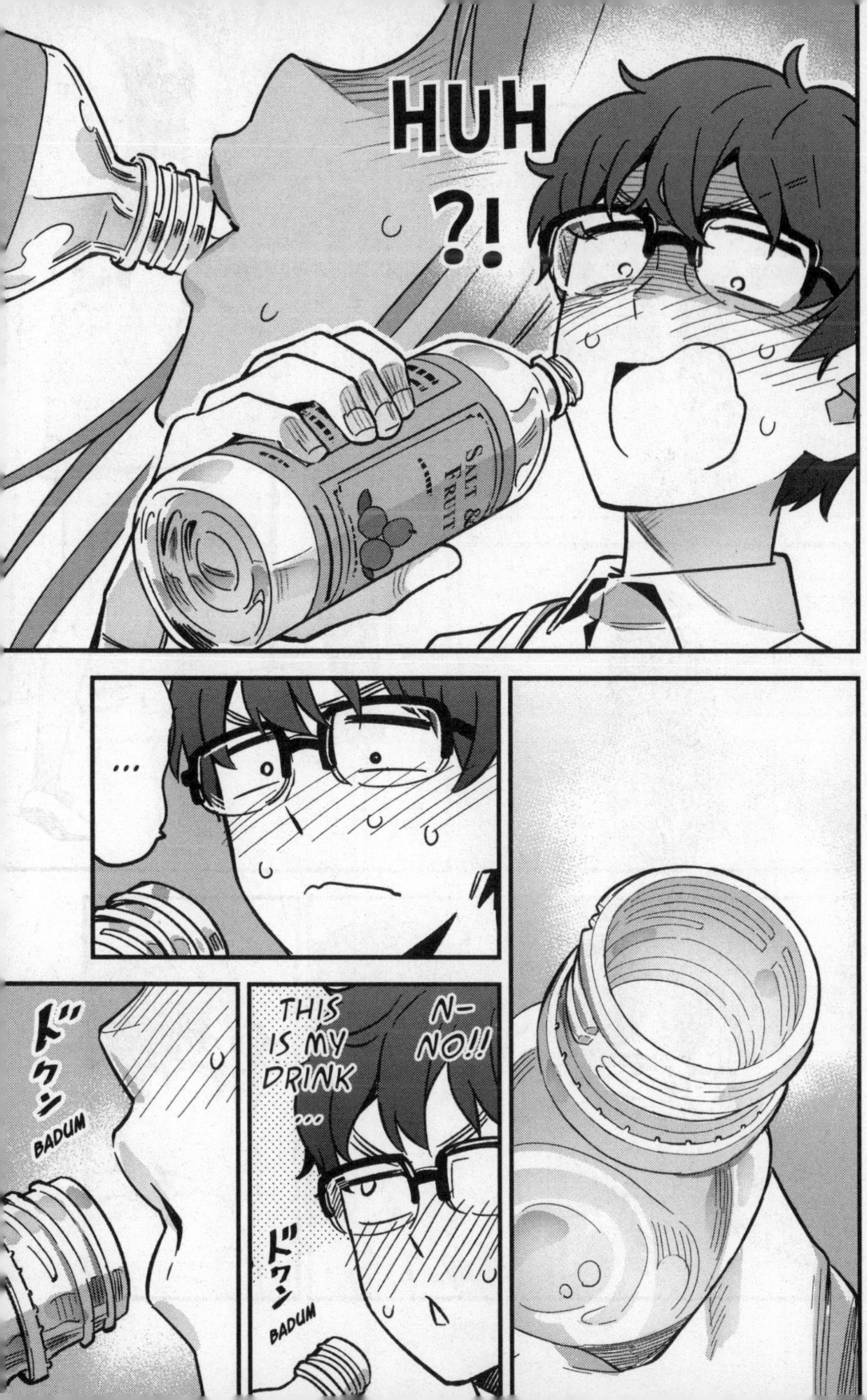
HUH
?!
...
N-NO!!
THIS IS MY DRINK...
ドクン
BADUM
ドクン
BADUM

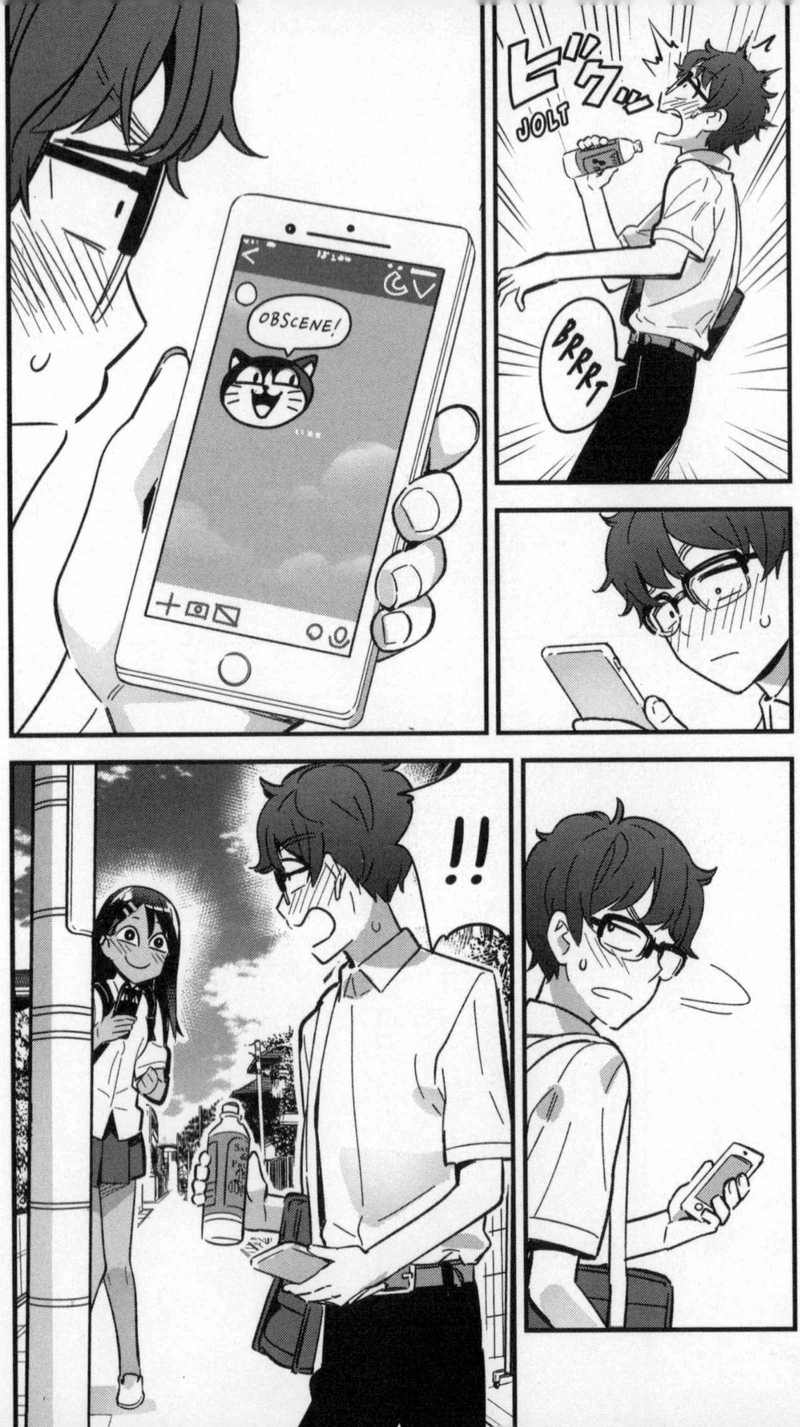
ビクッ
JOLT
BRRRT
OBSCENE!
!!

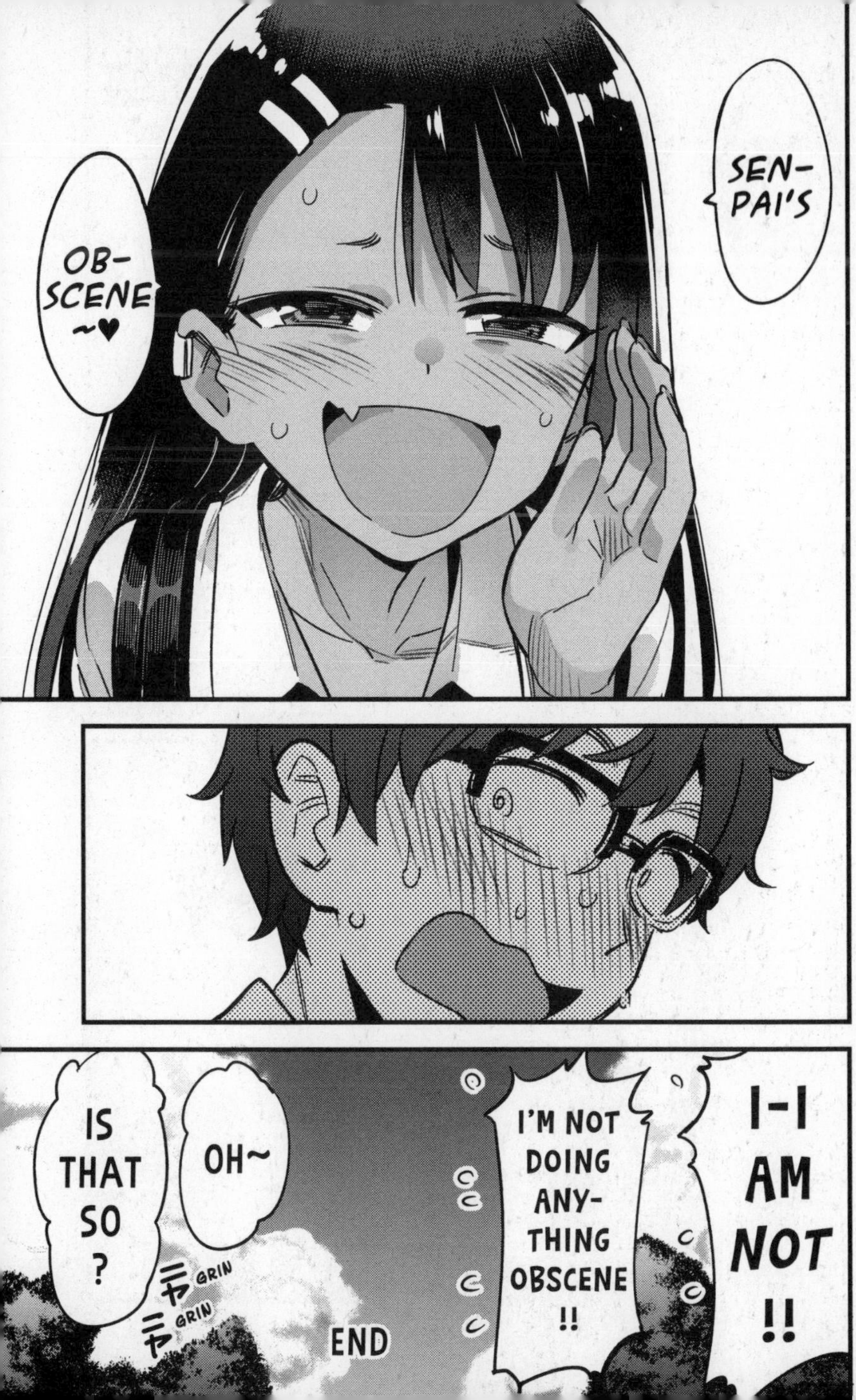
SEN-PAI'S
OB-SCENE~♥
I-I AM NOT!!
I'M NOT DOING ANY-THING OBSCENE!!
OH~
IS THAT SO?
ニヤ GRIN
ニヤ GRIN
END

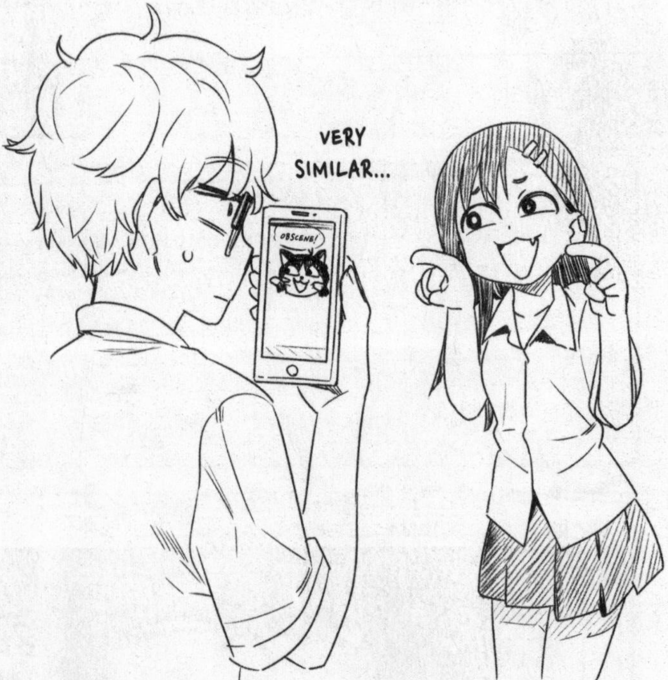
VERY SIMILAR...
OBSCENE!

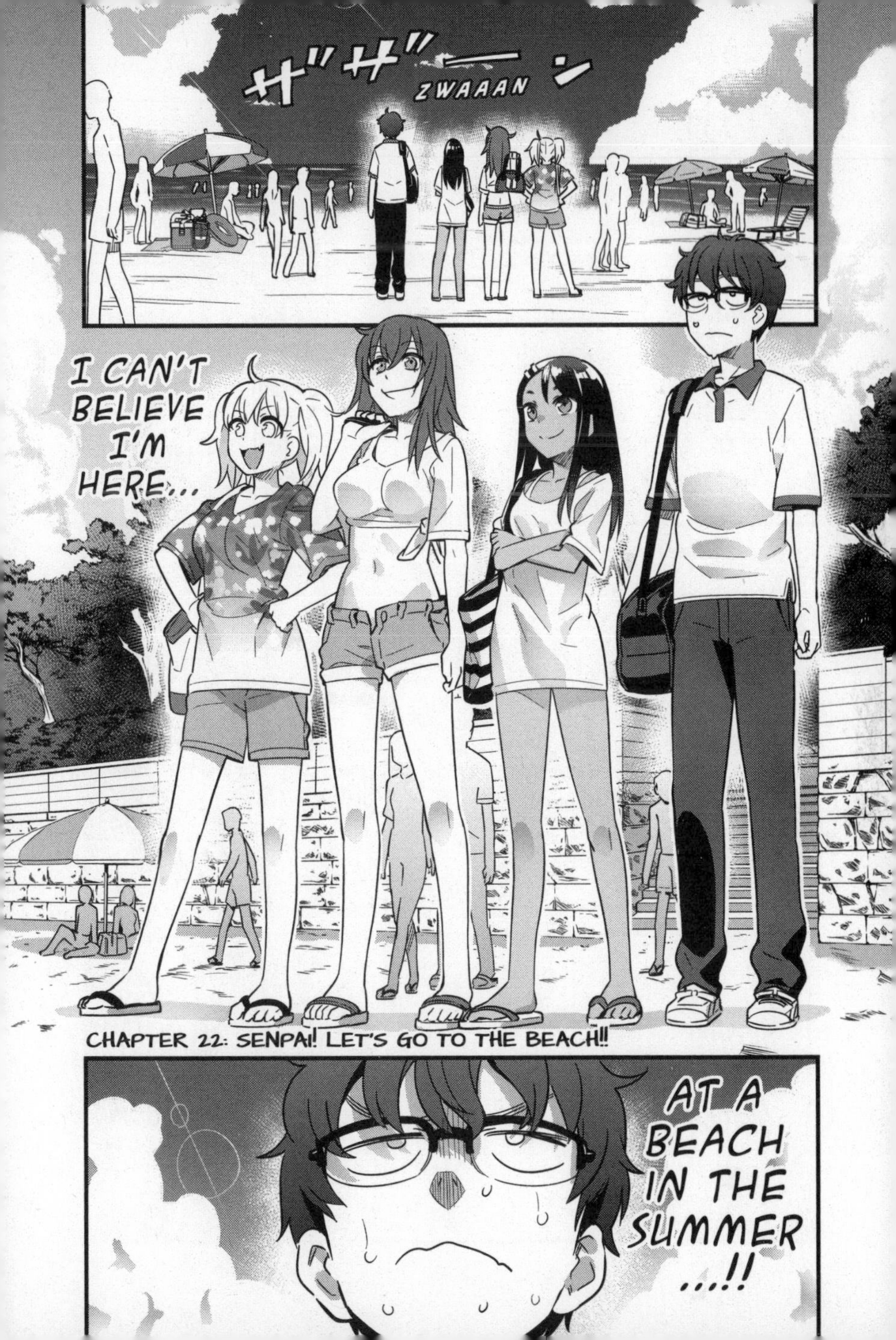
ザザーン
ZWAAAN
I CAN'T BELIEVE I'M HERE...
CHAPTER 22: SENPAI! LET'S GO TO THE BEACH!!
AT A BEACH IN THE SUMMER...!!

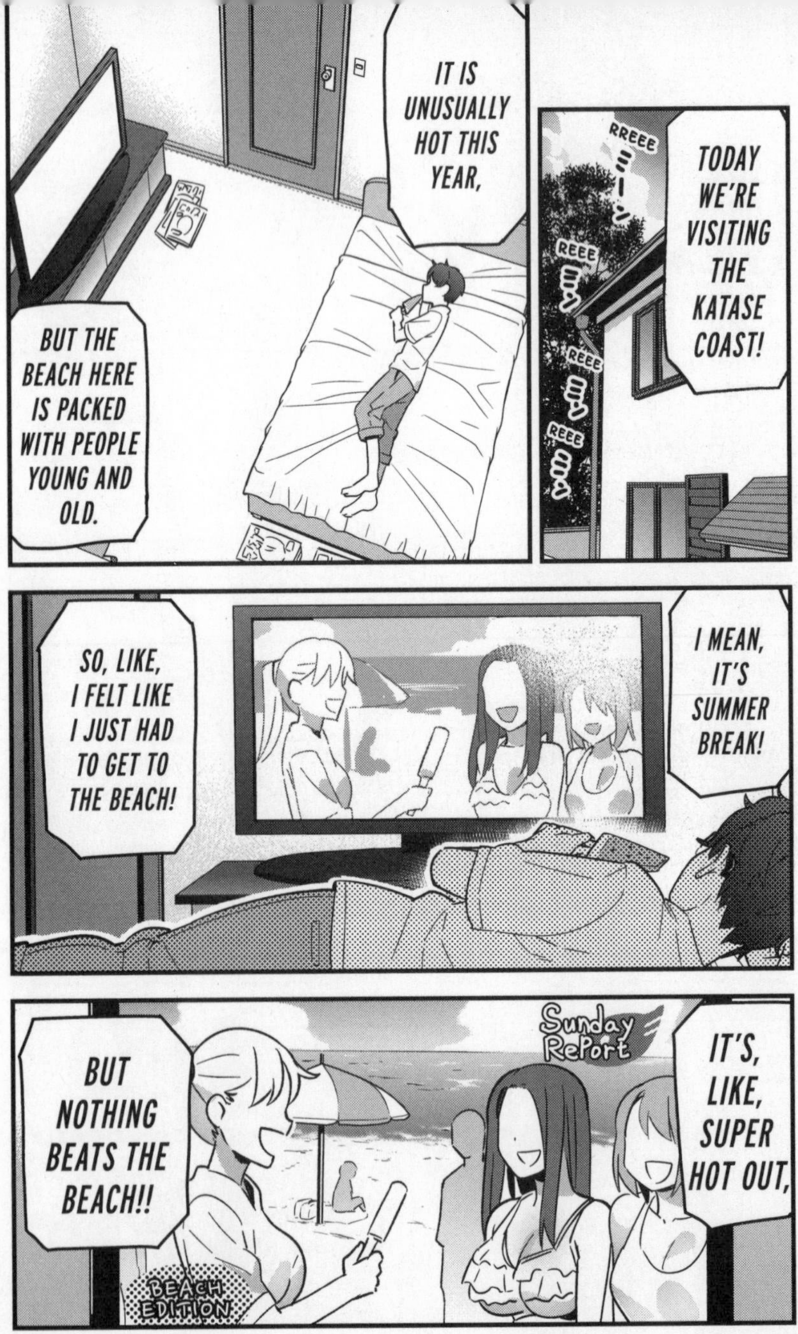
RREEE
REEE
REEE
REEE
TODAY WE'RE VISITING THE KATASE COAST!
IT IS UNUSUALLY HOT THIS YEAR,
BUT THE BEACH HERE IS PACKED WITH PEOPLE YOUNG AND OLD.
I MEAN, IT'S SUMMER BREAK!
SO, LIKE, I FELT LIKE I JUST HAD TO GET TO THE BEACH!
Sunday Report
IT'S, LIKE, SUPER HOT OUT,
BUT NOTHING BEATS THE BEACH!!
BEACH EDITION

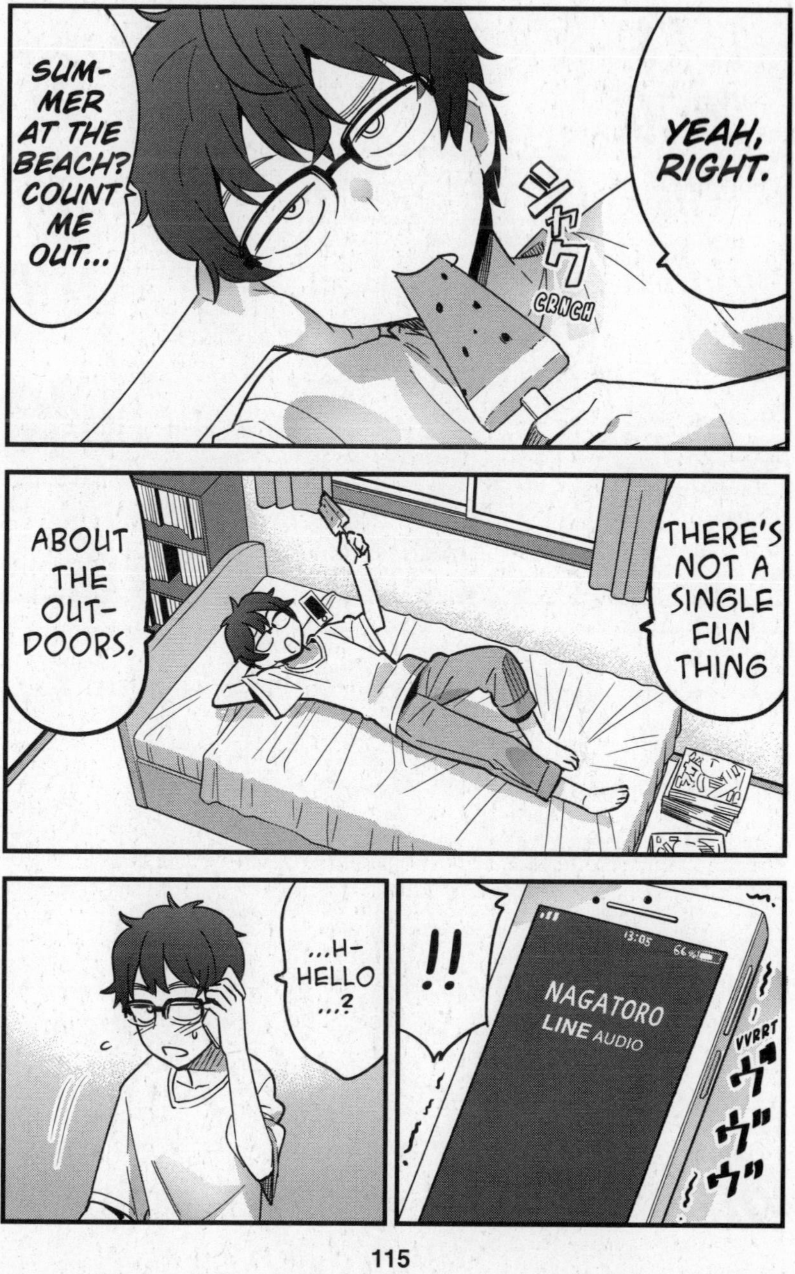
YEAH, RIGHT.
シャク
CRNCH
SUM-MER AT THE BEACH? COUNT ME OUT...
THERE'S NOT A SINGLE FUN THING
ABOUT THE OUT-DOORS.
!!
13:05
NAGATORO
LINE AUDIO
VVRRT
ヴヴヴ
...H-HELLO...?

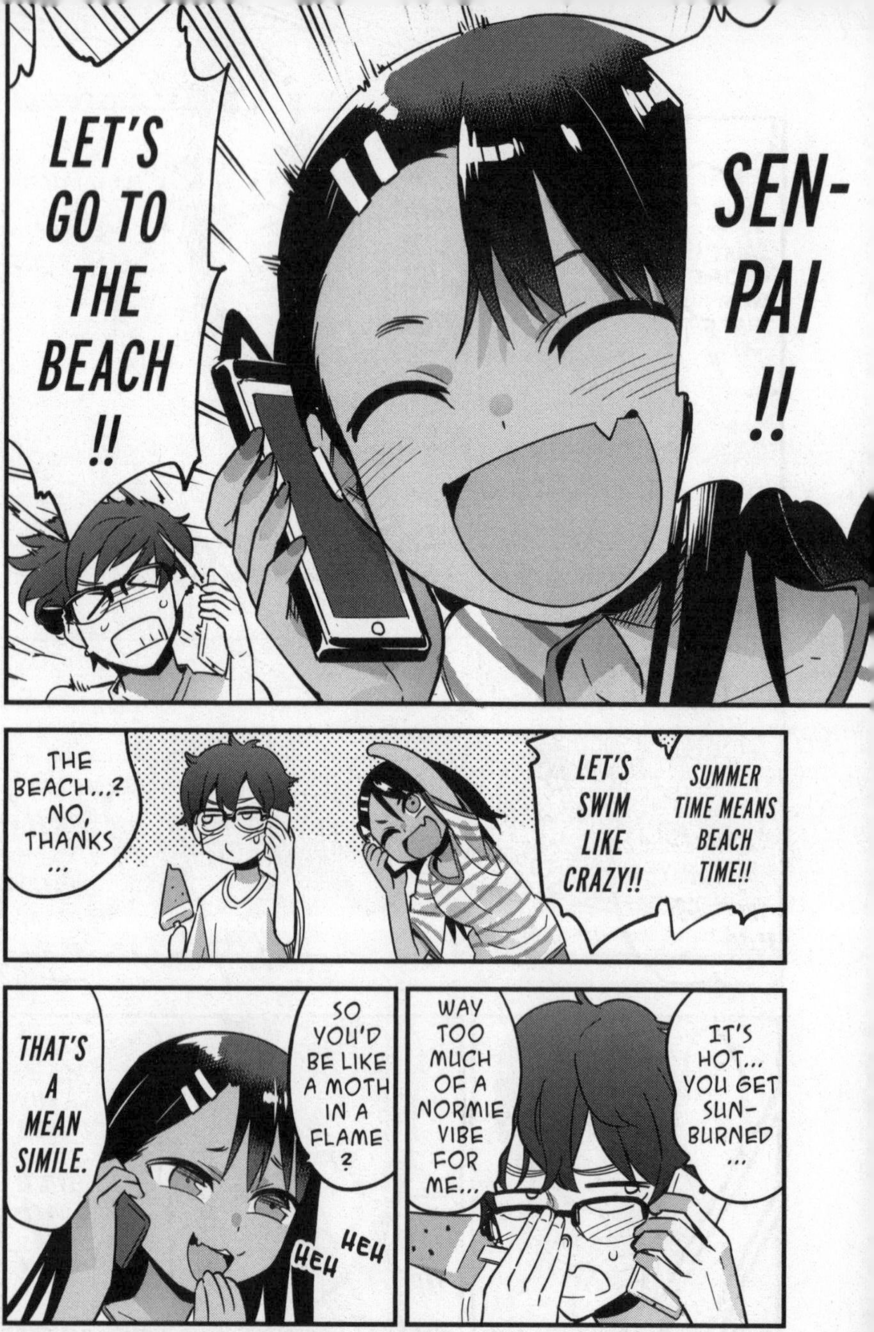
SEN-PAI!!
LET'S GO TO THE BEACH!!
SUMMER TIME MEANS BEACH TIME!!
LET'S SWIM LIKE CRAZY!!
THE BEACH...? NO, THANKS...
IT'S HOT... YOU GET SUN-BURNED...
WAY TOO MUCH OF A NORMIE VIBE FOR ME...
SO YOU'D BE LIKE A MOTH IN A FLAME?
THAT'S A MEAN SIMILE.
HEH HEH

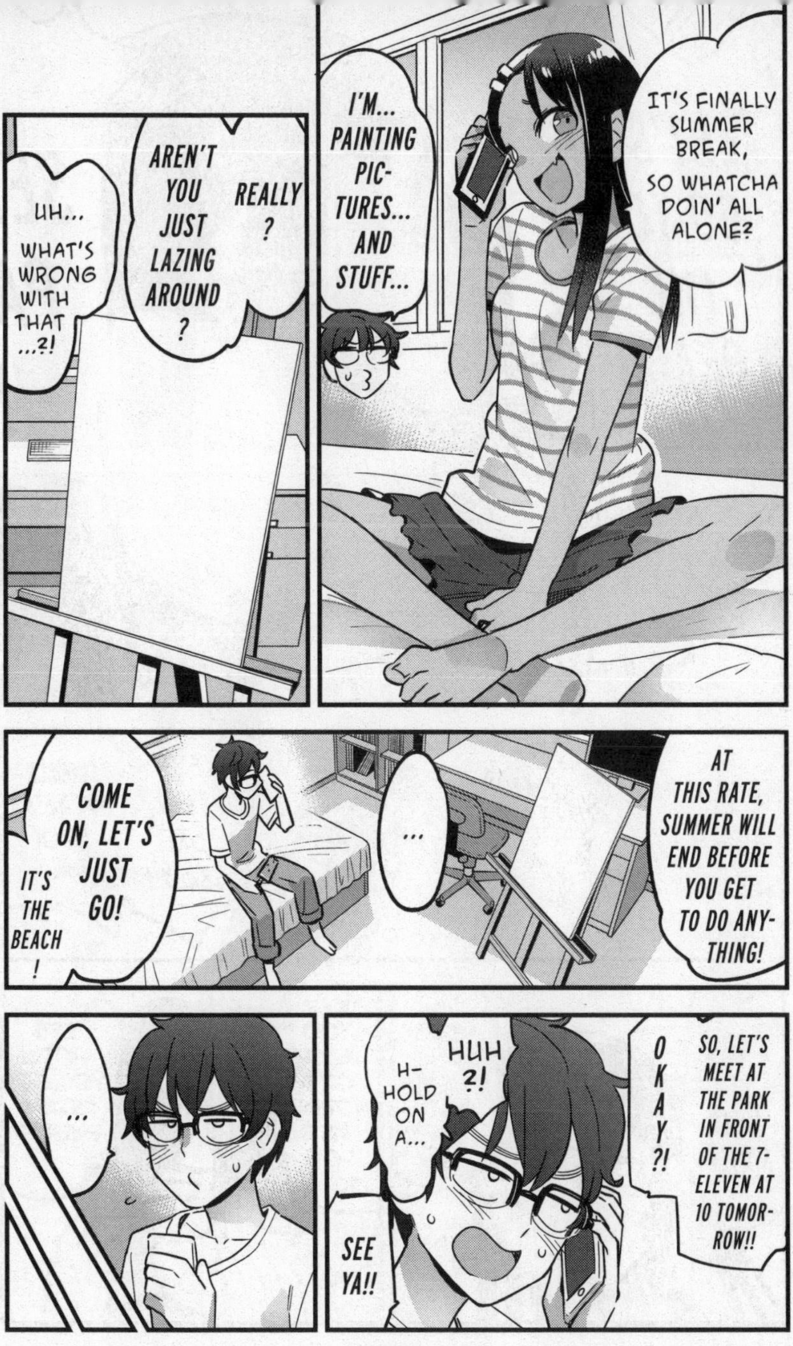
IT'S FINALLY SUMMER BREAK, SO WHATCHA DOIN' ALL ALONE?
I'M... PAINTING PIC-TURES... AND STUFF...
REALLY?
AREN'T YOU JUST LAZING AROUND?
UH... WHAT'S WRONG WITH THAT...?!
AT THIS RATE, SUMMER WILL END BEFORE YOU GET TO DO ANY-THING!
...
COME ON, LET'S JUST GO!
IT'S THE BEACH!
SO, LET'S MEET AT THE PARK IN FRONT OF THE 7-ELEVEN AT 10 TOMOR-ROW!!
OKAY?!
HUH?!
H-HOLD ON A...
SEE YA!!
...

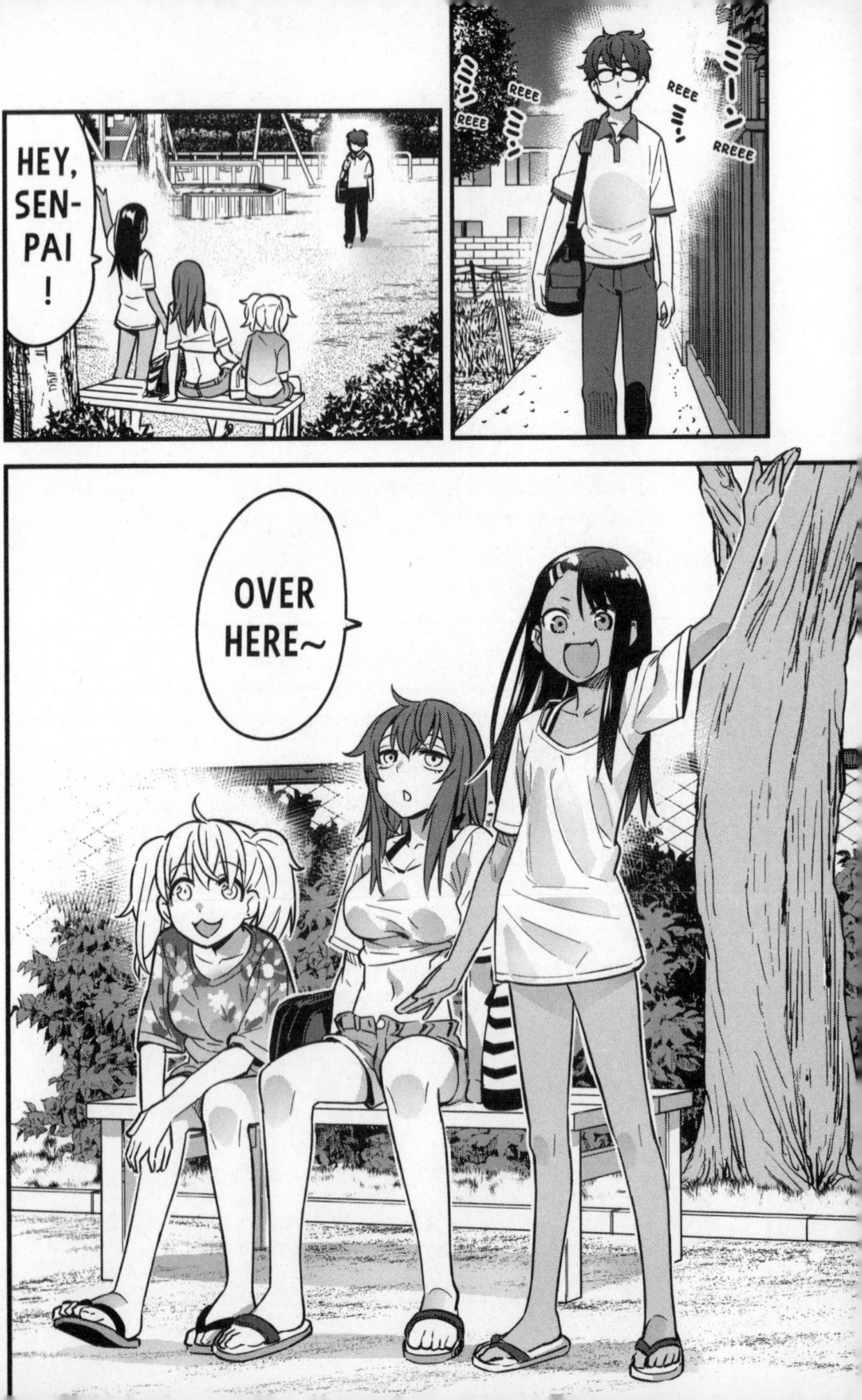
REEE
RREEE
REEE
REEE
HEY, SEN-PAI!
OVER HERE~

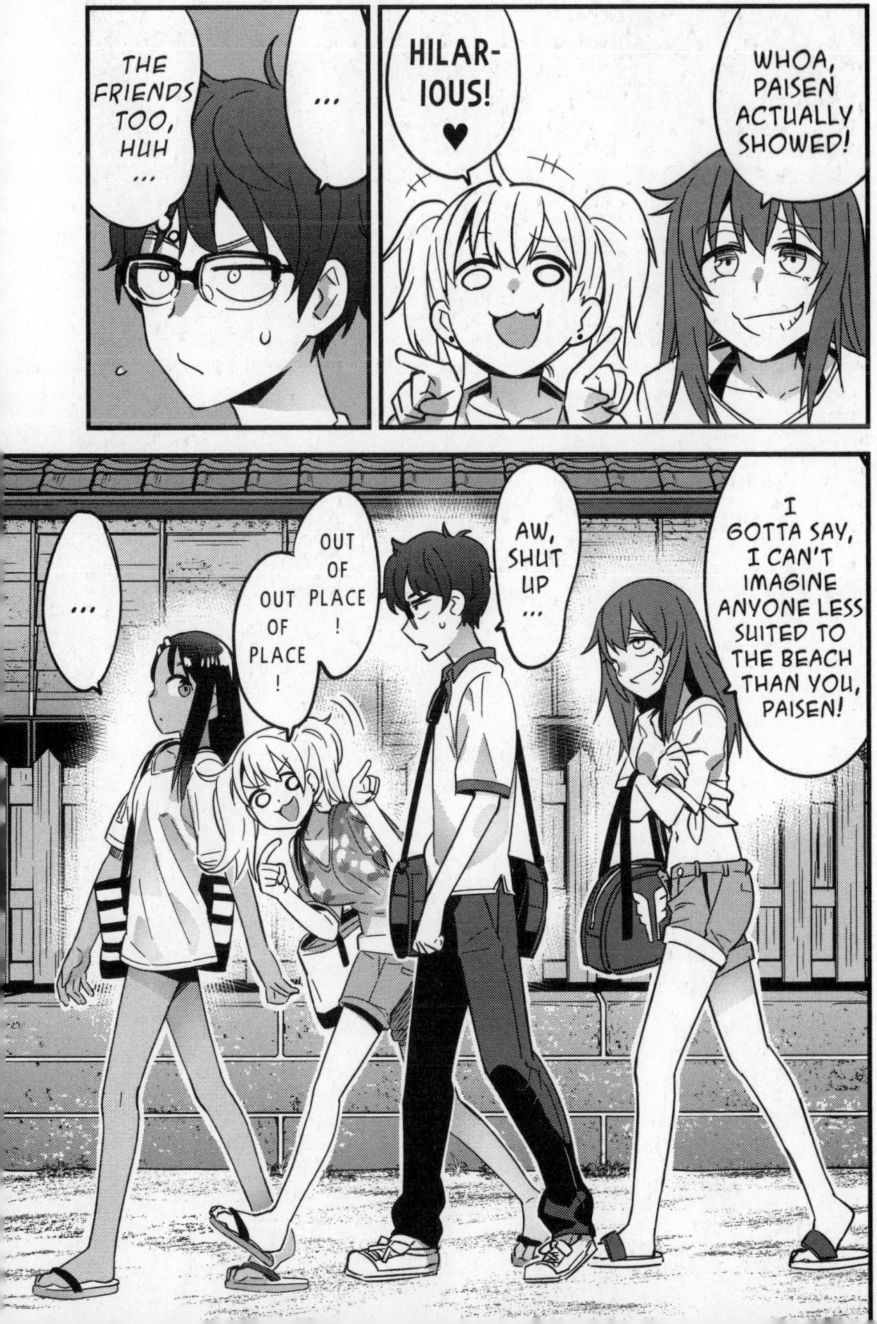
WHOA, PAISEN ACTUALLY SHOWED!
HILAR-IOUS! ♥
...
THE FRIENDS TOO, HUH ...
I GOTTA SAY, I CAN'T IMAGINE ANYONE LESS SUITED TO THE BEACH THAN YOU, PAISEN!
AW, SHUT UP ...
OUT OF PLACE !
OUT OF PLACE !
...

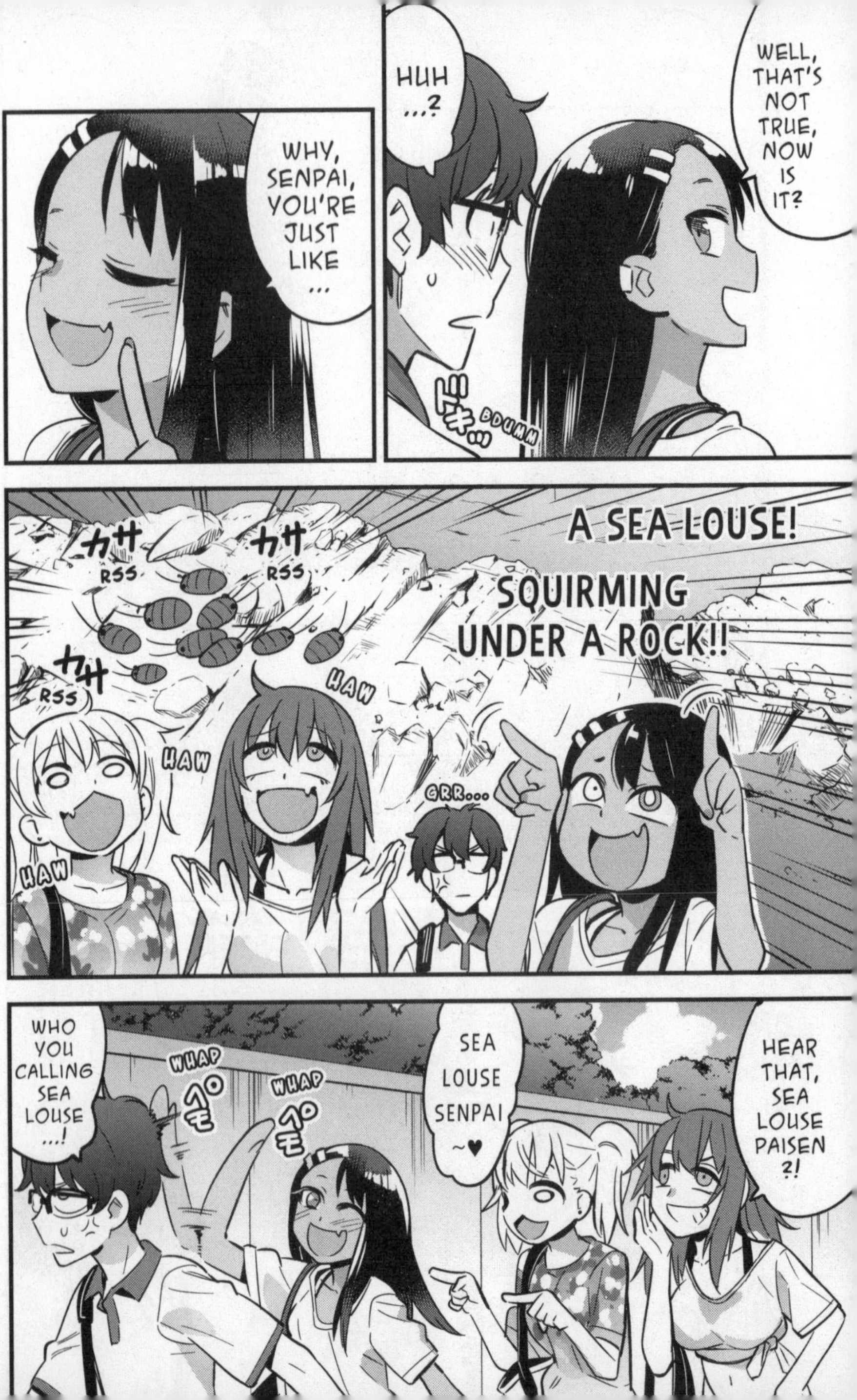
WELL, THAT'S NOT TRUE, NOW IS IT?
HUH ...?
ドキ
BDUMM
WHY, SENPAI, YOU'RE JUST LIKE ...
A SEA LOUSE!
SQUIRMING UNDER A ROCK!!
カサ
RSS
カサ
RSS
カサ
RSS
HAW
GRR...
HAW
HAW
HEAR THAT, SEA LOUSE PAISEN?!
SEA LOUSE SENPAI ~♥
ペモ
WHAP
ペモ
WHAP
WHO YOU CALLING SEA LOUSE ...!

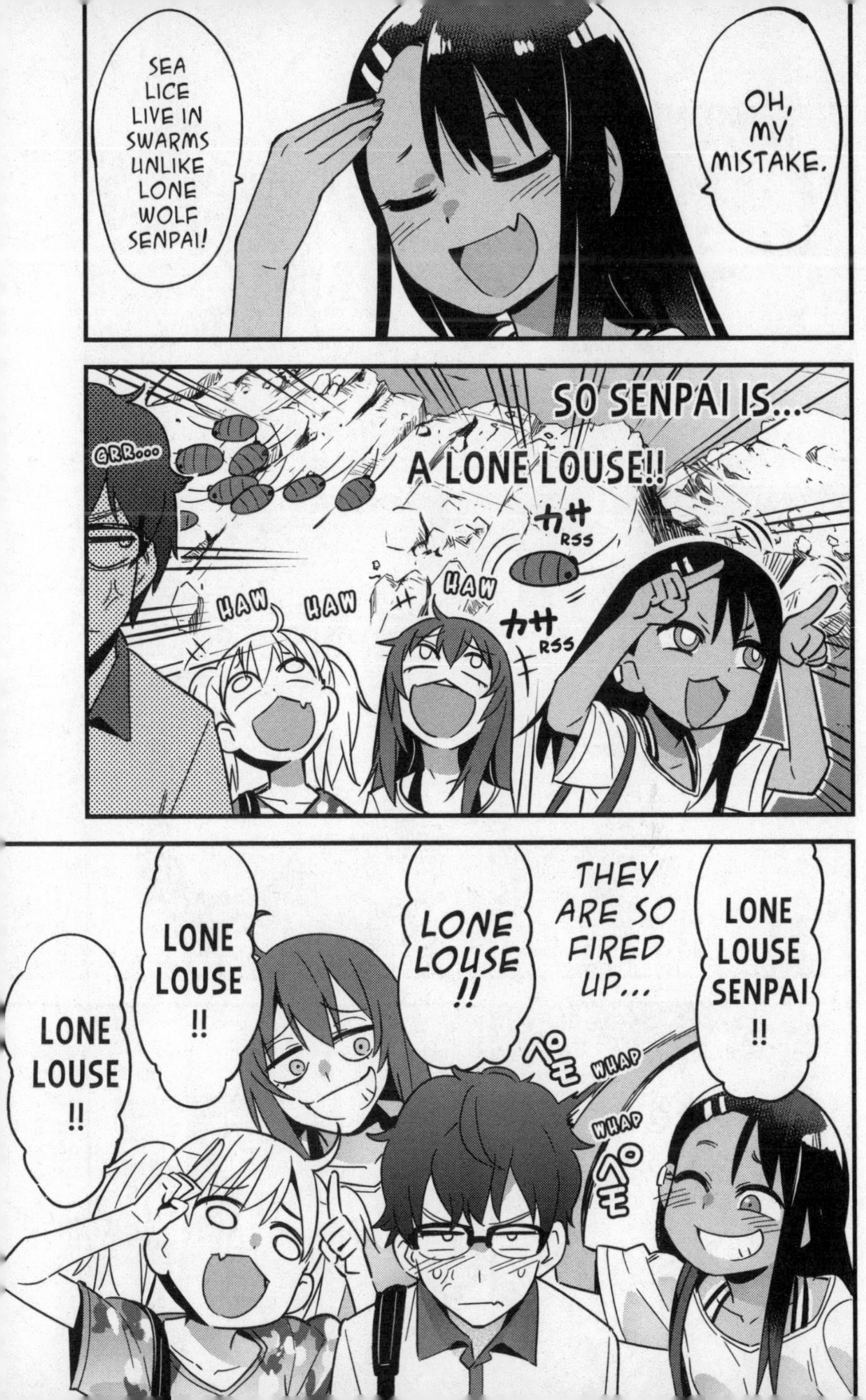
OH, MY MISTAKE.
SEA LICE LIVE IN SWARMS UNLIKE LONE WOLF SENPAI!
SO SENPAI IS...
A LONE LOUSE!!
カサ RSS
GRR...
カサ RSS
HAW
HAW
HAW
LONE LOUSE SENPAI !!
THEY ARE SO FIRED UP...
LONE LOUSE !!
ペモ WHAP
ペモ WHAP
LONE LOUSE !!
LONE LOUSE !!

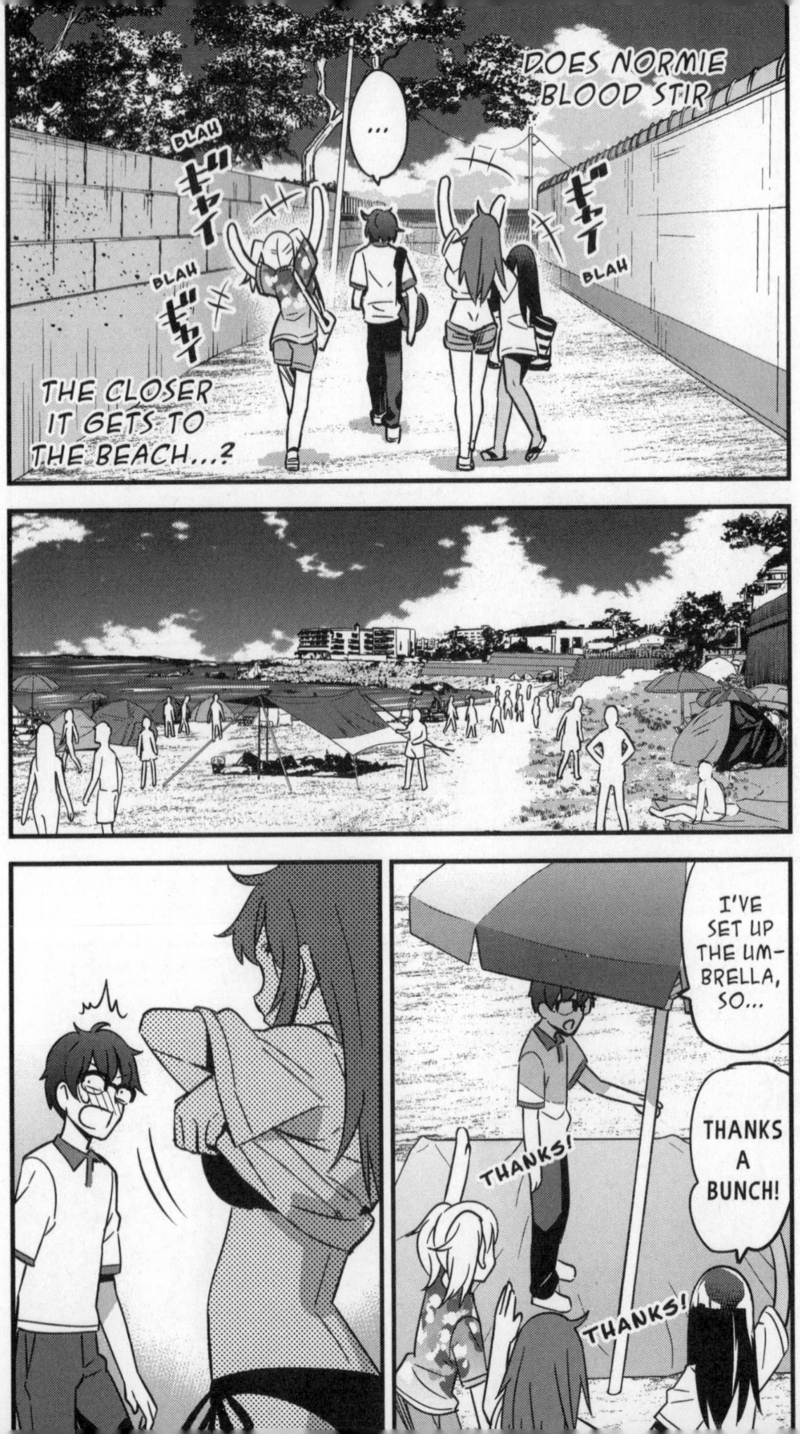
DOES NORMIE BLOOD STIR
...
BLAH
ギャイ
BLAH
ギャイ
BLAH
ギャイ
BLAH
ギャイ
THE CLOSER IT GETS TO THE BEACH...?
I'VE SET UP THE UM-BRELLA, SO...
THANKS A BUNCH!
THANKS!
THANKS!

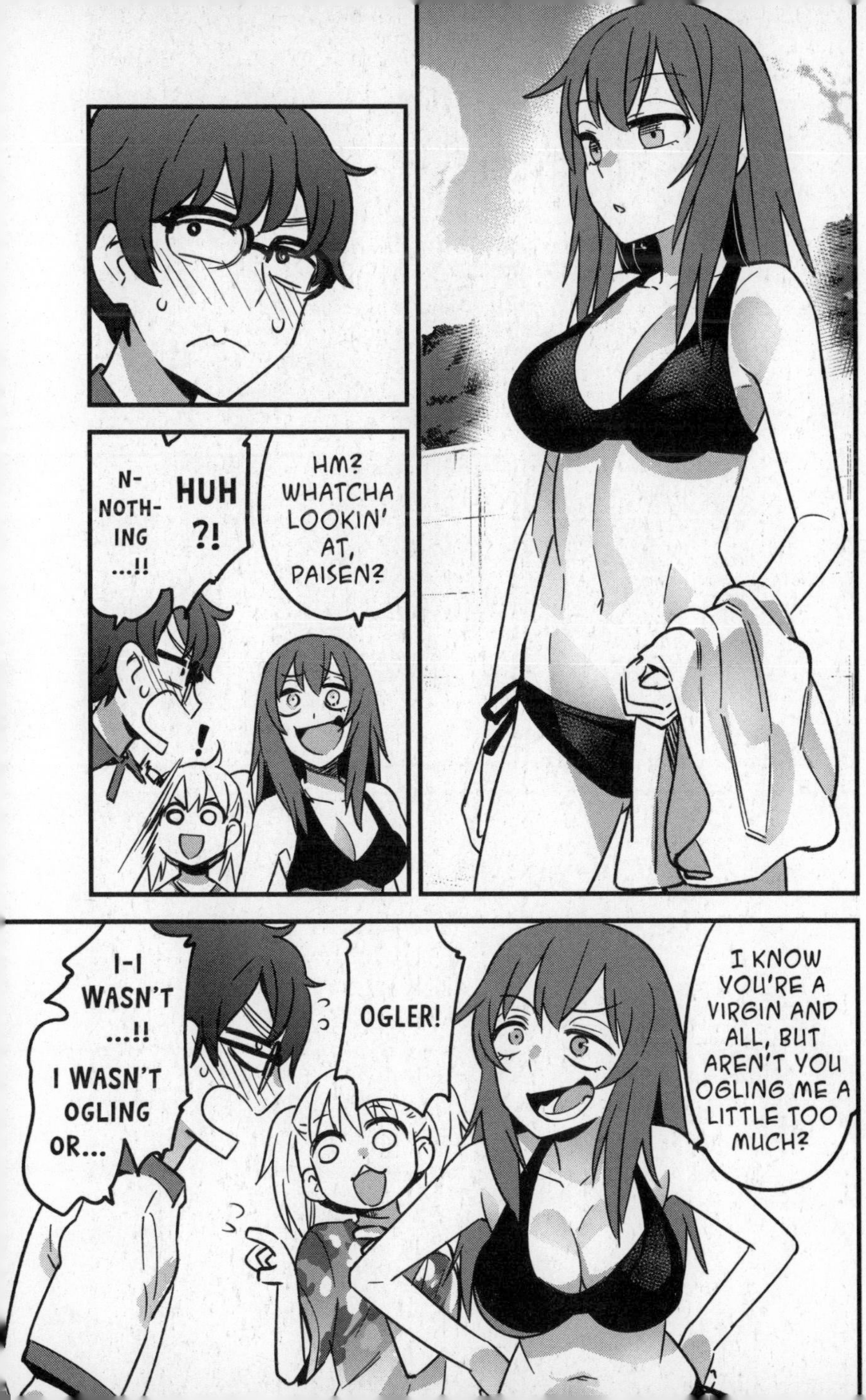
HM? WHATCHA LOOKIN' AT, PAISEN?
HUH ?!
N-NOTH-ING ...!!
!
I KNOW YOU'RE A VIRGIN AND ALL, BUT AREN'T YOU OGLING ME A LITTLE TOO MUCH?
OGLER!
I-I WASN'T ...!!
I WASN'T OGLING OR...

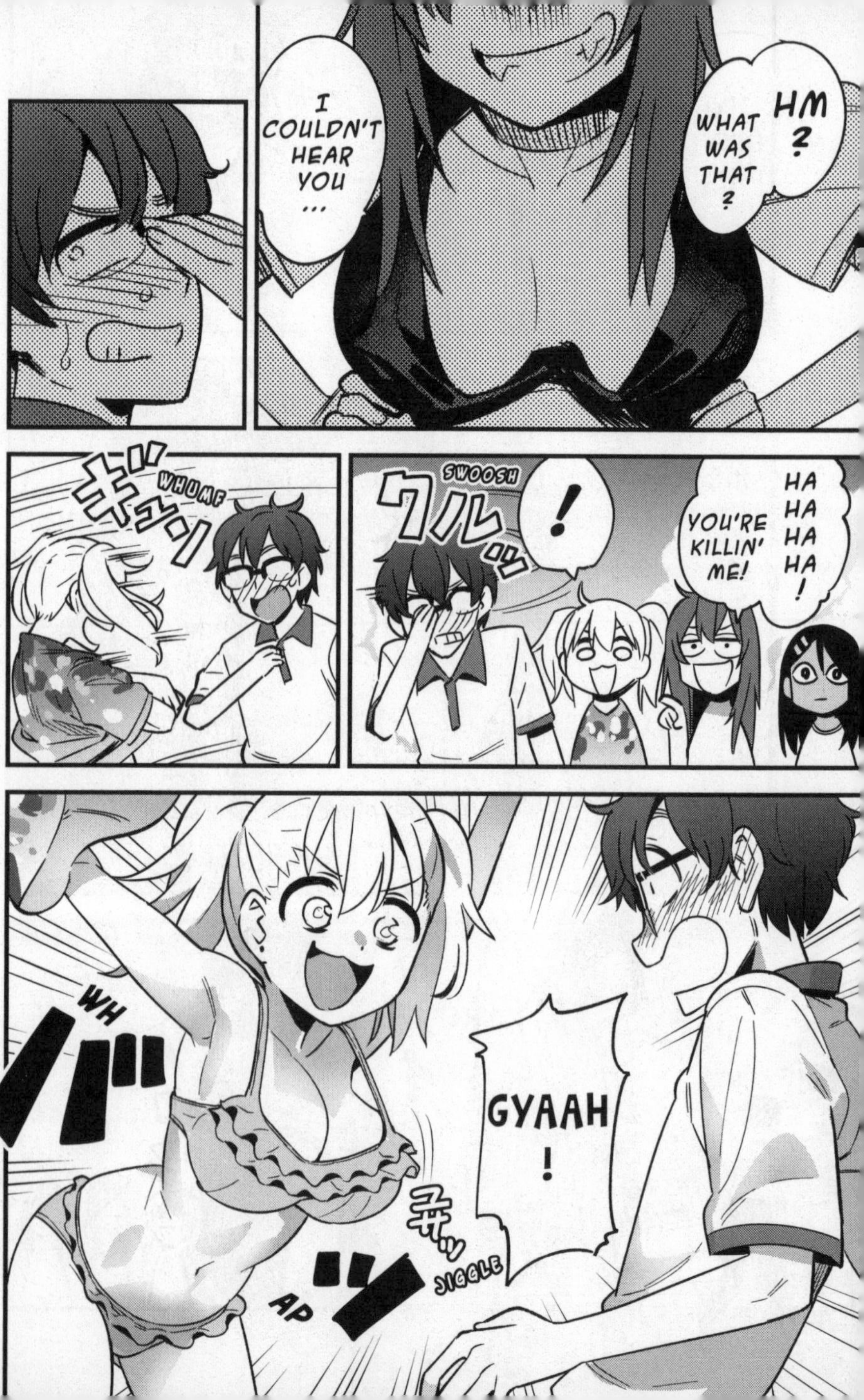
HM?
WHAT WAS THAT?
I COULDN'T HEAR YOU ...
HA HA HA HA!
YOU'RE KILLIN' ME!
!
クルッ
SWOOSH
ギュッ
WHUMF
GYAAH!
WH
AP
ユサッ
JIGGLE

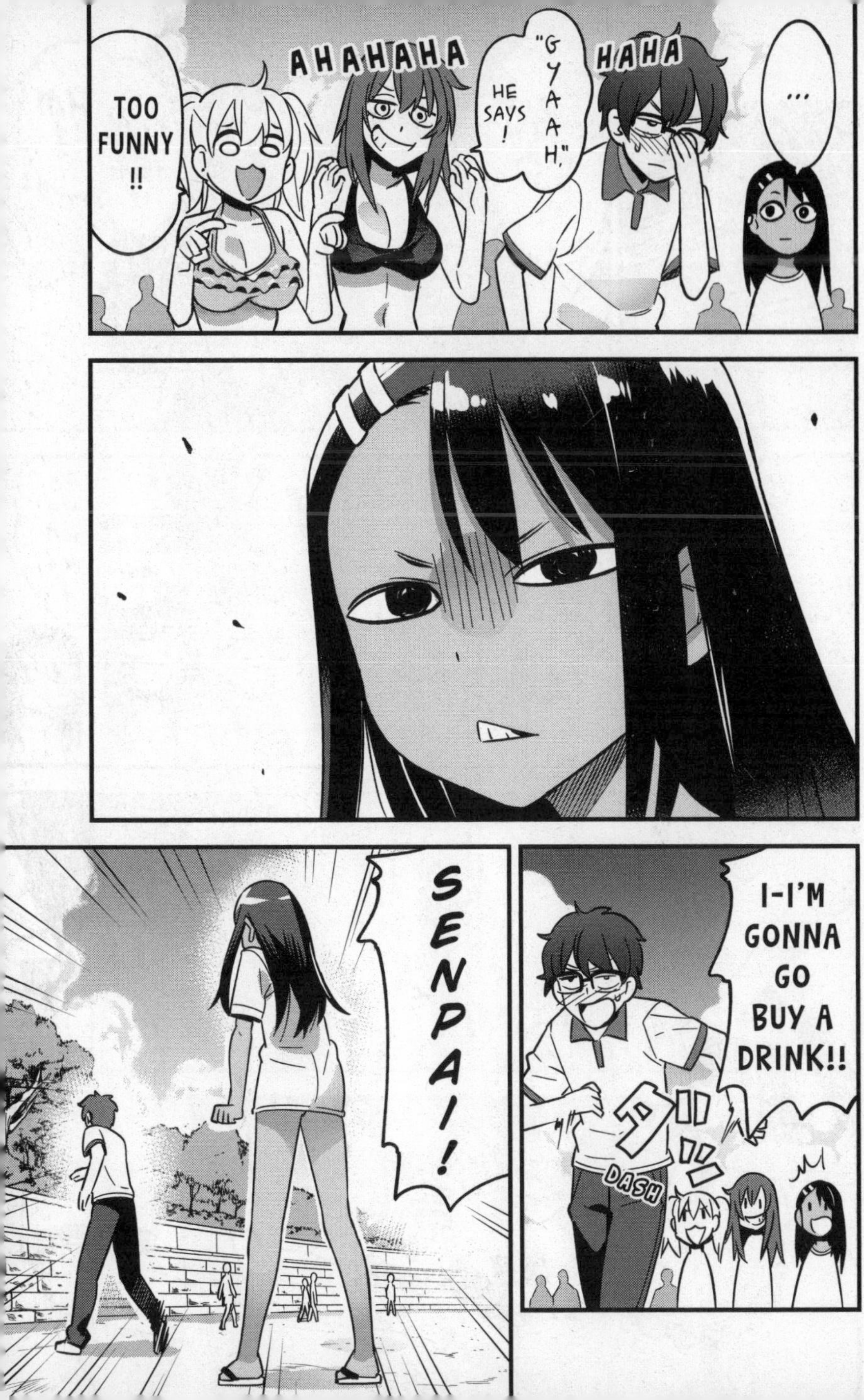
...
HAHA
"GYAAH," HE SAYS!
AHAHAHA
TOO FUNNY!!
I-I'M GONNA GO BUY A DRINK!!
DASH
SENPAI!

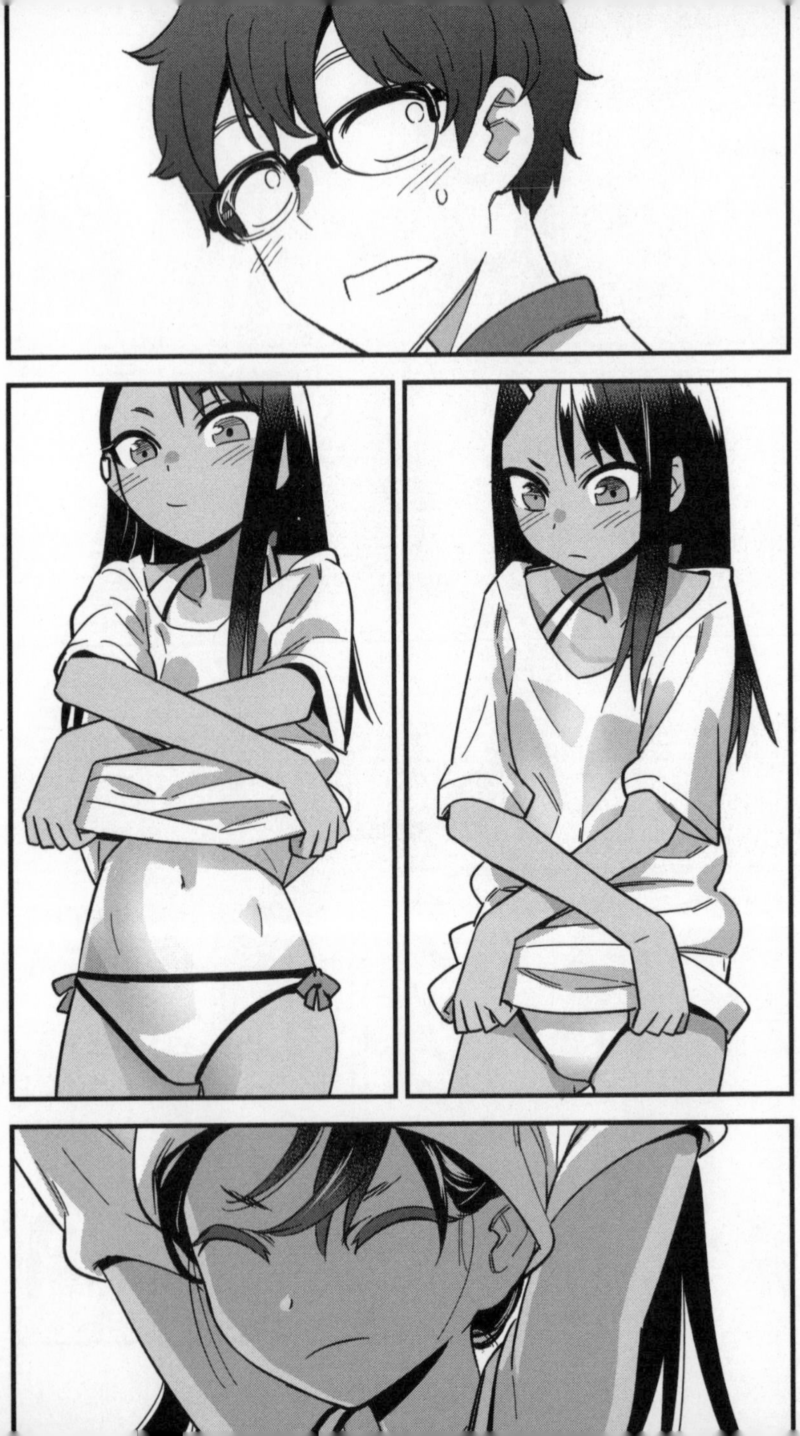

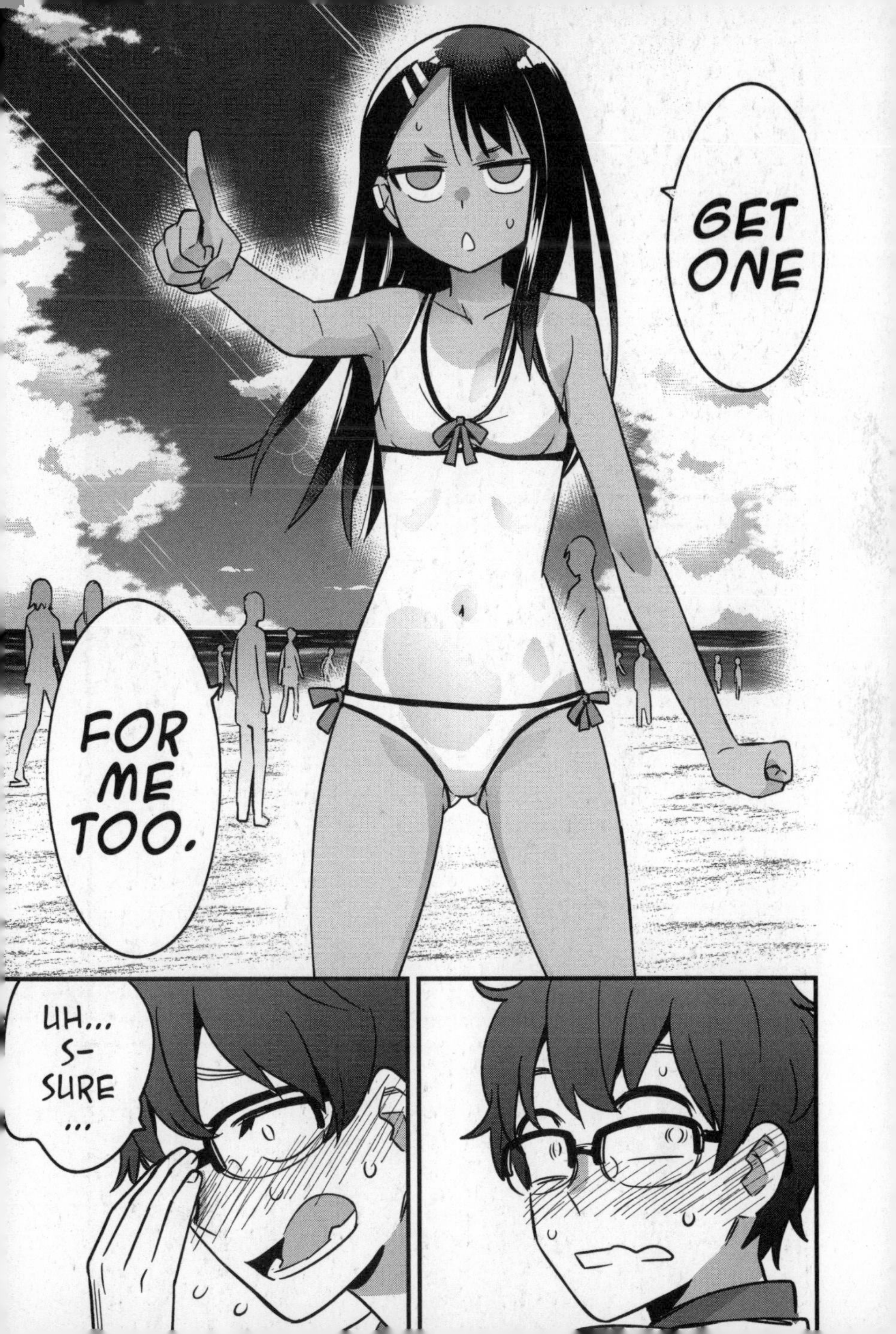
GET ONE
FOR ME TOO.
UH... S-SURE ...

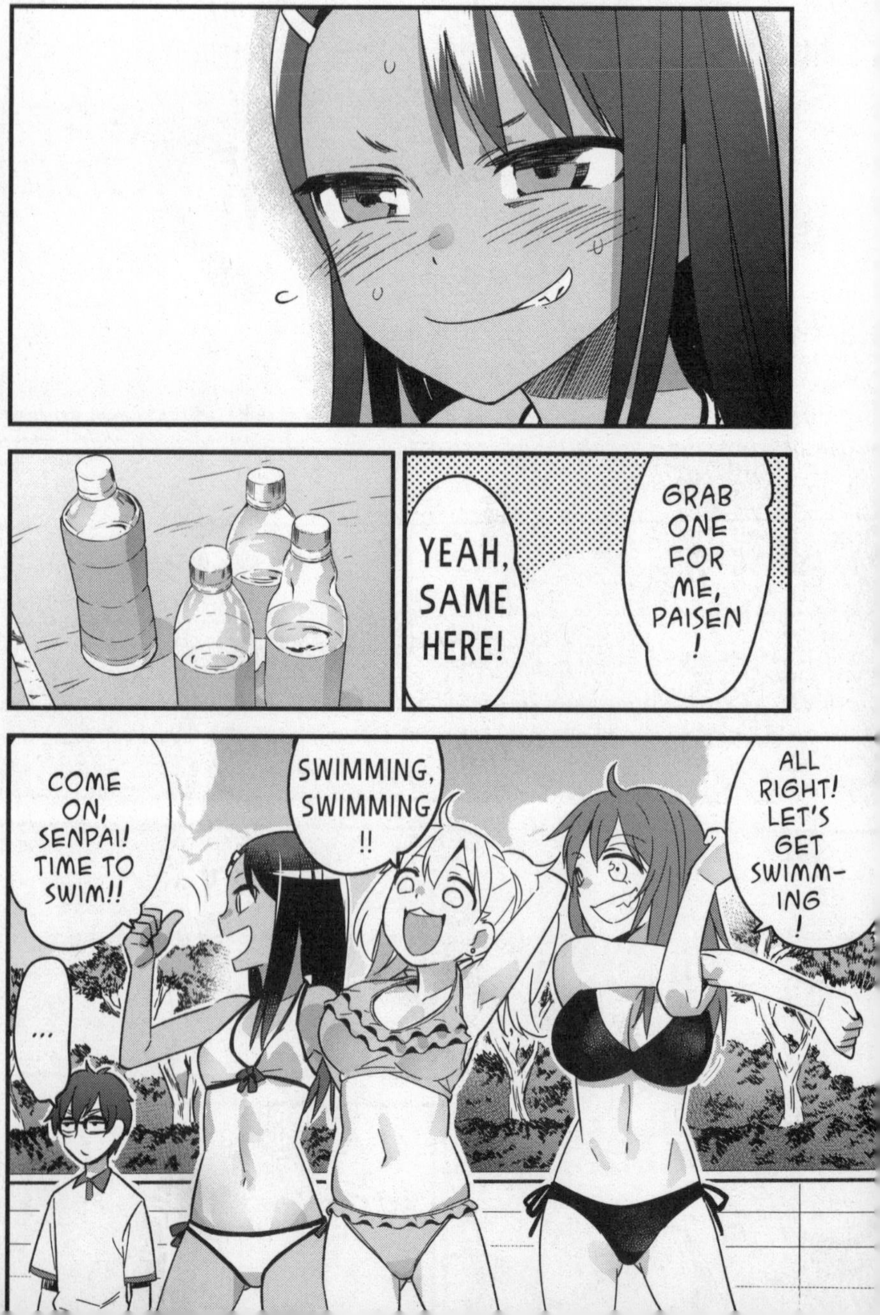
GRAB ONE FOR ME, PAISEN!
YEAH, SAME HERE!
ALL RIGHT! LET'S GET SWIMM-ING!
SWIMMING, SWIMMING!!
COME ON, SENPAI! TIME TO SWIM!!
...

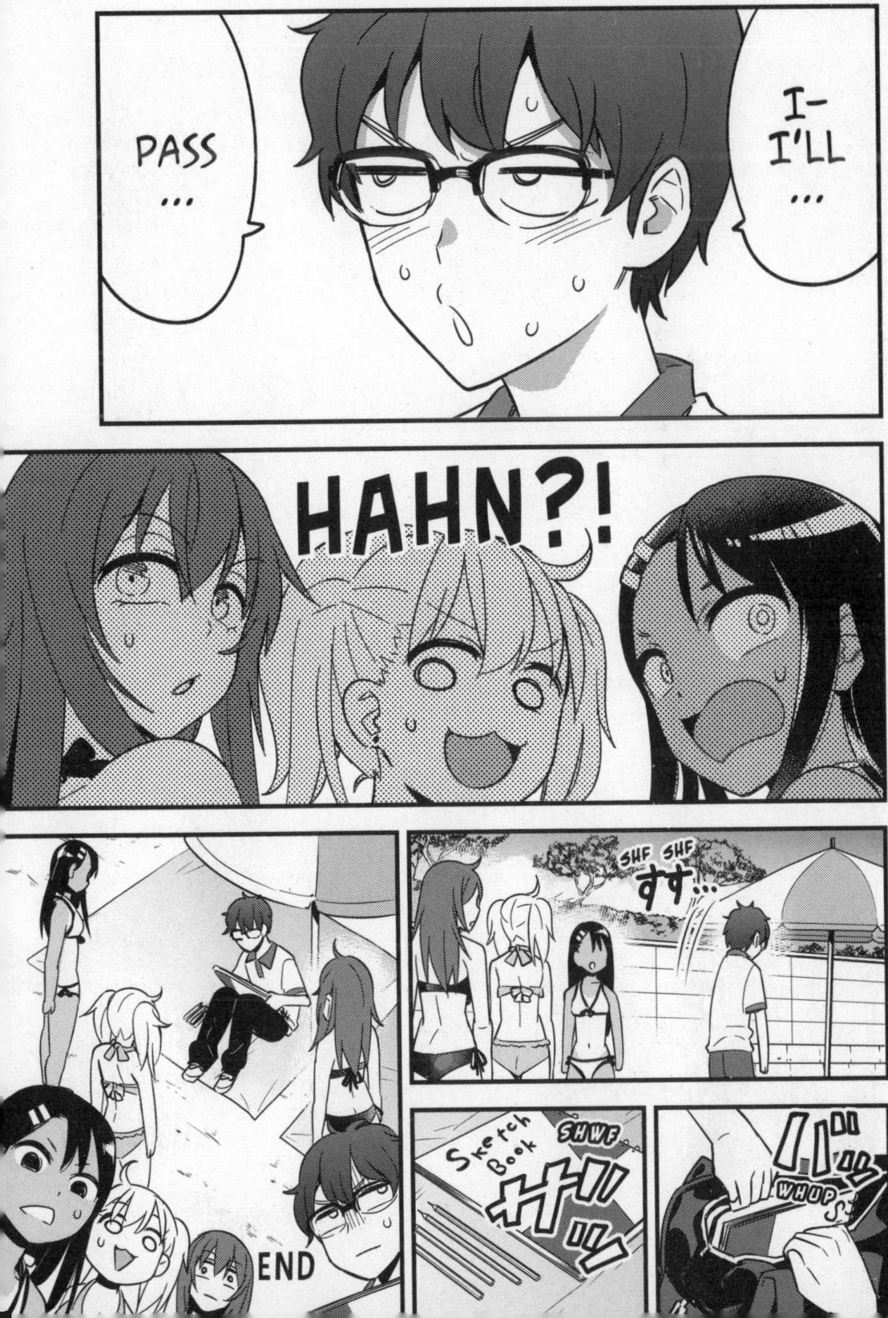
I– I'LL ...
PASS ...
HAHN?!
SHF SHF
すす...
WHUP
Sketch Book
SHWF
END

DON'T TOY WITH ME,
MISS NAGATORO

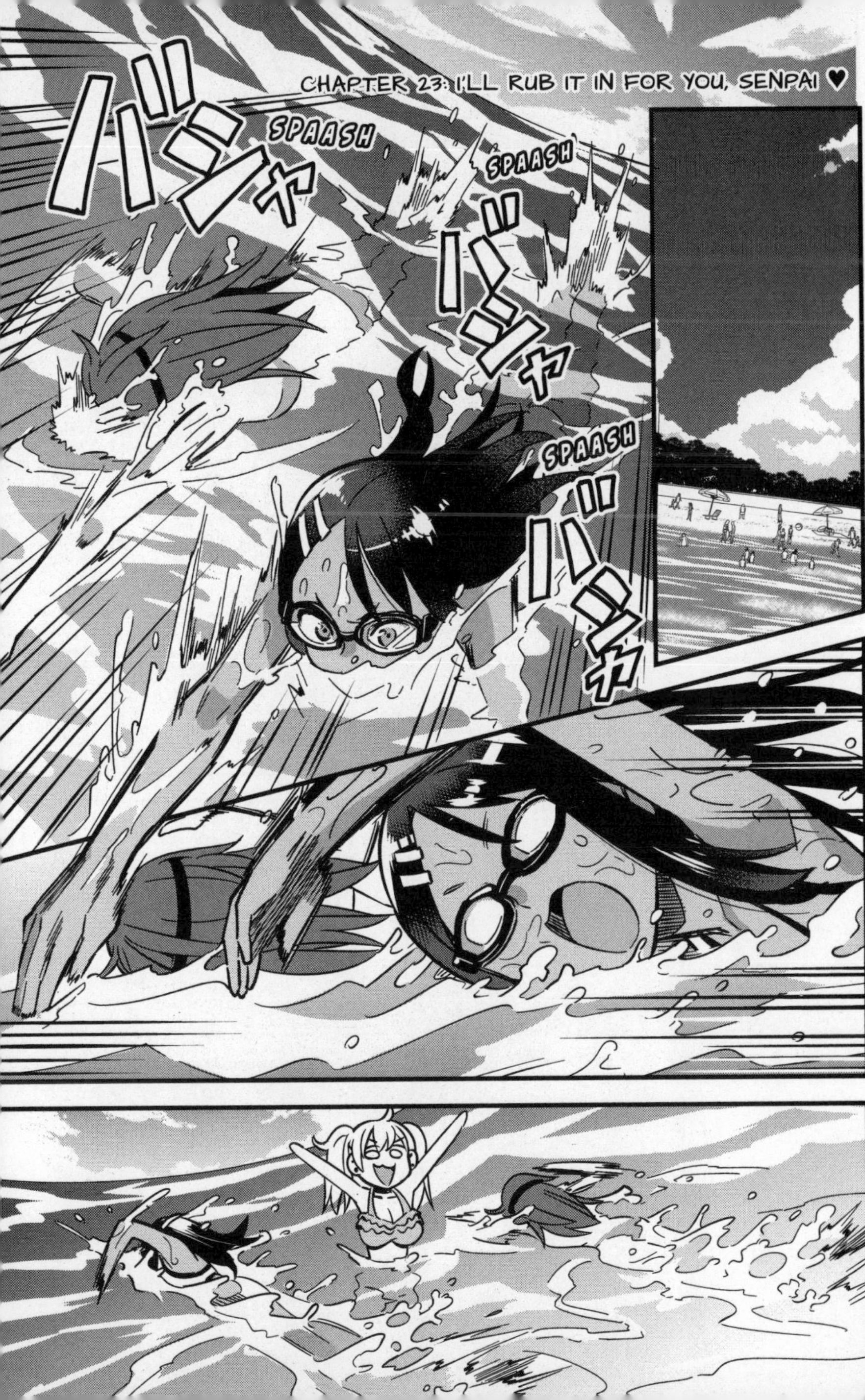
CHAPTER 23: I'LL RUB IT IN FOR YOU, SENPAI ♥
SPAASH
バーシャ
SPAASH
バーシャ
SPAASH
バシャ

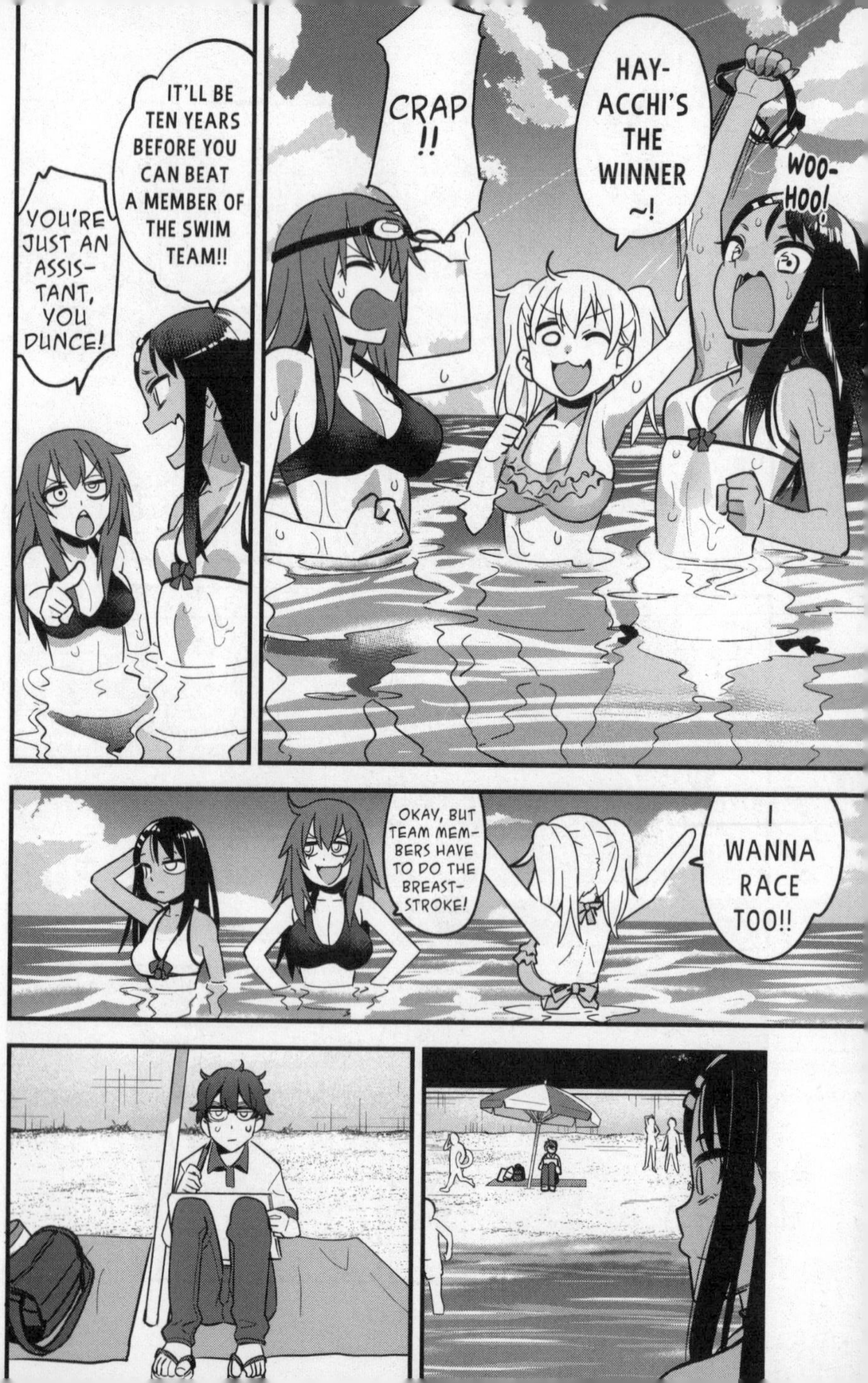
WOO-HOO!
HAY-ACCHI'S THE WINNER ~!
CRAP!!
IT'LL BE TEN YEARS BEFORE YOU CAN BEAT A MEMBER OF THE SWIM TEAM!!
YOU'RE JUST AN ASSIS-TANT, YOU DUNCE!
I WANNA RACE TOO!!
OKAY, BUT TEAM MEM-BERS HAVE TO DO THE BREAST-STROKE!

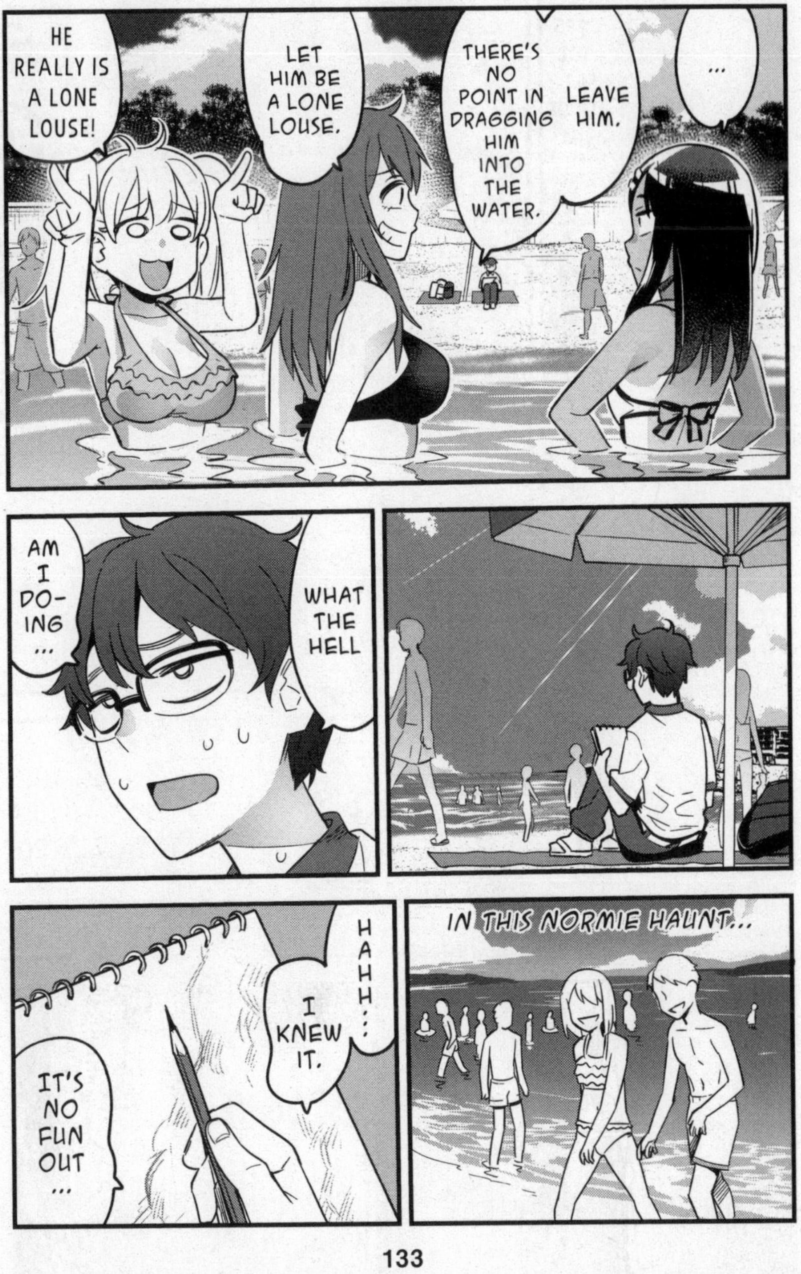
...
LEAVE HIM.
THERE'S NO POINT IN DRAGGING HIM INTO THE WATER.
LET HIM BE A LONE LOUSE.
HE REALLY IS A LONE LOUSE!
WHAT THE HELL
AM I DOING...
IN THIS NORMIE HAUNT...
HAHH...
I KNEW IT.
IT'S NO FUN OUT...

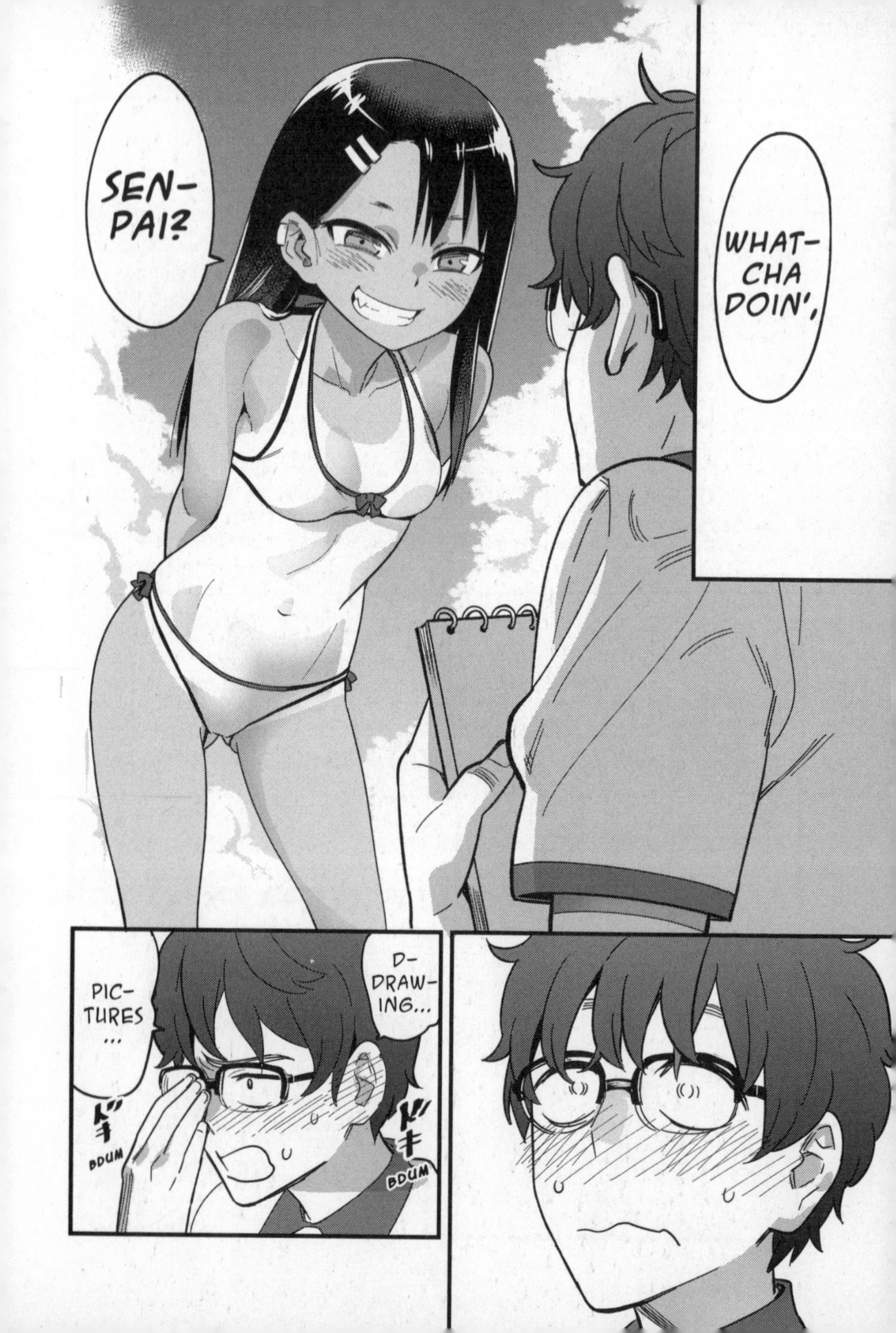
WHAT-CHA DOIN',
SEN-PAI?
D-DRAW-ING...
PIC-TURES ...
ドキ BDUM
ドキ BDUM

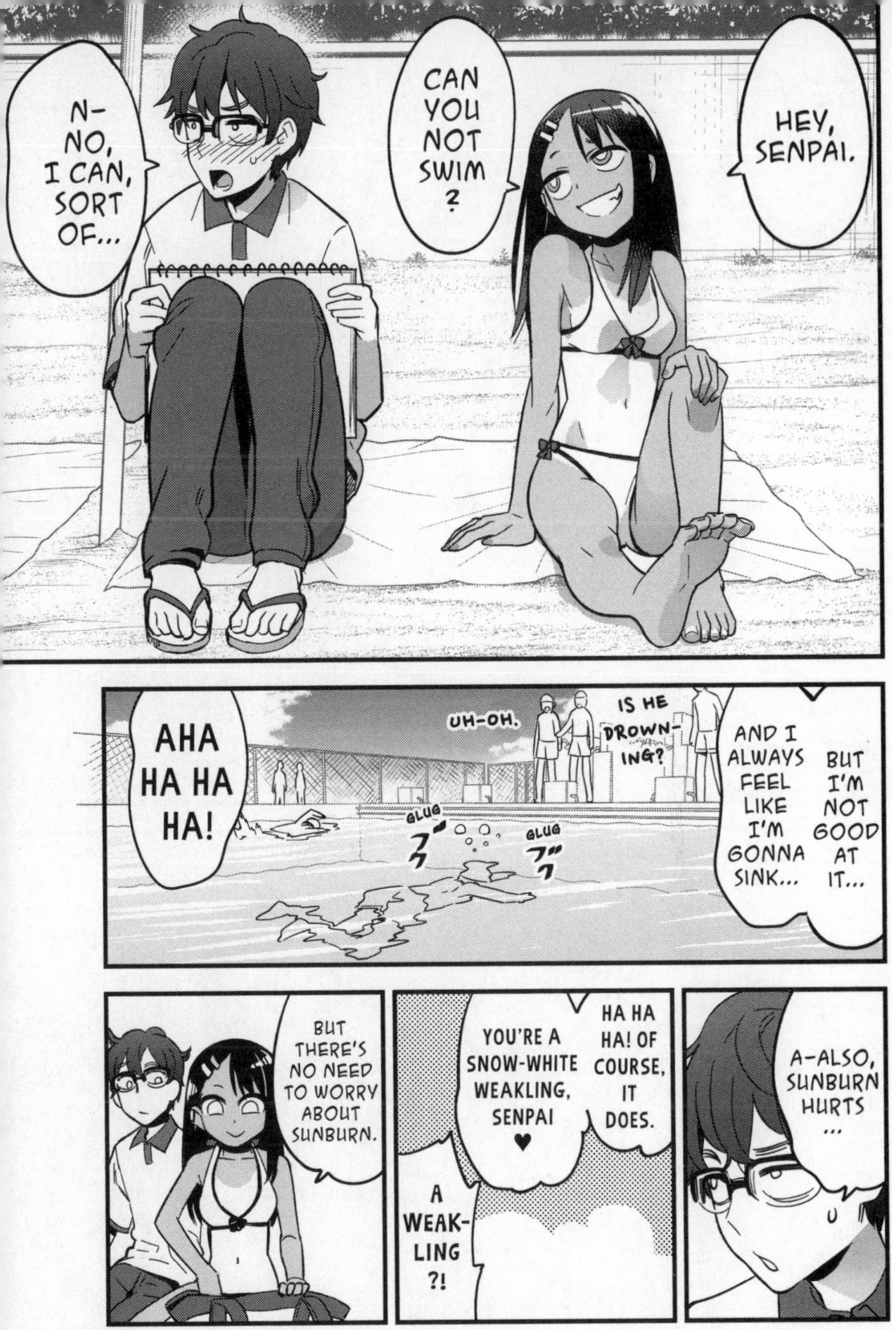
HEY, SENPAI.
CAN YOU NOT SWIM?
N-NO, I CAN, SORT OF...
BUT I'M NOT GOOD AT IT...
AND I ALWAYS FEEL LIKE I'M GONNA SINK...
IS HE DROWNING?
UH-OH.
GLUG
GLUG
AHA HA HA HA!
A-ALSO, SUNBURN HURTS...
HA HA HA! OF COURSE, IT DOES.
YOU'RE A SNOW-WHITE WEAKLING, SENPAI ♥
A WEAKLING?!
BUT THERE'S NO NEED TO WORRY ABOUT SUNBURN.

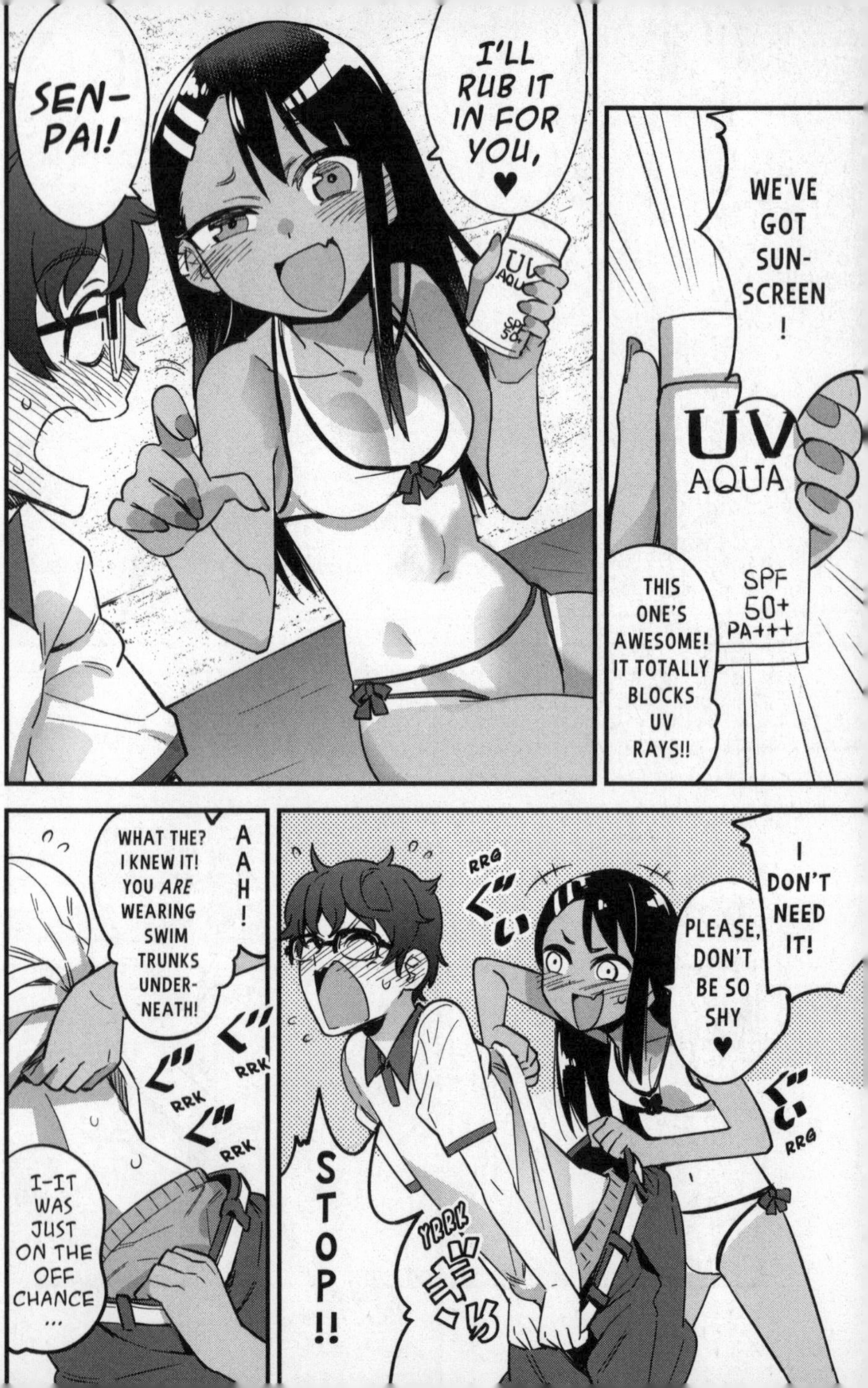
WE'VE GOT SUN-SCREEN!
THIS ONE'S AWESOME! IT TOTALLY BLOCKS UV RAYS!!
UV AQUA SPF 50+ PA+++
I'LL RUB IT IN FOR YOU, ♥
SEN-PAI!
I DON'T NEED IT!
PLEASE, DON'T BE SO SHY ♥
RRG
RRG
STOP!!
YRRK
AAH!
WHAT THE? I KNEW IT! YOU *ARE* WEARING SWIM TRUNKS UNDER-NEATH!
RRK
RRK
RRK
I-IT WAS JUST ON THE OFF CHANCE...

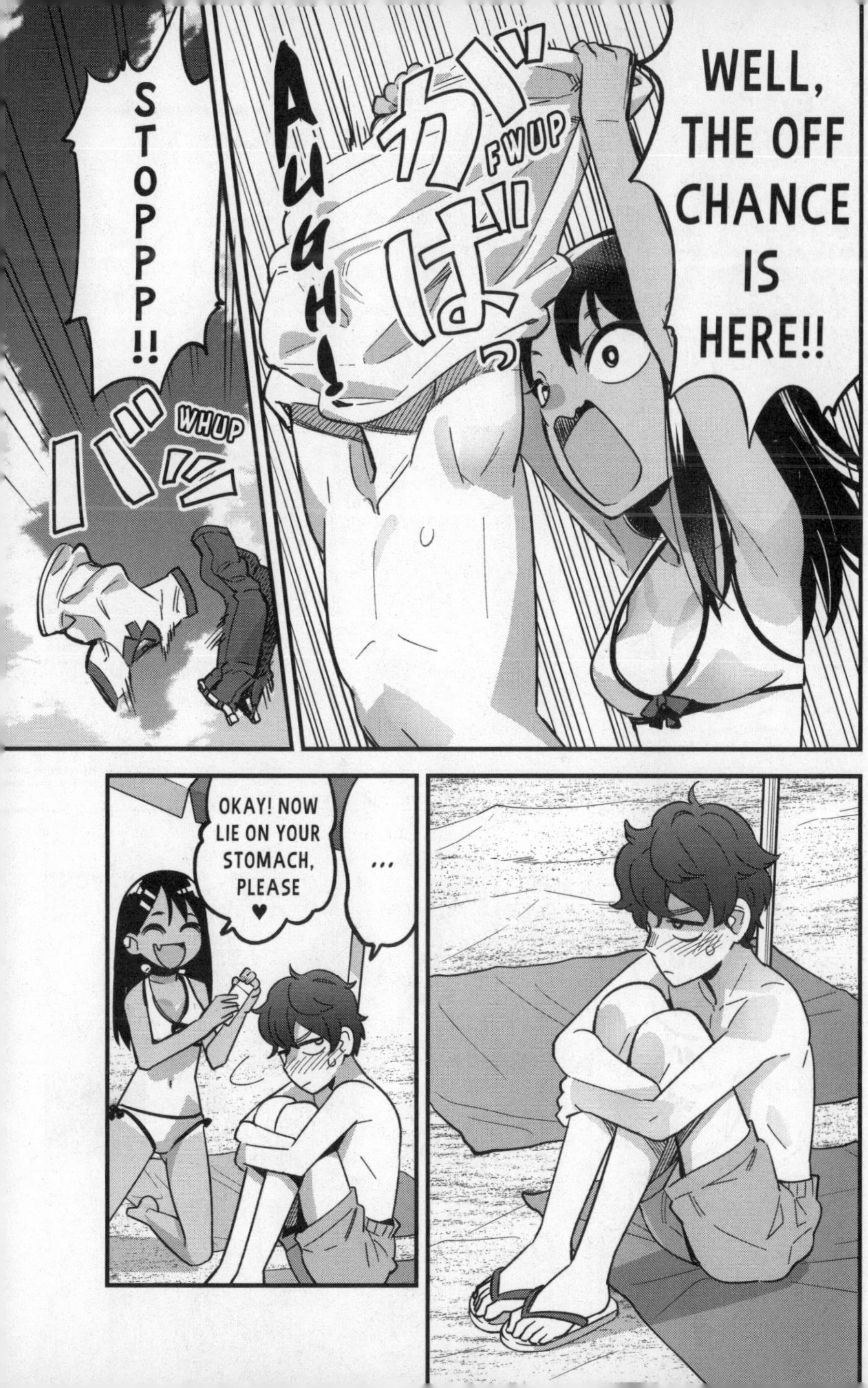
WELL, THE OFF CHANCE IS HERE!!
AUUGH!
ガばっ
FWUP
STOPPP!!
バッ
WHUP
OKAY! NOW LIE ON YOUR STOMACH, PLEASE ♥
...

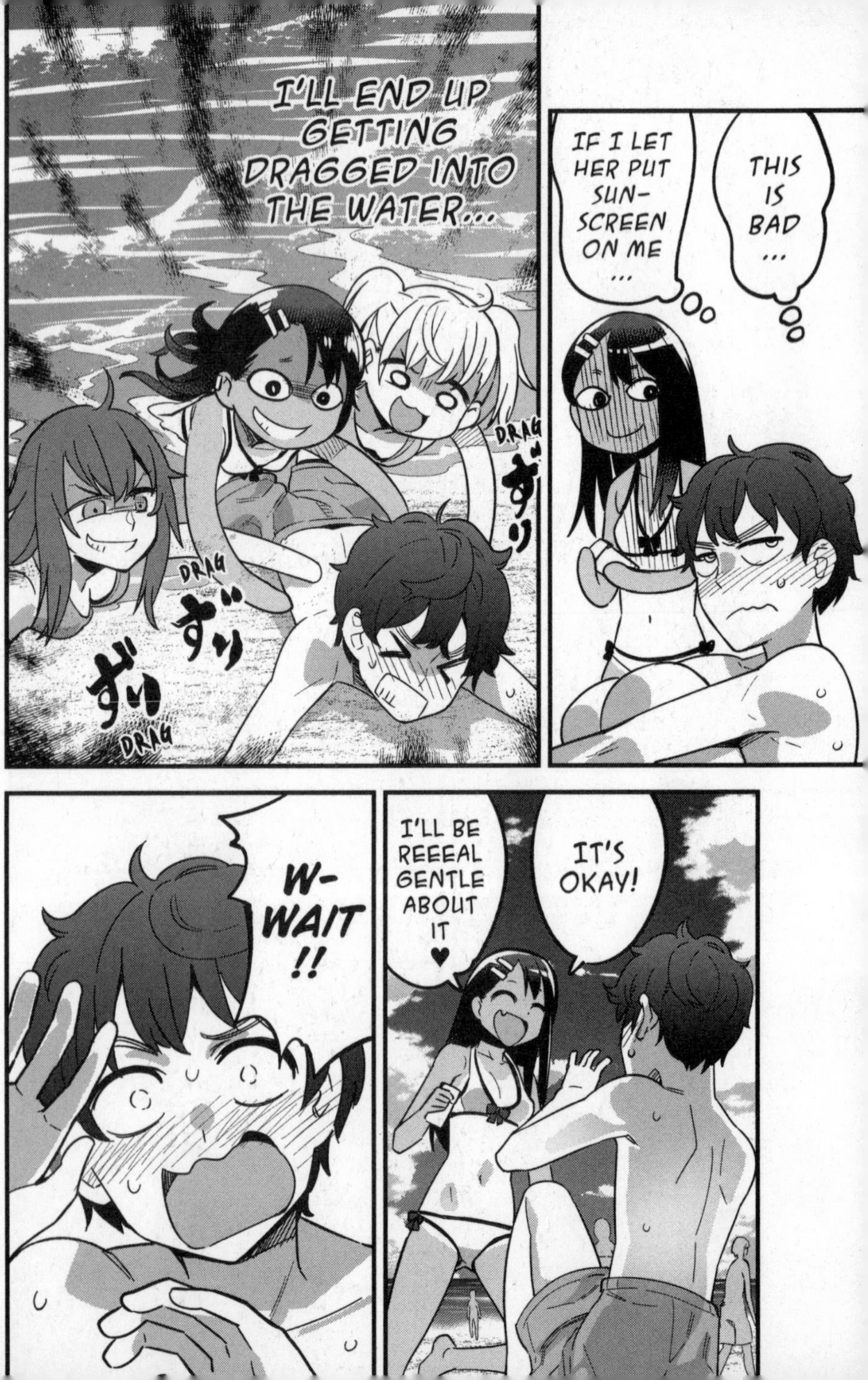
THIS IS BAD ...
IF I LET HER PUT SUN-SCREEN ON ME ...
I'LL END UP GETTING DRAGGED INTO THE WATER...
DRAG
ずり
DRAG
ずり
ずり
DRAG
IT'S OKAY!
I'LL BE REEEAL GENTLE ABOUT IT ♥
W-WAIT !!

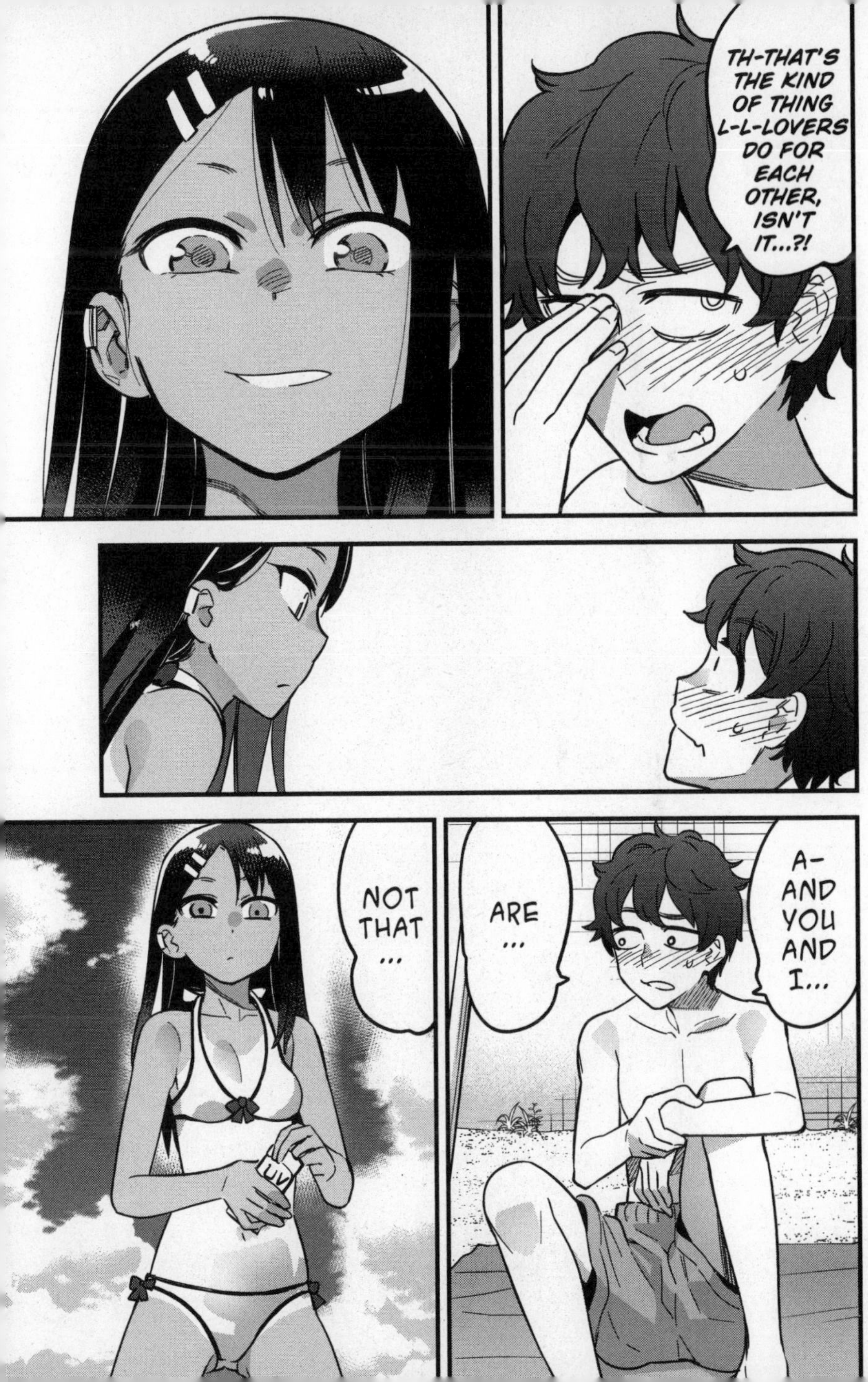
TH-THAT'S THE KIND OF THING L-L-LOVERS DO FOR EACH OTHER, ISN'T IT...?!
A- AND YOU AND I...
ARE ...
NOT THAT ...

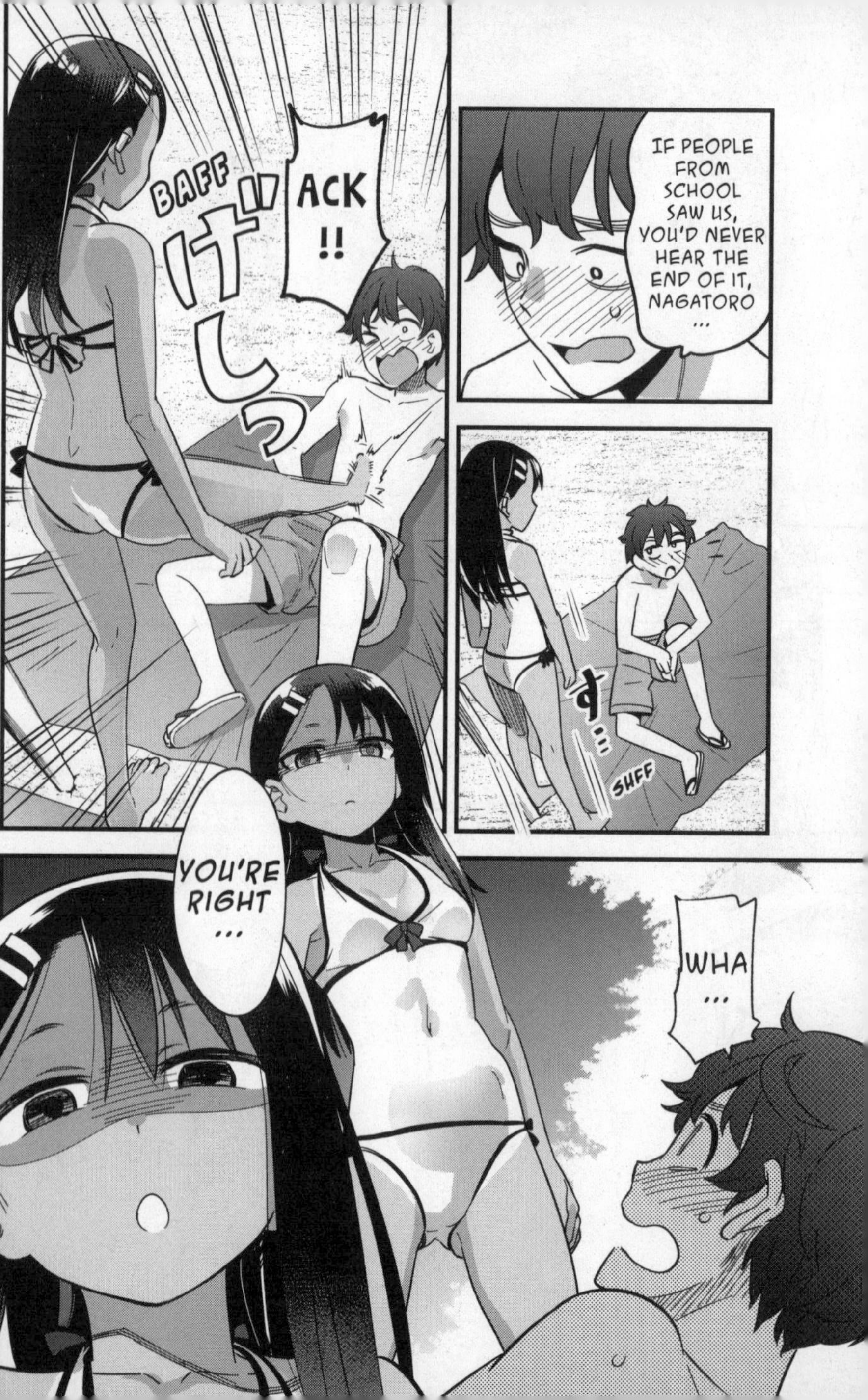
IF PEOPLE FROM SCHOOL SAW US, YOU'D NEVER HEAR THE END OF IT, NAGATORO ...
SHUFF
BAFF
ACK !!
YOU'RE RIGHT ...
WHA ...

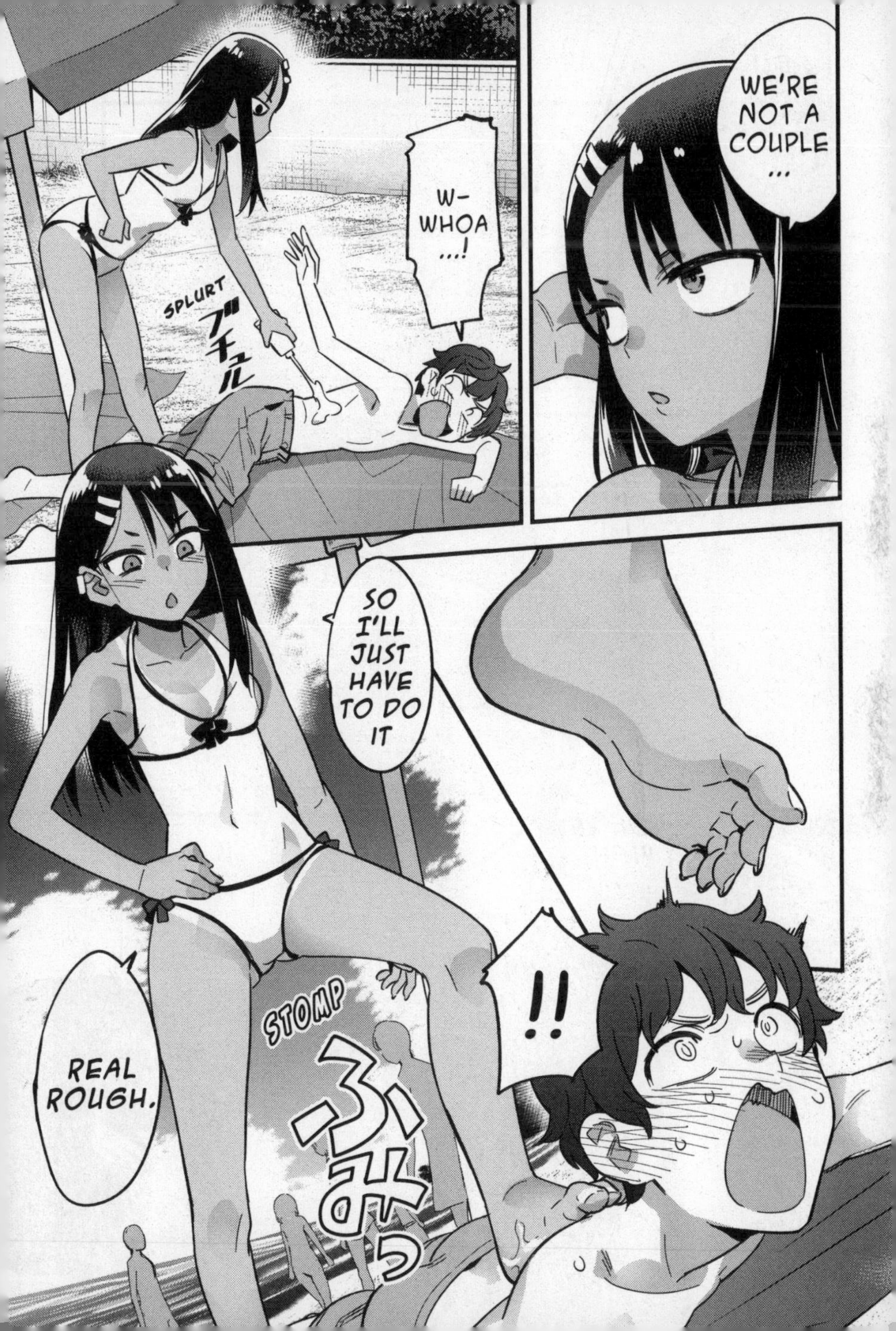
WE'RE NOT A COUPLE ...
W-WHOA ...!
SPLURT
ブチュル
!!
SO I'LL JUST HAVE TO DO IT
REAL ROUGH.
STOMP
ふみっ

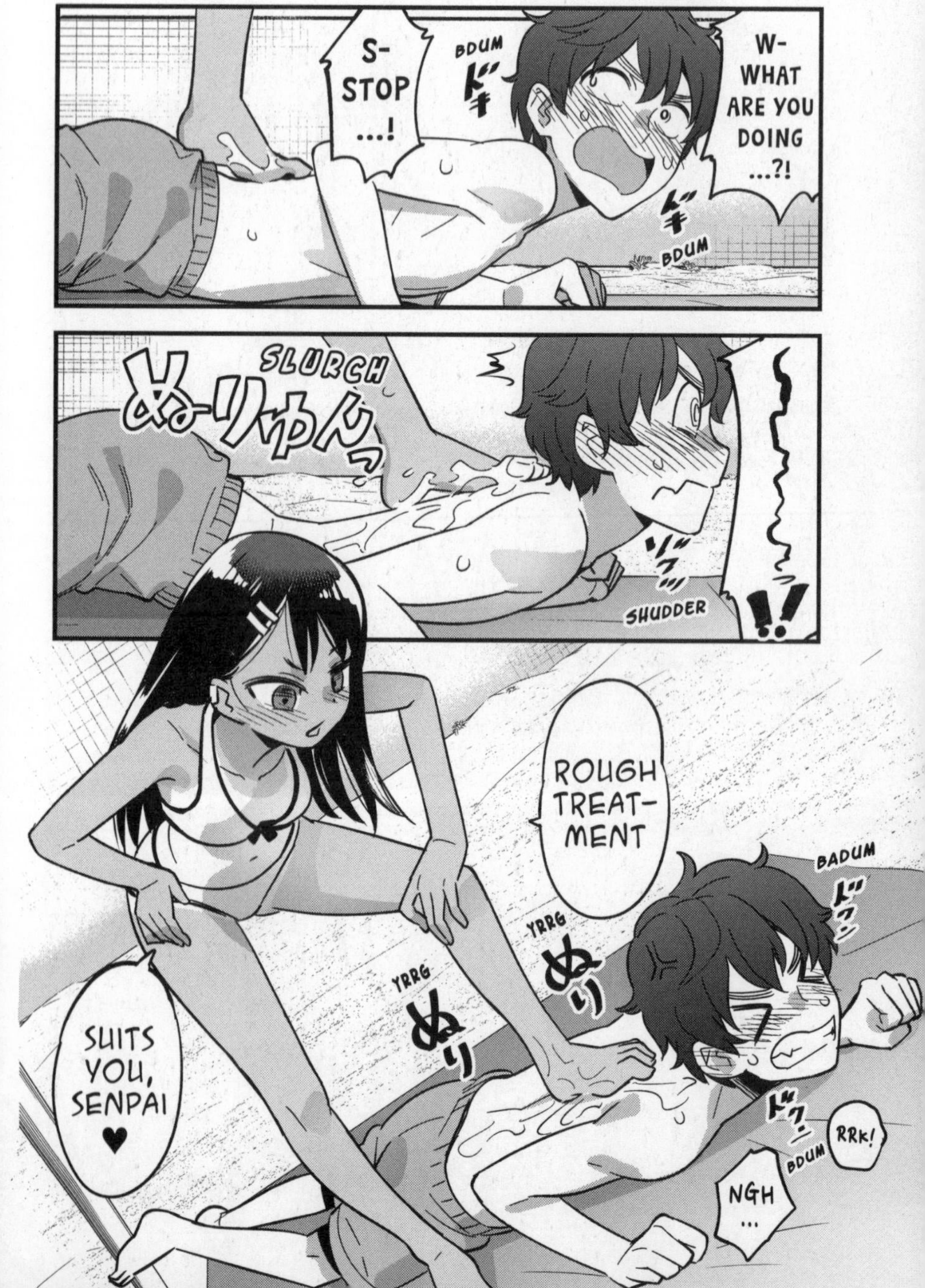

W-WHAT ARE YOU DOING ...?!
BDUM
ドキ
S-STOP ...!
ドキ
BDUM
!!
ゾクゾク
SHUDDER
SLURCH
ぬりゅんっ
BADUM
ドクッ
ROUGH TREAT-MENT
YRRG
ぬり
YRRG
ぬり
SUITS YOU, SENPAI ♥
ドクッ
BDUM
RRK!
NGH ...

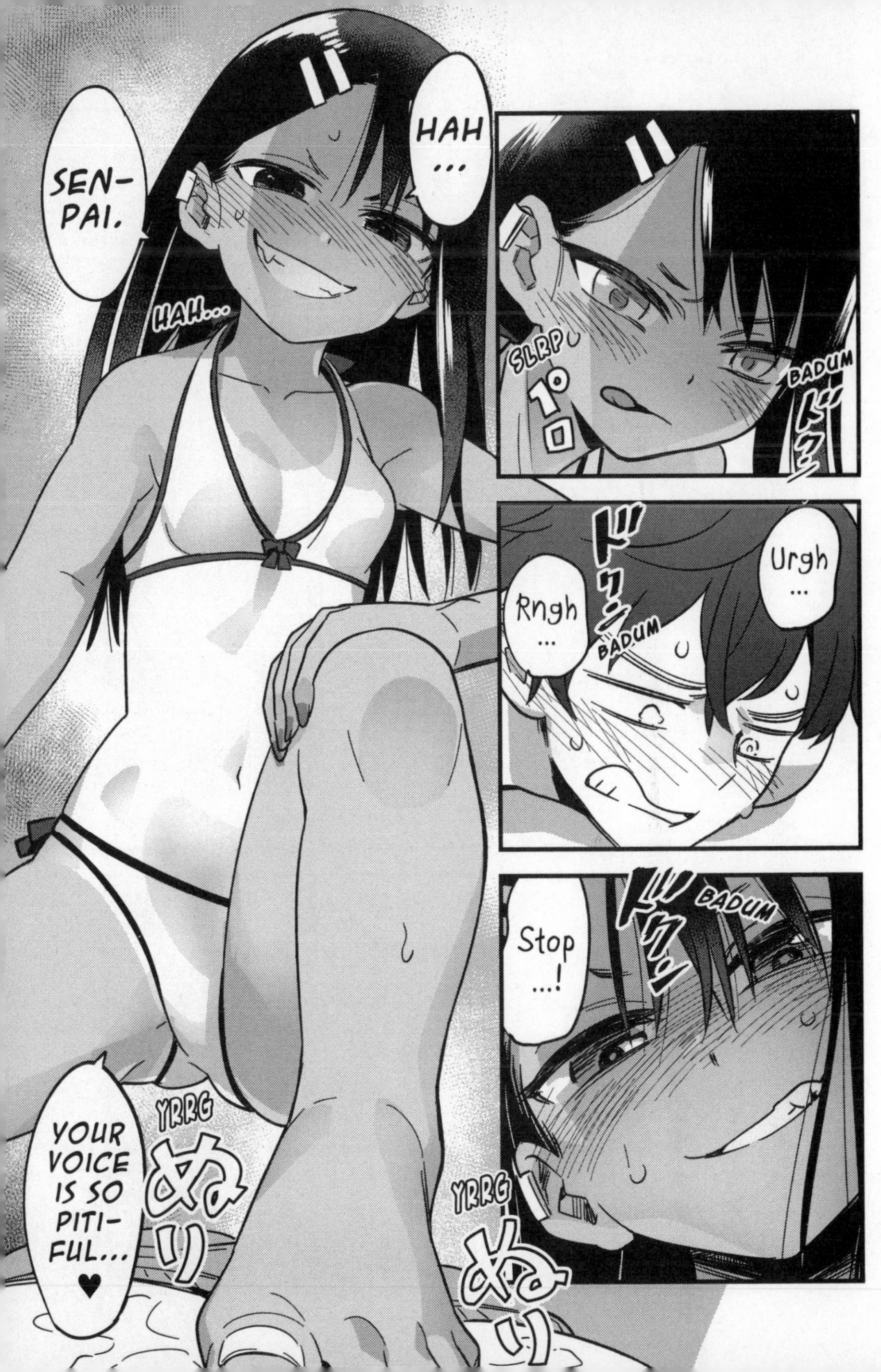
SLRP
BADUM
Urgh ...
Rngh ...
BADUM
BADUM
Stop ...!
HAH ...
SEN-PAI.
HAH...
YRRG
YOUR VOICE IS SO PITI-FUL... ♥
YRRG

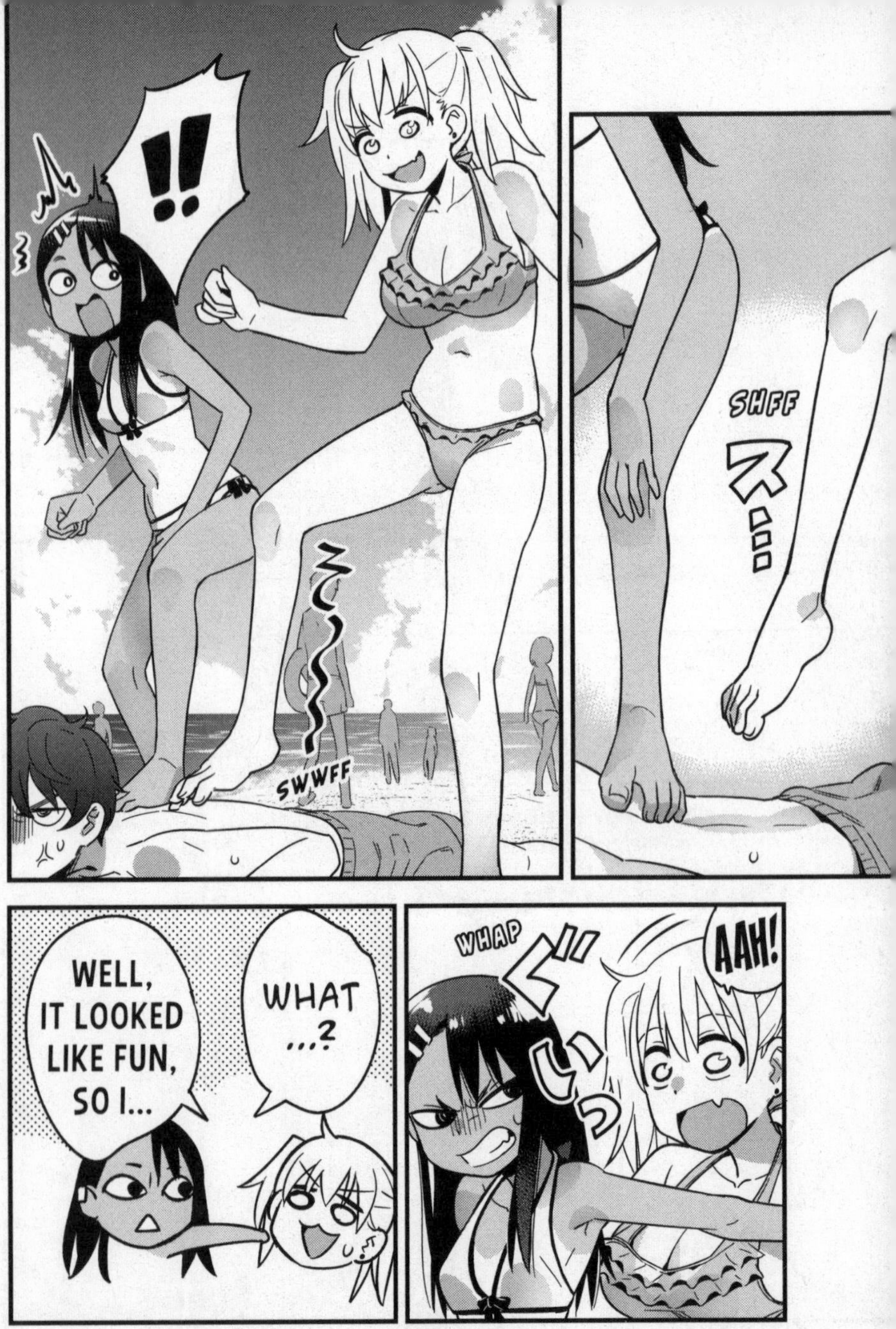
SHFF
!!
SWWFF
AAH!
WHAP
WHAT ...?
WELL, IT LOOKED LIKE FUN, SO I...

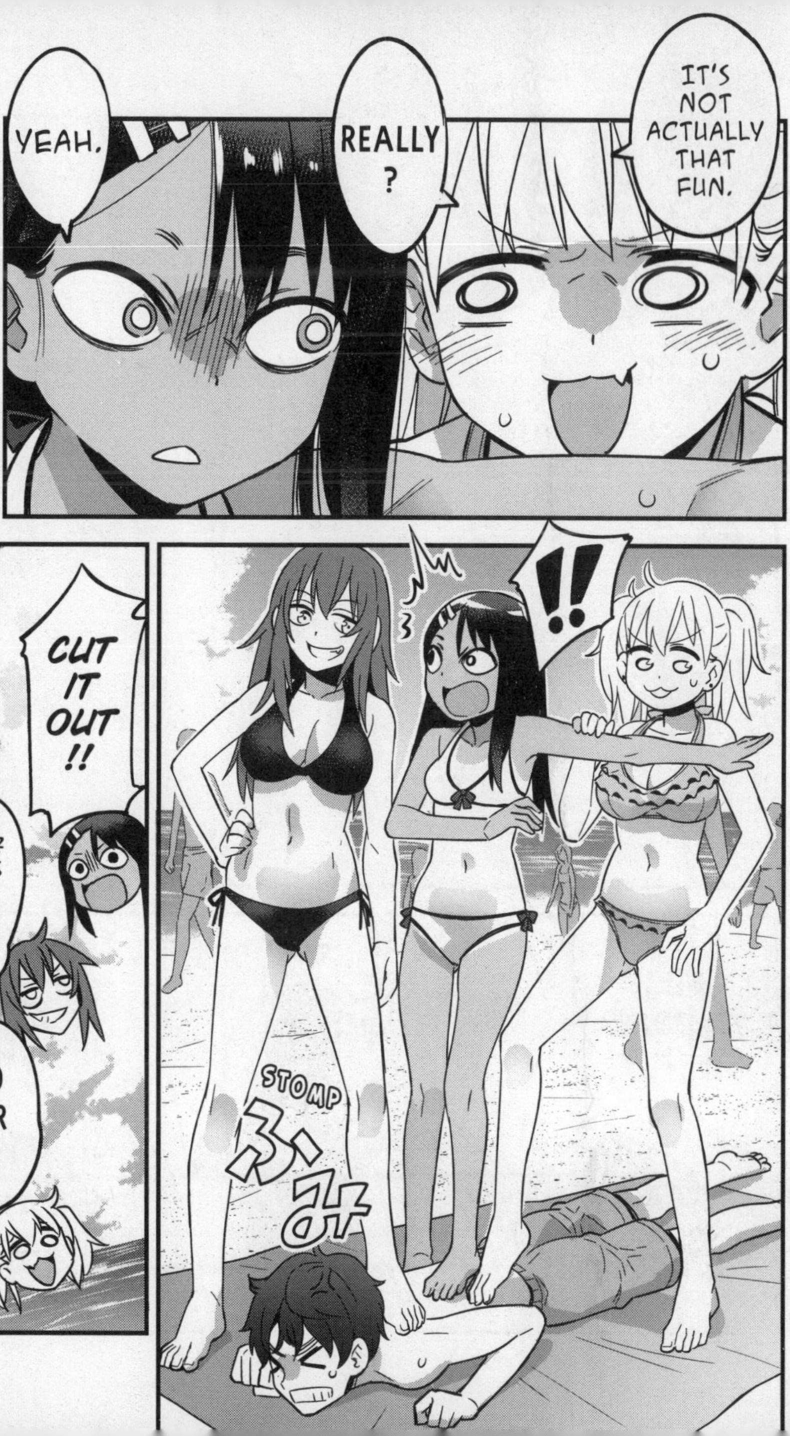
IT'S NOT ACTUALLY THAT FUN.
REALLY?
YEAH.
!!
STOMP
ふみ
CUT IT OUT!!
WHY? LET'S GO FOR IT.
GO FOR IT!

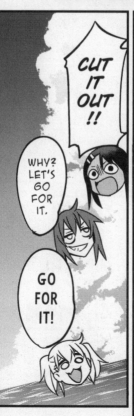

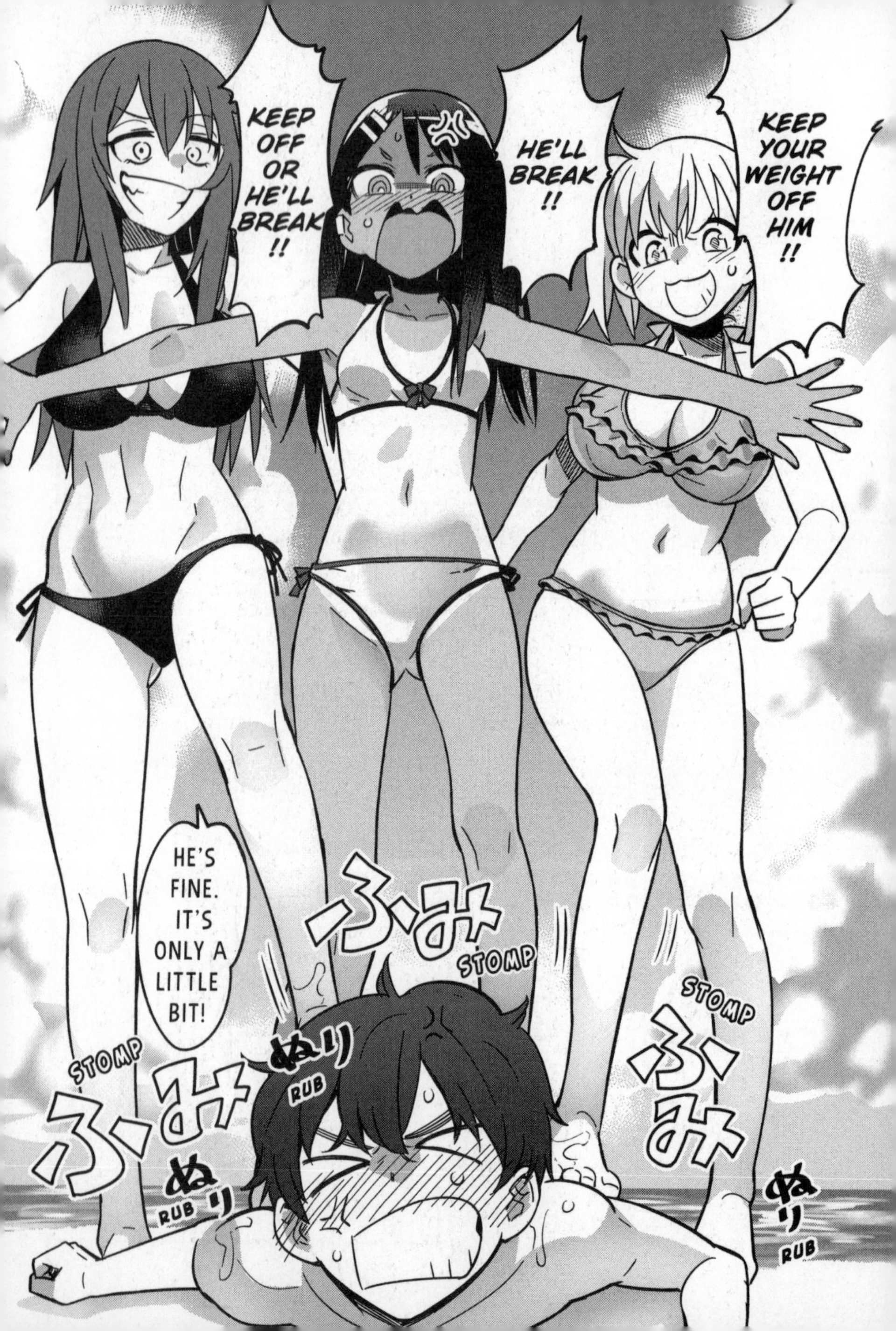
KEEP YOUR WEIGHT OFF HIM!!
HE'LL BREAK!!
KEEP OFF OR HE'LL BREAK!!
ふみ
STOMP
ぬり
RUB
ふみ
STOMP
HE'S FINE. IT'S ONLY A LITTLE BIT!
ぬり
RUB
ふみ
STOMP
ぬり
RUB

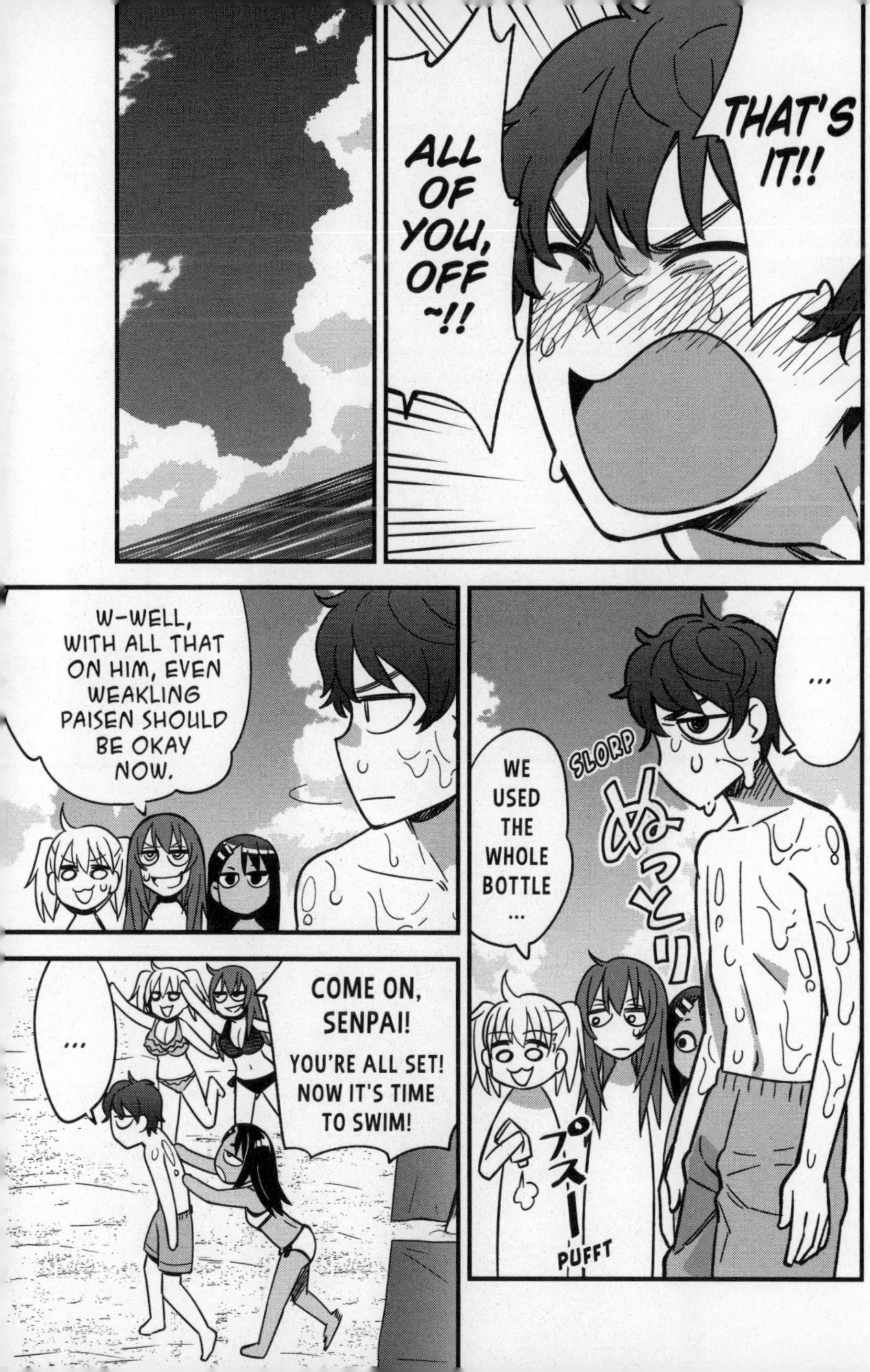
THAT'S IT!!
ALL OF YOU, OFF ~!!
...
SLORP
ぬっとり
WE USED THE WHOLE BOTTLE ...
プスー
PUFFT
W-WELL, WITH ALL THAT ON HIM, EVEN WEAKLING PAISEN SHOULD BE OKAY NOW.
COME ON, SENPAI!
YOU'RE ALL SET! NOW IT'S TIME TO SWIM!
...

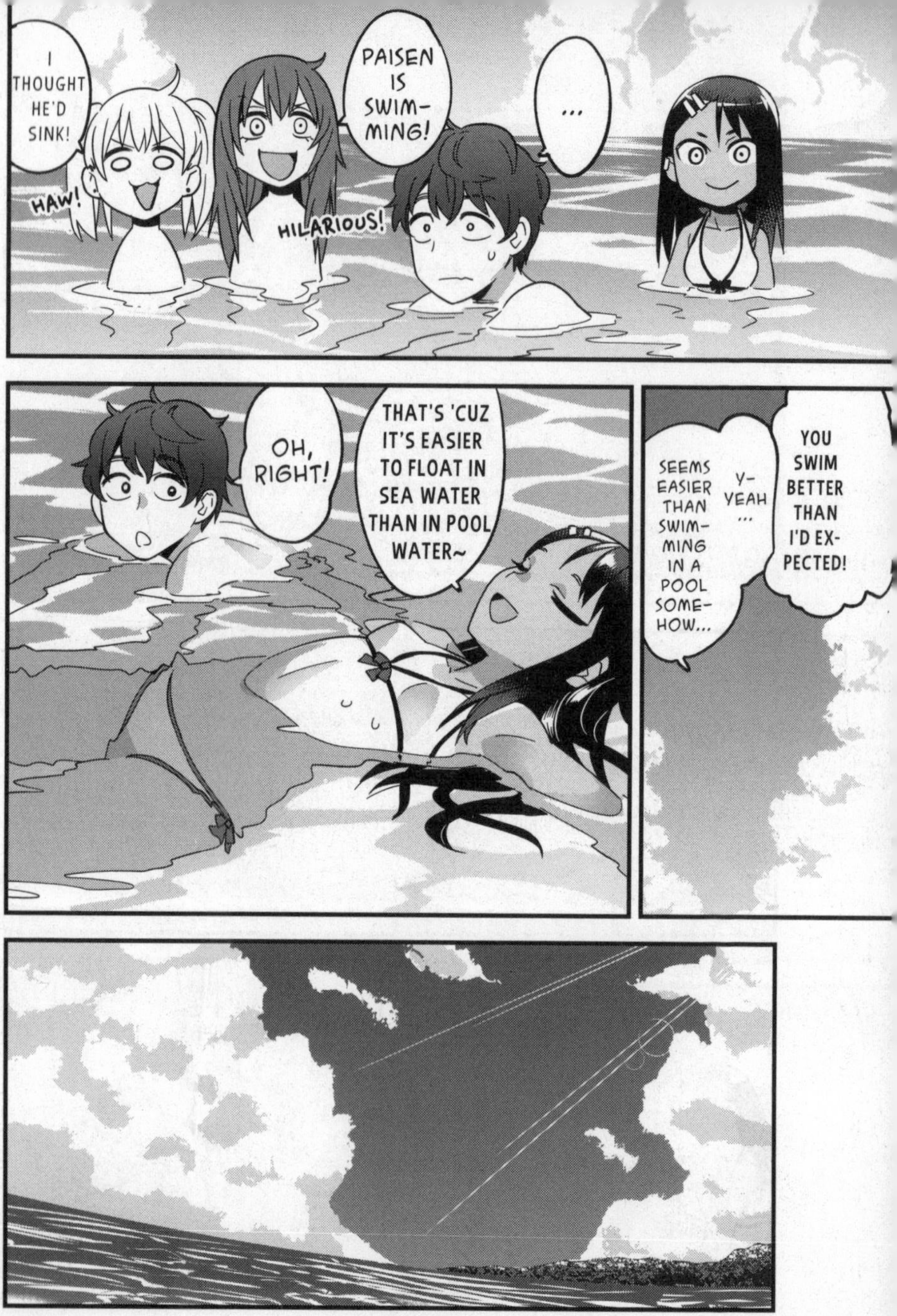
...
PAISEN IS SWIM-MING!
HILARIOUS!
I THOUGHT HE'D SINK!
HAW!
YOU SWIM BETTER THAN I'D EX-PECTED!
Y-YEAH...
SEEMS EASIER THAN SWIM-MING IN A POOL SOME-HOW...
THAT'S 'CUZ IT'S EASIER TO FLOAT IN SEA WATER THAN IN POOL WATER~
OH, RIGHT!

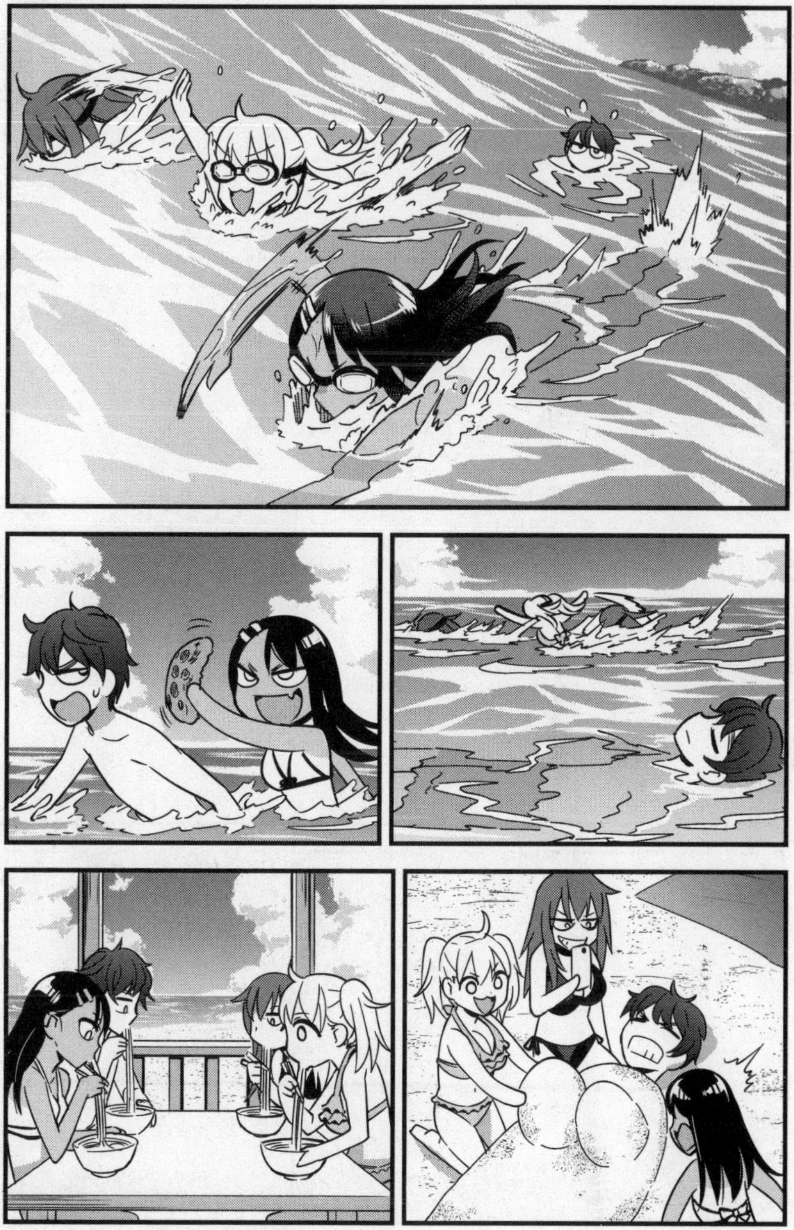

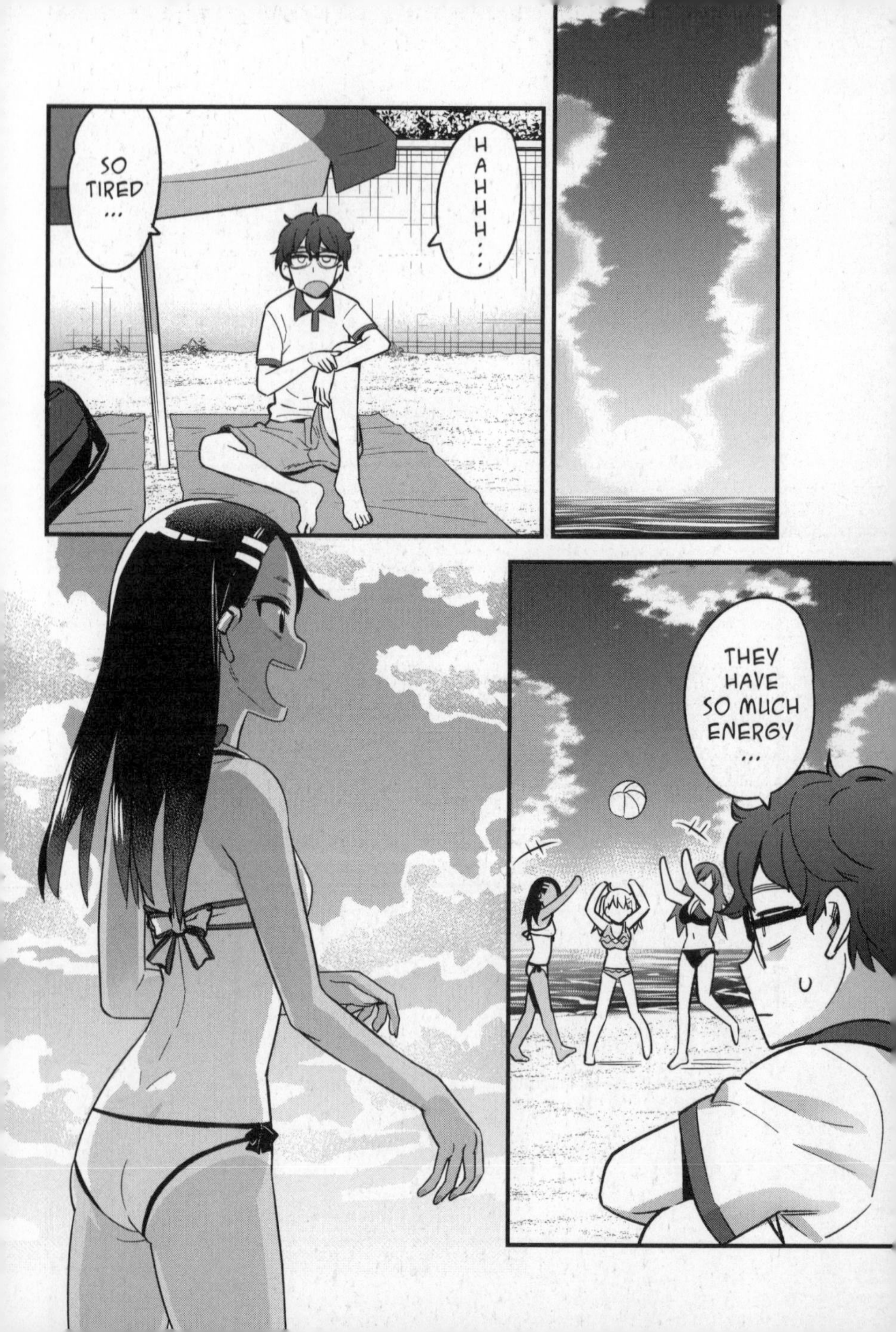
HAHHH...
SO TIRED ...
THEY HAVE SO MUCH ENERGY ...

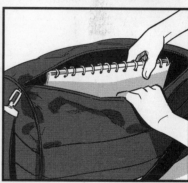

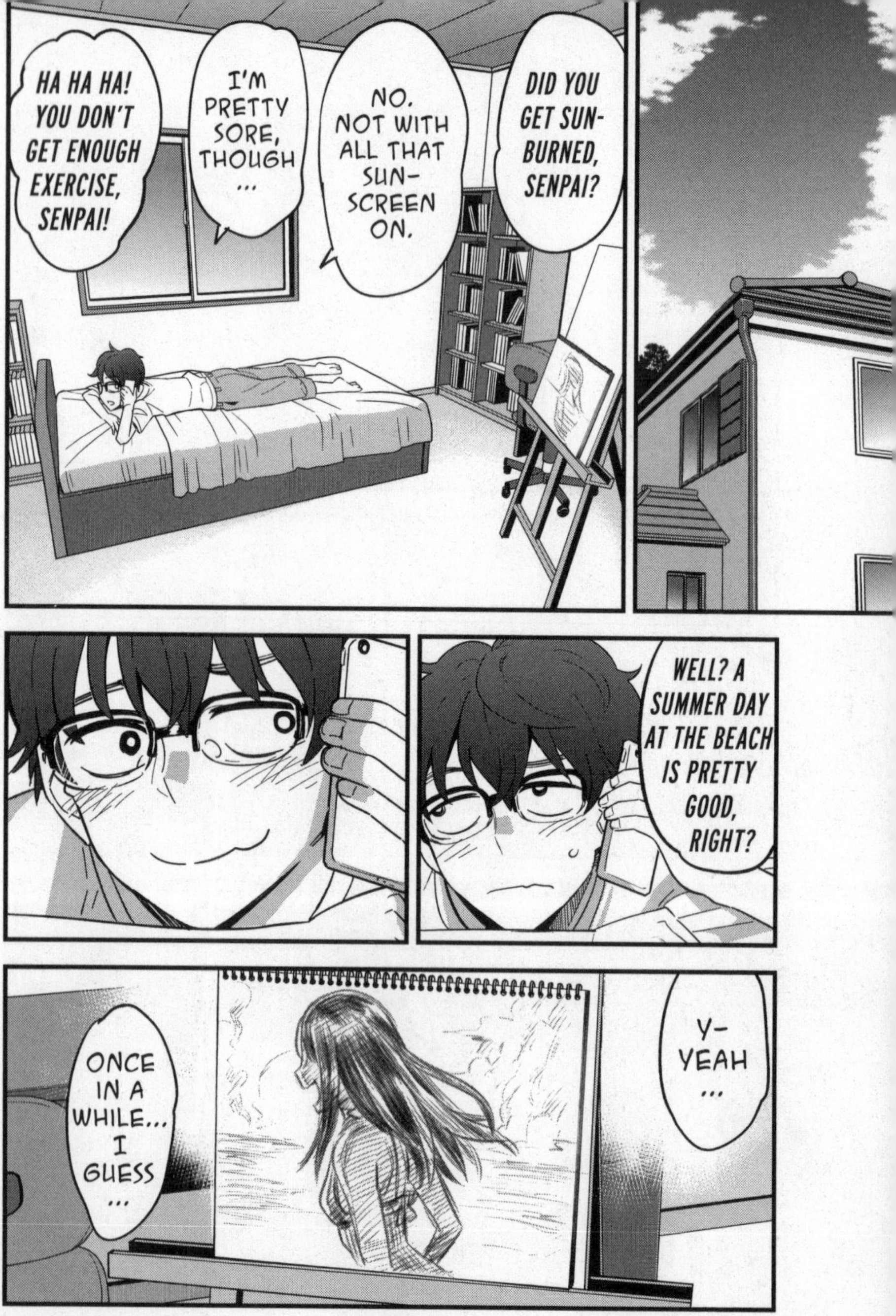
DID YOU GET SUN-BURNED, SENPAI?
NO. NOT WITH ALL THAT SUN-SCREEN ON.
I'M PRETTY SORE, THOUGH ...
HA HA HA! YOU DON'T GET ENOUGH EXERCISE, SENPAI!
WELL? A SUMMER DAY AT THE BEACH IS PRETTY GOOD, RIGHT?
Y-YEAH ...
ONCE IN A WHILE... I GUESS ...

END

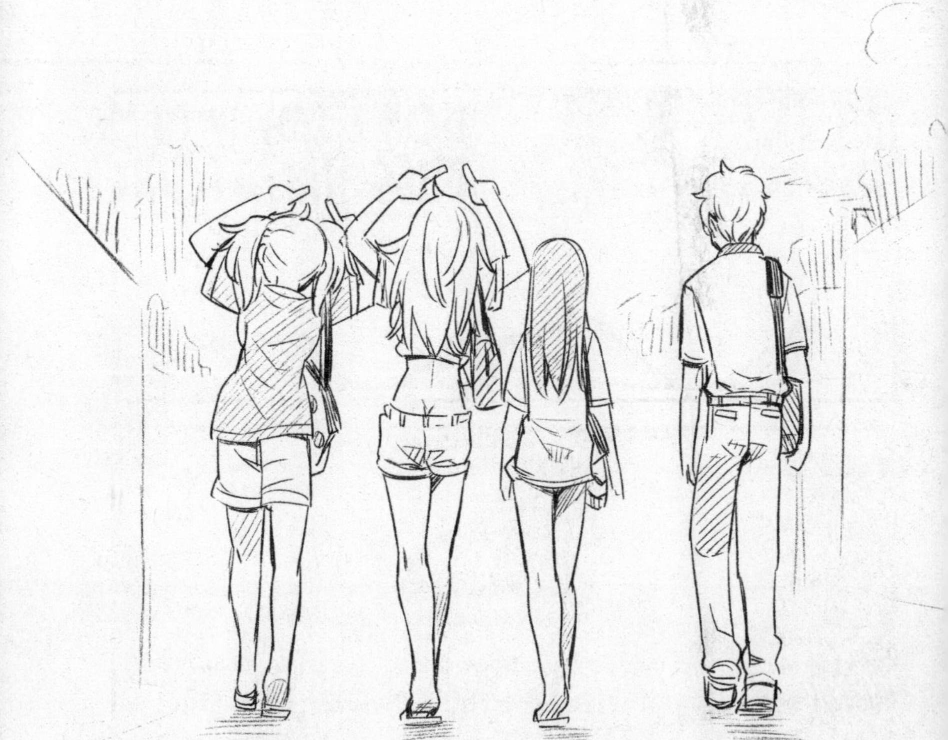

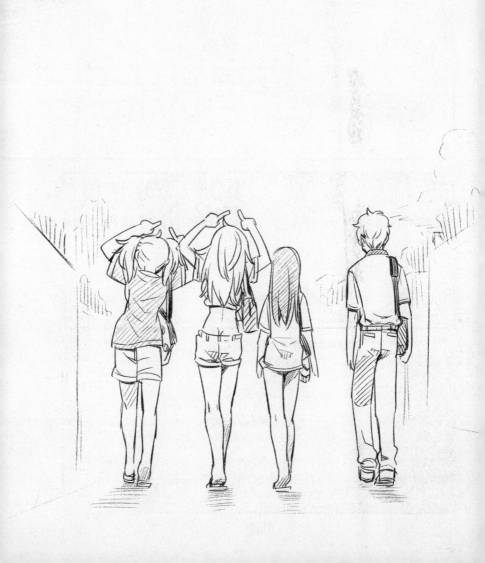

DON'T TOY WITH ME, MISS NAGATORO

←The following bonus manga were drawn based on selections from the **"I Want to be Toyed With Like This!" Twitter campaign.**

Thank you truly for all of your entries!!

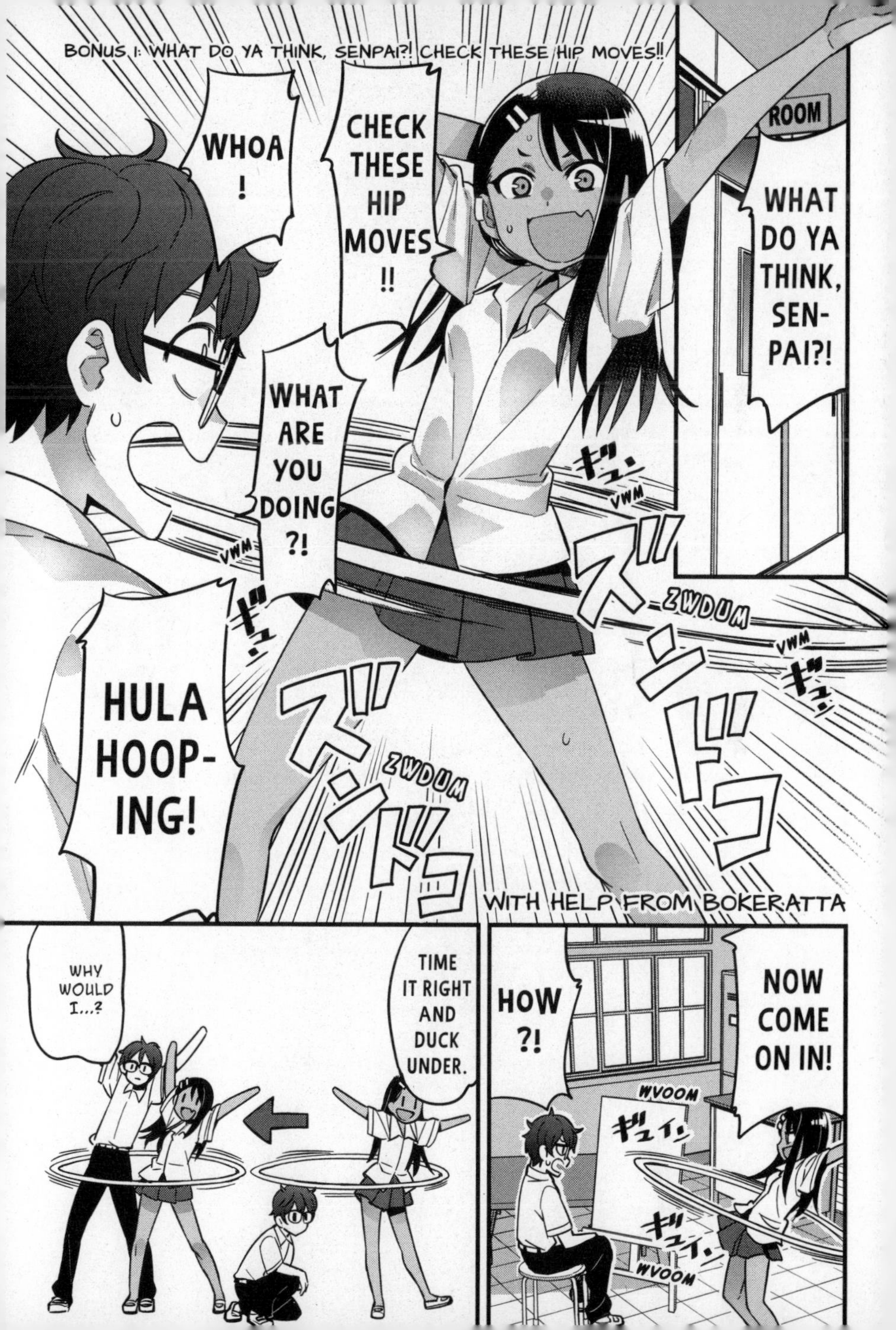
BONUS 1: WHAT DO YA THINK, SENPAI?! CHECK THESE HIP MOVES!!
ROOM
WHAT DO YA THINK, SEN-PAI?!
CHECK THESE HIP MOVES!!
WHOA!
WHAT ARE YOU DOING?!
VWM
VWM
HULA HOOP-ING!
ZWDUM
VWM
ZWDUM
WITH HELP FROM BOKERATTA
NOW COME ON IN!
HOW?!
WVOOM
WVOOM
TIME IT RIGHT AND DUCK UNDER.
WHY WOULD I...?

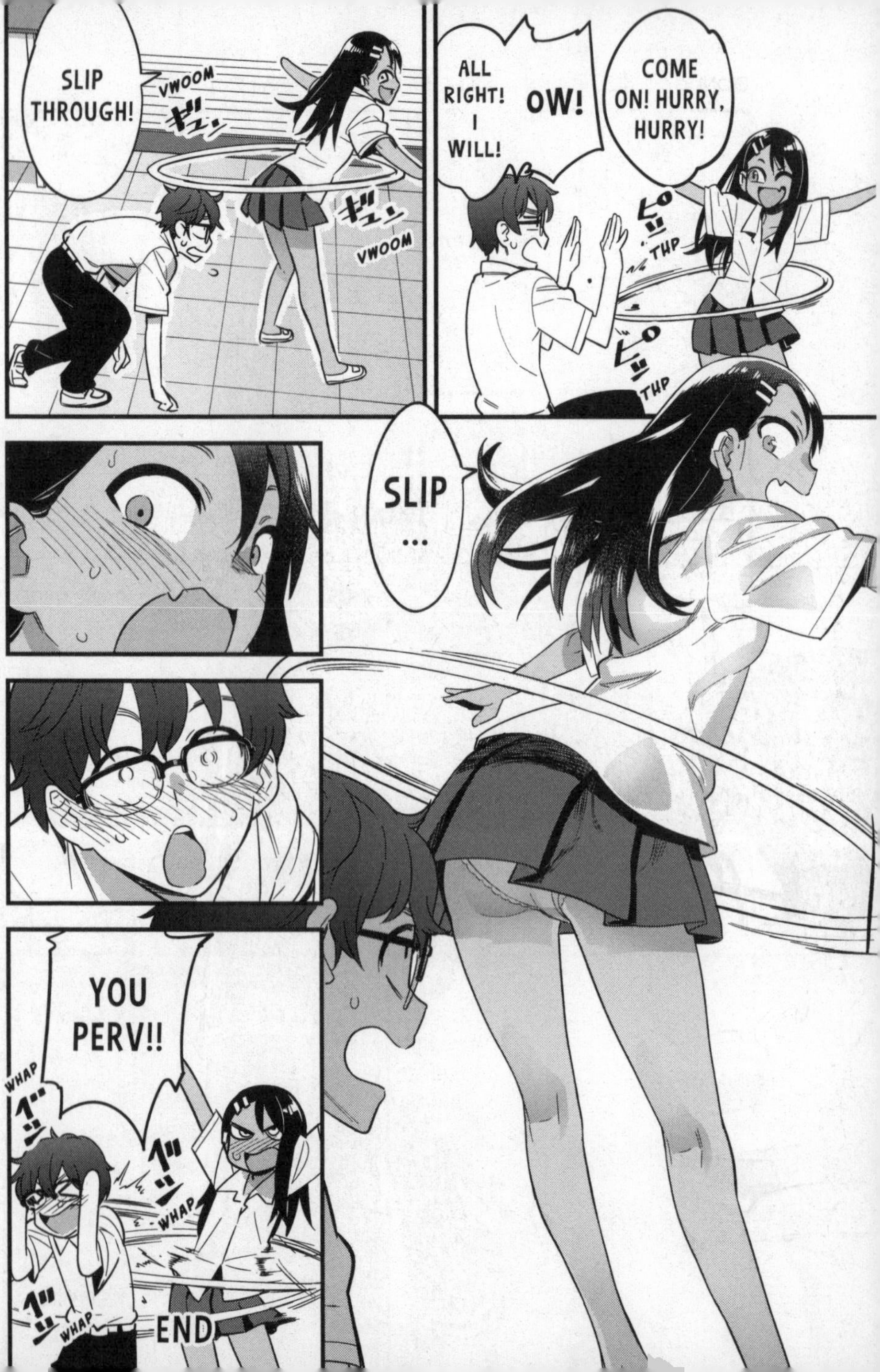

COME ON! HURRY, HURRY!
ALL RIGHT! I WILL!
OW!
THP
THP
SLIP THROUGH!
VWOOM
VWOOM
SLIP ...
YOU PERV!!
WHAP
WHAP
WHAP
END

BONUS 2: I'LL BOOST YOUR SPIRITS, SENPAI ♥

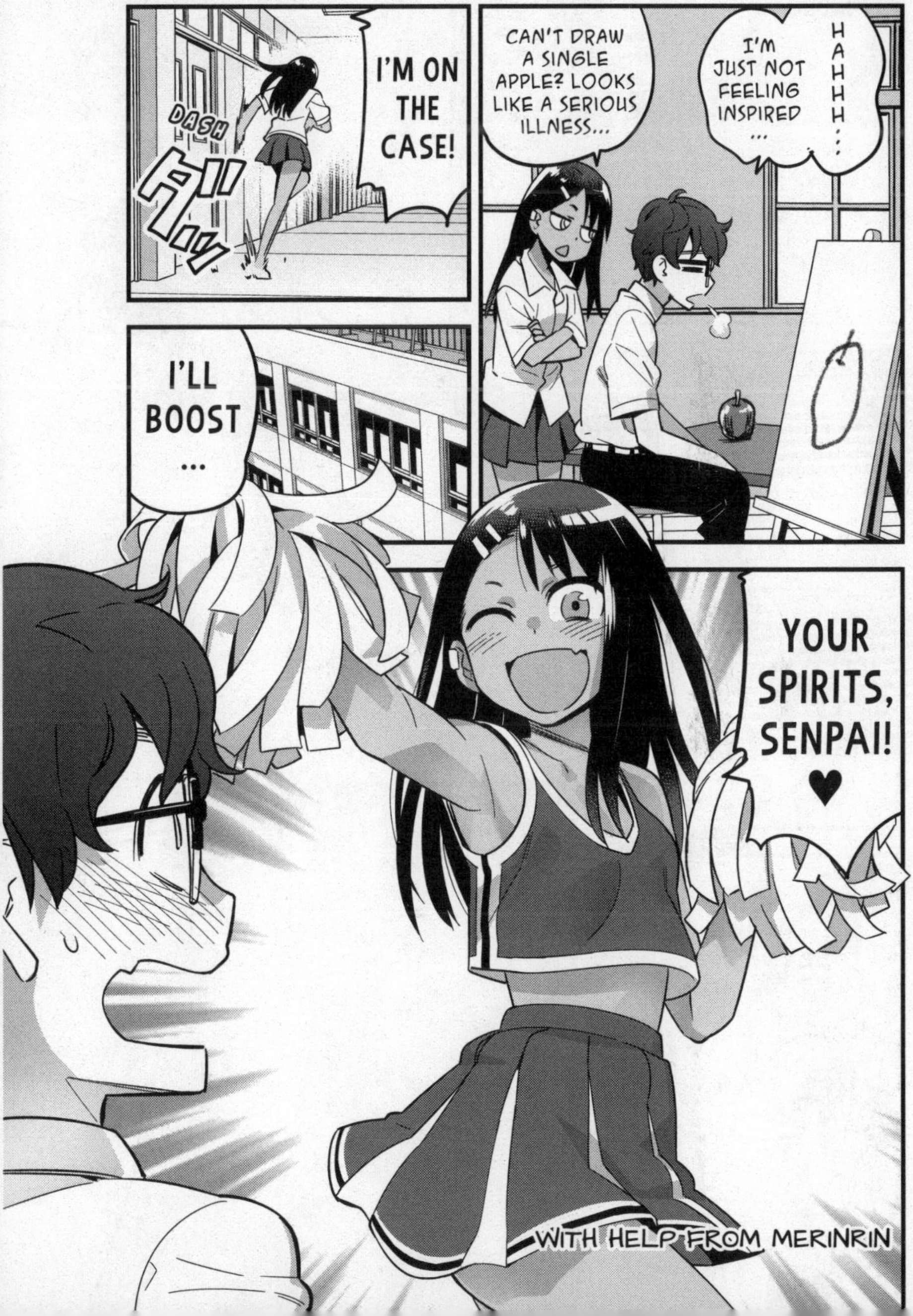
HAHHH...
I'M JUST NOT FEELING INSPIRED...
CAN'T DRAW A SINGLE APPLE? LOOKS LIKE A SERIOUS ILLNESS...
I'M ON THE CASE!
DASH
I'LL BOOST...
YOUR SPIRITS, SENPAI! ♥
WITH HELP FROM MERINRIN

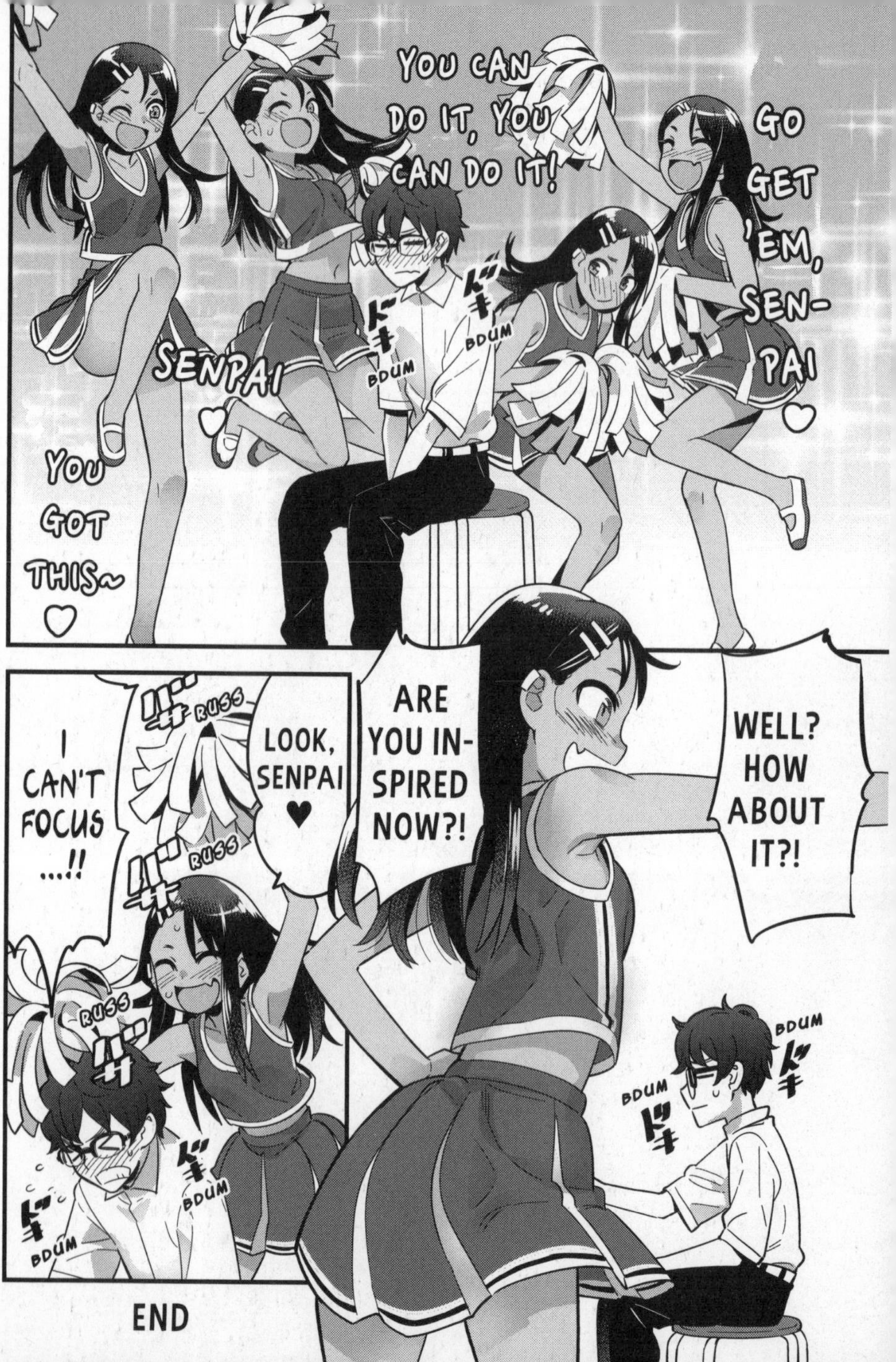
GO GET 'EM, SEN-PAI ♥
YOU CAN DO IT, YOU CAN DO IT!
BDUM
BDUM
SENPAI ♥
YOU GOT THIS~ ♥
WELL? HOW ABOUT IT?!
ARE YOU IN-SPIRED NOW?!
BDUM
BDUM
LOOK, SENPAI ♥
RUSS
RUSS
I CAN'T FOCUS ...!!
RUSS
BDUM
BDUM

END

STAY TUNED FOR THE NEXT VOLUME!!
- NANASHI

Don't Toy With Me, Miss Nagatoro 3

A Vertical Comics Edition

Editing: Kristi Fernandez
Translation: Kumar Sivasubramanian
Production: Risa Cho
Eve Grandt

First published in Japan in 2018 by Kodansha, Ltd., Tokyo
Publication rights for this English edition arranged through Kodansha, Ltd., Tokyo
English language version produced by Vertical Comics, an imprint of Kodansha USA Publishing, LLC

Translation provided by Vertical Comics, 2020
Published by Kodansha USA Publishing, LLC, New York

Originally published in Japanese as *Ijiranaide, Nagatorosan 3* by Kodansha, Ltd., 2018
Ijiranaide, Nagatorosan first serialized in *Magazine Poketto*, Kodansha, Ltd., 2017-

ISBN: 978-1-949980-10-3

Manufactured in the United States of America

First Edition

Fifth Printing

Kodansha USA Publishing, LLC
451 Park Avenue South
7th Floor
New York, NY 10016
www.kodansha.us

Vertical books are distributed through Penguin-Random House Publisher Services.